The Streak

Books by John Eisenberg

The Longest Shot

Cotton Bowl Days

From 33rd Street to the Camden Yards

Native Dancer

The Great Match Race

My Guy Barbaro

That First Season

Ten-Gallon War

The Streak

The Streak

Lou Gehrig, Cal Ripken Jr., and
Baseball's Most Historic Record

John Eisenberg

HOUGHTON MIFFLIN HARCOURT   BOSTON   NEW YORK   2017

For information about permission to reproduce selections from this book, write to trade.permissions@hmhco.com or to Permissions, Houghton Mifflin Harcourt Publishing Company, 3 Park Avenue, 19th Floor, New York, New York 10016.

www.hmhco.com

Library of Congress Cataloging-in-Publication Data is available.
ISBN 978-0-544-10767-0

Book design by Brian Moore

Printed in the United States of America
DOC 10 9 8 7 6 5 4 3 2 1

Contents

A consecutive game playing streak shall be extended if the player plays one half inning on defense, or if he completes a time at bat by reaching base or being put out. A pinch running appearance only shall not extend the streak. If a player is ejected from a game by an umpire before he can comply with the requirements of this rule, his streak shall continue.

— Major League Baseball rule

Man is a creature that can get accustomed to anything, and I think that is the best definition of him.

— Fyodor Dostoyevsky, *The House of the Dead*

Introduction

Several hours before the first pitch at Baltimore's Oriole Park at Camden Yards, Adam Jones strides through the spacious home clubhouse, brimming with upbeat energy. He jokes with teammates, banters with reporters, flashes an incandescent smile. The Orioles are contending for a playoff berth, and Jones, their star center fielder, is having another big year.

Wearing shower slippers, white baseball pants, and a tight black T-shirt that emphasizes his muscular torso, he drops into a recliner in front of his locker. Batting practice begins in 30 minutes; he has a few minutes to talk. "Whatcha got?" he asks. I tell him I want to know about his desire to play in every game. He nods and, before I ask a question, sprays a thought in rat-a-tat fashion.

"I'm never going to say to the manager, 'Hey, I need a day off.' I'm just never going to go into his office and utter those words," Jones says. "For me to not play, he's going to have to decide to leave me out of the lineup."

A first-round draft choice as an 18-year-old from Southern California and a major leaguer by 22, Jones, now in his early 30s, is the brightest of baseball lights. Every year he hits almost 30 home runs, plays defense worthy of a Gold Glove, and piles up runs batted in — and he does it all with a glib lightheartedness, romping through interviews, interacting with fans on social media, chomping gum and blowing bubbles as he plays. For many years, when teammates conducted television interviews on the field after a Baltimore victory, Jones snuck up and slammed them in the face with a pie from the clubhouse kitchen.

But he also is the rare modern player who respects baseball traditions that go back decades. He plays with the bottoms of his uniform pant legs cut near his knees, revealing more than a foot of his black-and-white stirrup socks — a fashion long out of style. He swings his bat ferociously, seemingly giving little thought to the statistical metrics that now guide how the game is played. He runs so hard on the bases, even on routine ground balls, that his cap flies off.

And he never wants to miss a game. Not one.

"There are days when I wake up sore and think, 'Oh, it would be a great day to not play, or to DH.' But once I get myself up and ready and I'm on my way to the ballpark, I want to play," Jones says. "If I'm not injured or not dealing with something that would bar me from playing, I don't see why I shouldn't be in the lineup."

The topic of playing every day is holy terrain in Baltimore, where Cal Ripken Jr., a shortstop for the Orioles, went more than 16 years without missing a game, setting the major league record for consecutive games played — 2,632. "The streak," as it is known, made Ripken a sports star of the highest eminence and resonated far beyond baseball's typical boundaries of renown. The president and vice president of the United States both saw him set the record in Baltimore on September 6, 1995. Political commentators suggested his work ethic symbolized all that was right and good about America.

Before Ripken, the consecutive-game record belonged to Lou Gehrig, the New York Yankees' powerful, ill-fated slugger, whose streak of 2,130 straight games was stopped by the onset of a fatal disease in 1939. Before Gehrig, Everett Scott, a slender shortstop for the Yankees and Boston Red Sox during and after World War I, held the record, and others such as the St. Louis Cardinals' Stan Musial, the Chicago Cubs' Billy Williams, and the Los Angeles Dodgers' Steve Garvey also compiled long streaks, stacking season after season of perfect attendance.

It is a complex achievement, widely admired yet also subjected to criticism at times. Gehrig's teammate Babe Ruth mocked Gehrig for playing so long without a day off, sneering that the Yankees did not pay him to do that. Miller Huggins, Scott's manager in New York, was annoyed that he had to keep playing the light-hitting shortstop simply because of a record. While in the process of setting the National League consecutive-game record in the 1960s, Billy Williams wondered aloud why he was bothering to do it. When Ripken went through slumps at the plate, newspaper columnists and radio talk-show callers practically screeched that he was being selfish for refusing to sit out a game and recharge.

They all played on despite injuries, illnesses, and fatigue to complete full seasons of 162 games (154 until the early 1960s); played with bruises, headaches, pulled muscles, even broken bones; played when they did not feel like it; yet always played well enough to keep their place in the lineup.

More recently, higher salaries, guaranteed contracts, advanced statistical analysis, and more sophisticated sports medicine have helped change baseball's philosophy on feats of endurance. Unlike in the eras of Scott, Gehrig, and even Ripken, few current players even attempt to play entire seasons without taking a break.

"I don't know that we'll ever see another guy get to a thousand games in a row, much less to how far Gehrig and Cal went," Garvey said in an interview for this book in 2015.

But endurance has remained a tradition and a priority in Baltimore since Ripken's retirement in 2001. Another Baltimore shortstop, Miguel Tejada, compiled the major leagues' longest consecutive-game streak of the twenty-first century. Nick Markakis, a taciturn right fielder, missed just 11 games over a five-year span beginning in 2007. Jones, who played alongside Markakis in the outfield starting in 2009, vowed to follow his teammate's lead. "I was like, 'Markakis is out there every day. Man, I want to be out there with him,'" Jones says.

From 2012 through 2014, Jones missed just 5 of 486 regular-season games, achieving perfect attendance in 2012 by playing in all 162. "I was exhausted," Jones admits. Injuries forced him out of several dozen games in 2015 and 2016, but Manny Machado, the team's young third baseman, caught the bug from Markakis and Jones. He was the only major leaguer to play a full season in 2015.

"We've got a bunch of guys on this team who want to play every day. It's a consensus around here," Jones says. "Maybe there are times when a day off can help you clear your head, but the competitor in me wants to get back out there because I think that day I might go 4-for-4. Every day when I go to the park I think I'm going to do something positive to impact the game, and that's why I want to play."

In 2012, the Orioles signed Jones to an $85.5 million contract extension, and he effectively became the face of the franchise, as Ripken was — and, in a way, still is. The two see each other around Baltimore, where Ripken still resides.

"Every time I see Cal, I ask him about playing every day for all of those years," Jones said. "I say it all the time to him. I go, 'Cal, how did you do that? Honestly, how in the hell did you do that?'"

Jones shakes his head.

"All Cal says is, 'I wanted to play.' He breaks it down as simply as that. 'I wanted to play.'"

Again, Jones shakes his head.

"I played in 162 once, and that's impressive, but to do it for 16 straight years, that's . . . that's . . . that's . . ."

For once, the loquacious Jones is at a loss for words.

The Streak

1

Ripken

A VICTORY LAP

The fans sent wave after wave of cheers into a warm, late-summer night by the Chesapeake Bay, their ovation lasting three minutes, five, eight . . . so long that the umpires finally decided not to try to restart the game until the noise subsided. The Baltimore Orioles and California Angels had only played 4½ in Baltimore on September 6, 1995. Their game was just half over. And the longer the fans cheered, the more Cal Ripken Jr., the Orioles' shortstop, whose historic feat was being celebrated, was becoming embarrassed about the length of the delay.

The Orioles were out of the American League playoff race, but the Angels had a shot at winning their division, so it mattered that they trailed Baltimore by two runs at the brick-and-wrought-iron ballpark known as Oriole Park at Camden Yards. Their pitcher, Shawn Boskie, had warmed up for the bottom of the fifth inning. He was ready to go. His teammates were at their defensive positions, also ready. But the cheering for Ripken was so persistent that the game could not possibly resume, and now Boskie was cooling down, seemingly a disadvantage.

Trying to quell the ovation, Ripken had twice emerged from the Orioles' dugout, waving his arms and patting his heart to acknowledge the cheers and indicate his appreciation. He was deeply touched. But he hoped his gesture would bring the celebration to a close, much like an actor's curtain call on a Broadway stage. He owed that to the Angels, he thought. But the fans just kept cheering. If anything, they were getting louder.

Ripken's teammates had convinced him to take the second curtain call, thinking that would end the ovation and enable the game to resume. But it did not, and now Ripken was back on the dugout bench, shaking his head, smiling, and wondering what he could do to stop the noise raining down from the stands.

"Hey, why don't you go run around the field or something?" shouted Rafael Palmeiro, Baltimore's first baseman, who stood in front of Ripken.

Ripken looked at him with a quizzical expression. Run around the field?

Palmeiro shrugged. "I don't know. Go out there and shake their hands," he continued. "Maybe that will get them to stop."

As Ripken pondered the idea, Palmeiro quickly repeated it, adding with a shout, "You need to go out there!"

Another veteran teammate, Bobby Bonilla, picked up on the suggestion. Seated next to Ripken on the bench, Bonilla leaned over and shouted in his teammate's ear, "Junior, if you don't go out there, we may never finish this game!"

Ripken gave a halfhearted smile, clearly unconvinced. Spontaneous gestures made him uncomfortable. He was a planner, a pragmatist. Whatever endeavor he undertook, on or off the baseball diamond, he researched it, reflected on it, devised an approach, and saw it through. "He wore a watch in batting practice to make sure everything ran on time. That's how organized and precise he was in everything he did," recalled Phil Regan, the Orioles' manager in 1995. And running around the field in the middle of this historic game was not in Ripken's plans.

Honestly, he thought it sounded ridiculous. Who had ever heard of such a thing? The game was his day at the office, a sacred time reserved for focusing on his job, his craft, his teammates and opponents. Interacting with fans was the last thing he should do, even on a night history was being made. Ripken's father, a crusty baseball lifer, had taught him the sport's sober code of conduct. *Respect the game. Let your performance do your talking. The game matters more than you.*

Running around the field and shaking hands with fans in the fifth inning was antithetical to everything Ripken believed. But Palmeiro was not interested in debating philosophy. He just wanted to get the game going again.

He grabbed Ripken by the shoulders and pulled the six-foot-four, 230-pound shortstop up the dugout steps. Bonilla joined in, holding Ripken's left arm. They pulled him onto the field, dragged him a few steps, and playfully shoved him down the right-field foul line. Ripken, laughing, offered no resistance.

"Pushing him out of the dugout wasn't planned. We didn't talk about it beforehand or anything," Palmeiro recalled. "The fans were just so incredibly into the situation. It was a nonstop ovation. As long as Cal sat in the dugout, we might still be sitting there. When we said, 'Go run around the field or something,' he wouldn't do it. So we pushed him out there."

The fans roared at the sight of Ripken back on the field. He took several wandering steps, hugged one of the Orioles' coaches, and waved. Palmeiro's idea echoed in his mind. Run around. Shake hands with them.

"OK," Ripken thought. "I'll try it."

It was the strangest of baseball celebrations when you thought about it — not the product of an awe-inducing home run barrage, prodigious career hit record, or any of the kinds of spectacular achievements that usually generated acclaim. Ripken was in the spotlight for the simplest of baseball acts: Just being on the field. Playing. As opposed to not playing.

His repertoire of talents included much more than just his enduring presence, of course. A sure-handed fielder and reliably productive hitter, he would earn two American League Most Valuable Player awards and make 15 All-Star Game appearances by the end of his 21-year major league career. The first shortstop to accumulate 3,000 hits and 400 home runs, he would alter basic notions about his position. Once he came along, a shortstop could hit for power and anchor a lineup as well as solidify his team's infield defense. When Ripken was eligible for induction into the National Baseball Hall of Fame in Cooperstown, New York, in 2007, an overwhelming 98.6 percent of the Baseball Writers' Association of America's voters said he belonged.

Yet the most outstanding aspect of his career was the fact that he played in 2,632 straight games, all for the Orioles.

For more than 16 years, from May 30, 1982, through September 19, 1998, he was ever present in Baltimore's lineup. The Orioles' fortunes careened through soaring highs, such as a World Series triumph, and appalling lows, such as a season-opening 21-game losing streak. Ripken never rested. They made seven managerial changes, including the hiring and firing of Ripken's father. He continued to play. The United States went through four presidential election seasons, electing Ronald Reagan in 1984, George H. W. Bush in 1988, Bill Clinton in 1992, and Clinton again in 1996. Ripken never missed a game.

Along the way, he badly sprained an ankle, twisted a knee in a brawl, bowled over catchers in home-plate collisions, was hit by dozens of pitches, fought the flu, developed a serious back ailment, and grew from a callow youngster to a middle-aged father of two. But he never suffered an injury that forced him to stop playing, and he never said he was so tired that he needed to take a game off.

No major leaguer had ever played so continuously without interruption, and his consecutive-game streak eventually earned a place on baseball's list of iconic feats, alongside such achievements as Joe DiMaggio's 56-game hitting streak, the home run records of Babe Ruth and Hank Aaron, and the accomplishments of such legends as Cy Young and Ty Cobb. But unlike the others, Ripken did not have to hit a home run, reach base, or perform extraordinarily in any way in a game to further his record. In fact, he could strike out four times, boot ground balls, and draw boos. As long as he fulfilled the requirements for being credited with playing, he added another game to his streak and perpetuated his reputation for earnest dependability.

He just had to play.

Why pursue this unusual challenge, something of a crazy uncle in the family of baseball feats? Ripken steadfastly denied he was purposefully pursuing *anything*, especially the major league record for consecutive games played, held by Lou Gehrig, the slugging first baseman who played in 2,130 straight games for the New York Yankees, stopping only when he was diagnosed with a fatal illness in 1939. No, Ripken said, he was not doing this just to pass Gehrig and polish his own star of individual glory. He contended it was his job to be available and his Baltimore managers actually created the streak by continually putting him in the lineup. His part in the streak's complex calculus, he said, was simply wanting to play.

Some found that explanation simplistic at best and disingenuous at worst. At times, his hitting slumped to the point that it seemed logical for him to want to take a break, miss a game or two, and collect himself —a tactic many players use when trying to end slumps. When Ripken persisted, seeking to play his way out of his slumps, some fans and analysts accused him of valuing his streak more than his team's best interests. In 2009, Buster Olney, an ESPN analyst who covered the Orioles for the

Baltimore Sun in the 1990s, told journalism students at Bowdoin College in Maine that Ripken was "without a doubt the most selfish athlete I ever covered, and it's not even close." Within a few years of the end of Ripken's streak, few major leaguers would attempt to play every game of even one season, much less many in a row. Baseball's philosophy on endurance experienced a tectonic shift. It no longer seemed practical to play every day for so long.

Ripken abhorred accusations of selfishness both when he played and long after, believing the Orioles always benefited from his presence in a game, regardless if he hit two home runs or struck out four times. He quarterbacked the defense, altered how other Orioles were pitched to, provided a foundation on which the team was built. There were always ways for him to put his experience and knowledge to work. When playing with inexperienced pitchers and catchers late in his career, he occasionally called the pitches for them from his perch in the middle infield.

If he truly were selfish, Ripken said later, he would have asked out of the lineup when the Orioles faced dominant pitchers such as Randy Johnson or Roger Clemens, who frustrated many batters and caused their averages to drop. "I would argue that the real selfish guys were the ones ducking Roger or Nolan Ryan, coming up with an injury or something so they didn't have to play that day. I saw that multiple times in my career, guys thinking about themselves, not the team. My brother always went out there, even on tough days for him, because he thought he could help the team," said Bill Ripken, Cal's younger brother, who played for four teams, including the Orioles, during a 12-year major league career.

Ripken's teammates and managers supported his contention that he should play every game. Even though he was 35 years old in 1995, he batted .262 that season and drove in 88 runs, and his manager never doubted whether he belonged on the field. "Cal was still outstanding, on top of his game. It was a pleasure to play him every day," Phil Regan recalled. "He was enthusiastic. He wasn't tired. His arm was still good. And the biggest thing was, he knew the American League so well. You didn't have to position him. He knew every player by heart. He directed the whole infield. The team accepted what he was doing as something very special."

As Ripken approached Gehrig's record in 1995, the criticism of him dwindled to a murmur, then was extinguished entirely. Controversy gave way to a nearly unanimous appreciation of his achievement. Ripken had stayed healthy enough and played well enough to keep his place in the lineup for what seemed an eternity. The odds against this were astronomical; even the best players usually were relegated to the bench now and then. How could you not be awed by Ripken's strength, consistency, and determination?

When he passed Gehrig and established a new consecutive-game record of 2,131 games on September 6, 1995, Ripken received baseball's version of a royal coronation. President Bill Clinton came from Washington to watch, as did Clinton's vice president, Al Gore. The evening compared with other historic baseball moments, such as the night in 1974 when Hank Aaron became the game's all-time home run leader, or the night in 1985 when the Cincinnati Reds' Pete Rose became the all-time leader in base hits. The home fans cheered until they grew hoarse. Millions watched ESPN's broadcast.

Arguably, Ripken engineered even more adulation than Rose or Aaron. His was truly the common man's record, one to which the public could relate. Fans could not bash home runs like Aaron or bang out hits like Rose, but they went to work every day, as Ripken did. "That's how he saw himself, through a blue-collar lens," said Richie Bancells, a trainer for the Orioles who worked with Ripken for a quarter century. "He equated playing shortstop every day to being a welder who went to work every day, or a guy punching a clock at a factory."

It was Ripken's populist ethos that drew the president and vice president to Camden Yards to see him pass Gehrig. And Ripken, as always, just had to play that night. Still, it was important that he somehow make the occasion memorable. Baseball desperately needed the positive message his record generated.

A year earlier, the game had experienced one of its darkest moments when the major league season was halted in August because of a labor impasse. When team owners and the players' union could not agree on a collective bargaining agreement, the rest of the 1994 regular season and the playoffs were canceled. For the first time in 92 years, there was no World Series matching the American League and National League winners. Millions of fans reacted furiously, claiming they would never again support such selfish players and owners. Major league attendance declined after the dispute ended in time for the 1995 season to proceed.

Although Ripken was a loyal union member and one of the sport's highest-paid players, he was widely viewed — correctly, according to his agent — as an outlier among his peers, a throwback to a time when men played baseball because they loved it, not because it made them rich. "I'm not going to say he didn't want to make the good money, but that never impacted his approach to the game. He loved it as much as anyone I have known," said Ron Shapiro, a Baltimore attorney who represented many major leaguers, including Ripken, beginning in the 1970s.

As Ripken passed Gehrig, his achievement amounted to a gift from baseball to its angry fans, a peace offering reaffirming the game's ability to excite and amaze. It was no exaggeration to suggest, as some commentators would, that Ripken carried his sport's good name on his broad shoulders as he began circling the field and celebrating with fans in the middle of the fifth inning that night in Baltimore.

There was no plan, no script. Ripken had no idea how long he would be out there, or what he would do. Whatever happened, he hoped it would eventually quell the ovation.

He jogged toward the tiered bank of field-level seats down the right-field line. The eyes of the fans in the front rows widened. They were excited just to be at Camden Yards to see history being made, but now Ripken was coming toward them. Was this really happening?

Ripken stopped at the railing with his right hand extended. A fan grabbed it for a shake. Ripken moved down the line, jogging lightly, almost skipping, shaking more hands and slapping palms. His white home uniform glinted in the stadium lights, as did his spikes of close-cropped gray hair. Fans from the higher rows rushed to the railing, hoping to shake his hand. It was as if he were a politician at a rally, or the pope after his Wednesday service at the Vatican.

Fred Roussey, a sergeant with the Baltimore police, was among a cordon of officers within feet of Ripken, standing by the foul line. Roussey had worked hundreds of Orioles games and would work hundreds more in the coming years. "Normally when you have a rush of fans to the railing like that, there's trouble, but the crowd that night was unlike any other," Roussey recalled. "No one was going to fight. Everyone was so ecstatic just to be there, so happy for Cal. When he started going down the line, the atmosphere was pure excitement."

Ripken had the same thought. Two decades later, recalling what would become known as his "victory lap" around Camden Yards, he said he was staggered by the emotional wallop of celebrating with the fans as the noise in the park swirled. "My initial reaction was, 'OK, I'm trying this to see if I can get the game started again,'" he recalled. "But once I began making my way around the field, I didn't care if the game started again or not."

Now that he was close to the fans, actually *with* the fans, he could sense their connection to him and his achievement. Ripken was one of them, a native of Aberdeen, Maryland, just north of Baltimore. Like many reaching for his hand, he had grown up supporting the Orioles, his father's employer, and also followed the Colts, Baltimore's National Football League team for many years. His hometown was a workingman's city without the sniffy airs of nearby Washington, D.C., a city where professors from Johns Hopkins University sat at games alongside bus drivers and steelworkers. Ripken fit right in. His father had raised him to be a baseball foot soldier, not a king.

At one point, Baltimore had brimmed over with sports successes, its teams winning titles and developing ardent followings, the Colts' crowds so enthusiastic a sportswriter referred to their games as "the world's largest outdoor insane asylum." But a pro basketball team, the Bullets, left for Washington in the 1970s, and the Colts' owner, Robert Irsay, an alcoholic air-conditioning magnate described by his own mother as a "devil on earth," failed to obtain funding for a new stadium and moved the team to Indianapolis in 1984, devastating fans and leaving them with just one team to root for, the Orioles, who then exacerbated the city's hurt by entering a steep decline soon after the Colts left.

Ripken had come along in these turbulent years, debuting with the Orioles in 1981 and catching the last out of their World Series victory in 1983, then playing through a long, dismal run of losing seasons, in the process becoming just about all Baltimore had to cheer for. On the night he passed Gehrig, the city's pride was palpable. Its teams had not won anything in a while, but its native son was making history, and he was an athlete to be proud of, not cocky or boastful, his priorities seemingly in order. Before embarking on his victory lap, he took off his jersey and game cap and presented them to his wife, Kelly, and their two young children, five-year-old Rachel and two-year-old Ryan, who were seated in the front row by the Orioles' dugout. Underneath his jersey, he wore a black T-shirt with the inscription 2,130 + HUGS AND KISSES FOR DADDY.

"He could have been elected mayor of Baltimore, governor of Maryland, really anything he wanted," recalled Al Clark, a veteran American League umpire who was on the field that night.

The Orioles had spent weeks preparing for the home games when he would tie and break the record, hoping to stage events that lived up to an occasion fans had waited years to see. The night before, when Ripken tied Gehrig's record, hitting a home run in an Orioles victory, there had been a postgame ceremony on the field during which he received gifts and testimonials from sports and entertainment celebrities such as Tom Selleck, a baseball-loving actor; David Robinson, a basketball star from northern Virginia; and Bonnie Blair, an Olympic speed skater who had won gold medals.

Now, a night later, the game was official in the middle of the fifth inning, Ripken owned the record, and he had hit another home run, delighting the crowd. There would be another ceremony later, more speeches, more gifts, more testimony, all culminating in a speech by Ripken.

But nothing planned in advance could match what unfolded on his impromptu lap around the field. "It turned out to be the best 'human moment' of my career," Ripken recalled. "Catching the last out of the World Series was my best baseball moment, because that's what every kid dreams of, and I experienced it. But the victory lap was my best human moment."

Having started in a counterclockwise direction around the edge of Camden Yards' natural-grass field, he quickly reached the right-field corner, where the stands were situated well above him. He jumped up to slap hands with fans, then continued across the outfield warning track toward center field, acknowledging the cheers with waves and shaking hands with several members of the grounds crew, who had emerged from the shed where they sat during games and stood on the grass, applauding. Several policemen watching the crowd also slapped hands with Ripken as he passed by.

Seated in the second row of an outfield section, Al Fultz, a 37-year-old federal disability claims examiner from Catonsville, a Baltimore suburb, reached out to touch Ripken. "There was quite a rush of fans to the front row, people trying to shake his hand. Obviously no one expected him to come so close to where we sat, in the bleachers," Fultz recalled.

Fultz had bought five tickets to the game six months earlier and resisted offers from potential buyers as the big night neared. His wife, two of their three young daughters, and his brother-in-law were with him, and already, by the middle of the fifth, they knew it would be an unforgettable night. Fultz and his wife and daughters had made up white T-shirts with single numbers on the front spelling out 2,131 when they stood together. "Total strangers had been taking our picture all night," Fultz said. Then, in the second inning, his brother-in-law had caught a Palmeiro home run, breaking a finger in the process.

Shaking Ripken's hand on the victory lap would have provided Fultz, a lifelong Orioles fan, with the ultimate memory. "But where we were, Cal was just too far down," Fultz said. "But everyone there experienced something special. As he was on his lap, I reflected on how it must feel to know you're making so many people happy."

There was bedlam in the ballpark as Ripken jogged through deep center field. One fan leaned too far forward and tumbled out of the stands. Several others dangled on the outside of the outfield fence with their hands outstretched. Ripken jumped up, slapped their palms, and continued his trek along the fence, encountering teammates, the Orioles' relief pitchers, who spent games in the bullpen beyond left-center field. Like the fans, they had lined up along the fence with their hands extended. Ripken reached over and gave each a shake, stopping to clasp hands in a special embrace with Elrod Hendricks, the Orioles' jocular bullpen coach, a Baltimore fixture who had known him since he was a boy.

Leaving Hendricks behind, Ripken entered deep left field, where the stands were within easy reach. A sea of arms reached for him. He slowed down, shook some hands, waved, jogged several feet, shook more hands. Noticing a small girl amid the human crush, he reached in and made sure she received a handshake. One fan accidentally dropped a pen onto the field. Ripken picked it up and tossed it back into the crowd. Other fans held up signs reading THE HOUSE THAT CAL BUILT and PRESIDENT CLINTON, CAN YOU HELP ME GET CAL'S AUTOGRAPH?

After Ripken passed through the left-field corner, he turned toward home plate, now just walking as he continued to shake hands, point at some fans, and even speak to a few. It was as if he knew everyone. One man reached across the railing and touched his chest. Unafraid, Ripken grabbed the man's hand and shook it, then stepped back and waved to the crowd, first with one arm, then both.

As he came down the third-base side of the park and neared the Angels' dugout, two of the four umpires working the game intercepted him — Larry Barnett, the crew chief, who was behind home plate that night, and Al Clark, the second-most-senior ump on the crew, who was working third base. Barnett shook Ripken's hand and shouted congratulations. Ripken nodded. "Then I shook his hand," Clark recalled, "and Cal bent over to me and said, 'God, am I tired.' He was practically leaning on me. I said to him, 'Cal, you can stay here as long as you want.'"

When the ovation for Ripken had started after the top of the fifth, Barnett and Clark briefly looked at each other with their eyebrows raised, wondering what to do. "Part of our job is to keep the game moving. We thought about reining him in," Clark said. "Then we looked at each other and said, 'Are you fucking kidding me?' There was no way in the world we were going to stop what was going on."

As the victory lap unfolded, all four umpires joined the fans in cheering the Orioles shortstop.

"It was the only time in my 26 years in the majors that I saw the umpires applaud the efforts of a player," Clark said. "But we respected the hell out of what Cal did, playing in all those games. We don't care who wins and loses, but we care about baseball, and with a strike canceling the World Series the year before, our game had been dealt a terrible blow. Everything was negative, and then here came Cal, and everything was positive — his work ethic, his approach, the way he interacted with fans. It all came together that night. I felt tremendous pride just being in the same sport with him. I remember thinking, 'This is what's going to bring our game back.'"

Having circled most of the field, Ripken entered the visitors' dugout on the third-base side. The Angels were lined up on the top step, anticipating his arrival. Ripken shook hands and exchanged words with every player and coach. He embraced Rod Carew, the team's hitting coach, a brilliant contact hitter from the 1970s, now in the Hall of Fame. Rene Gonzales, a former teammate in Baltimore, grasped him in a hug.

Years later, Ripken would single out his interactions with the Angels as an especially memorable aspect of his record-breaking evening. "How often are you ever going to see something like that in the middle of a game?" he said.

The Angels' catcher, Jorge Fabregas, had warmed up Boskie for the bottom of the fifth and then joined the line of Angels waiting to offer congratulations in the dugout. Dressed in his catching garb, right down to his mask, Fabregas shook hands with Ripken and jogged back to his spot behind the plate.

Rex Hudler, the Angels' second baseman, watched the dugout scene enviously from the middle of the infield. Although he also was playing in the game, like Fabregas Hudler thought it would look strange for him to sprint to the dugout just to congratulate Ripken. "It was one time in my career when I wished I wasn't playing. Man, I wanted to be in that dugout," Hudler recalled.

A 35-year-old journeyman, Hudler had briefly played with Ripken on the Orioles in the 1980s. "I was there when Cal's dad managed. He was a rough old bird, man. On the team plane he'd come walking up the aisle and slap me right in the chest. I learned that meant he liked me!" Hudler said. "So I knew Junior, and to be on the field as this happened, I basically became a kid again — a young kid in a big league uniform."

Hudler had warmed up for the bottom of the fifth by taking some ground balls, then watched with astonishment as the cheering started and continued for so long that Ripken embarked on his journey around the field. "No one went, 'Oh no, look what he's doing.' The reaction was, 'He's going to high-five everyone here! This is the coolest thing ever!'" Hudler recalled.

As the lap ended, Hudler looked down and saw he was standing not by second base, but on the pitching rubber, some 40 or 50 feet from his position. "It was like I had been in a trance, just wandering around out there on the field," he said. "It was like I was dreaming."

When Ripken finished with the Angels, he stepped out of the dugout and greeted several people behind home plate. "Not bad, huh?" he said as he hugged his agent, Ron Shapiro.

Watching from a private suite overlooking the field, Ripken's 58-year-old father, Cal Ripken Sr., could scarcely believe what he had seen. Senior, as he was known, was out of baseball now after having worked for the Orioles from the 1950s through 1992. In all his years as a minor league player, minor league manager, scout, major league coach, and major league manager, he had never imagined he would see a player, especially his son, circle the field during a game.

This ovation was a hell of a thing, though, Senior had to admit. Before the victory lap, his son had located him and waved while acknowledging the cheers, and Senior had waved back—a father-son moment Hollywood could have scripted.

"I locked eyes with him. He was a man of few words when it came to how he felt about his son. But that look said a million words to me," Junior recalled.

Senior could scarcely believe his son had gone all the way around the field shaking hands and the fans still were applauding.

Within a few years, the way the world celebrated important moments would change dramatically. But in 1995, none of the fans at Camden Yards held a smartphone aloft, enabling them to film the scene or pose for selfies; all the emotion was directed at Ripken. Smartphones would not come along until the new century, and neither would social media, so Ripken's victory lap was not subjected to snarky comments on Facebook or Twitter.

"No one was second-guessing whether Cal should have taken the lap," wrote John Maroon, the Orioles' director of media relations in 1995, in an essay published 20 years later. "Social media has been an amazing tool that has changed our world, but some things, I believe, are best left to our memories and allowed to unfold the way we see them and recall them, rather than the way they are interpreted by others."

When the lap ended and he had no hands left to shake, Ripken lumbered down the Orioles' dugout steps, plopped on the bench, and blew out a breath, obviously winded. A trainer threw him a towel, and he wiped the sweat from his face. His teammates surrounded him, slapped him on the back. He exchanged wordless smiles with Palmeiro, who had suggested he take the lap.

"When anyone remembers that night, that's what they remember, that victory lap," Palmeiro recalled. "It was Cal's way of saying thank you to the fans. What a way to do it, man."

After a minute on the bench, Ripken abruptly jumped up, climbed the dugout steps, and stepped back onto the field to take yet another curtain call. The crowd continued to buzz. Ripken tapped his heart, mouthed the words "thank you," and shook his head, seemingly in disbelief at the persistence of the cheers. ESPN showed a close-up of his wife, Kelly, dabbing a tear.

Bill Ripken stood beside Kelly in a front-row seat behind home plate. A former Oriole, he knew his older brother was authoring an indelible sports moment. Baseball fans across the country would remember his one-of-a-kind victory lap. In Baltimore, it would rank with the exploits of Johnny Unitas, the famous Colts quarterback, who once threw at least one touchdown pass in 47 straight NFL games; and Brooks Robinson, the Orioles' Hall of Fame third baseman, whose fielding was so slick that fans nicknamed him "the Human Vacuum Cleaner."

"Baltimore fans had always connected with guys like Johnny and Brooks because it's a blue-collar town and they were so humble. If you saw them out somewhere, you could talk to them," Bill Ripken said. "That night, with Junior, the connection was even more intense. Here was an actual native son getting cheered just for doing his job. During that victory lap, what you saw was true gratitude. It was perfect."

2

Gehrig

THE GHOST OF 2,131

Soon after the last out in the top of the fifth, when it became official that Ripken had broken Lou Gehrig's record, silence enveloped ESPN's broadcast booth at Camden Yards. Chris Berman and Buck Martinez, the announcers calling the game, recognized that the images being captured by their network's cameras were more powerful than any words. They just watched Ripken circle the field, leaving the crowd's cheers as a soundtrack.

Berman ordinarily dominated the air with his booming baritone and gregarious character, spewing a rat-a-tat litany of nicknames, puns, and historical references while fulfilling his play-by-play duties. To prepare for this broadcast, he had read a Gehrig biography, helping him understand the enormity of Ripken's feat. But he said later he and Martinez, a former major league catcher, could not speak because they were shedding tears as Ripken hugged his wife and kids, waved to his father, and celebrated with the fans as he toured the field.

It was an emotional scene with inescapable significance. Baseball had broken its promise to its public by ending its season prematurely the year before, but now Ripken was literally extending his hand to the fans, as if to try to right the wrong by himself.

"People were mad, and they had a right to be," Ripken recalled. "But people were in tune with the streak. It helped bring the game back. I think I played a part in that."

During the stoppage in the game, which lasted 22 minutes, ESPN's producers occasionally cut away from the field to shots of Ripken's family members and some of the famous baseball figures in the crowd, all of whom were standing and applauding. There was Earl Weaver, the feisty bantam who had managed the Orioles in their heyday, which included the first years of Ripken's streak. There was Frank Robinson, an iconic Orioles outfielder from the 1960s, who also managed Ripken at one point. There was Carew, a Hall of Famer still in uniform.

Then there was the handsome, white-haired man watching in a private suite, a vision of elegance in a dark suit, his hair practically shimmering. ESPN cut to him once, again, a third time, underscoring his importance. Who was he? Many viewers knew, even without an introduction from Berman. His face was familiar to older fans from his years as a baseball star. Younger generations knew him as a television commercial pitchman.

It was Joe DiMaggio.

The New York Yankees star from a bygone era was more than just a great ballplayer in the canon of American celebrity. Taciturn and dignified, he was an emblem of graceful manhood, a defining figure of his epoch. In the 1950s, millions of men fantasized about Marilyn Monroe, the sultry actress. DiMaggio married her. When she died, he brought flowers to her grave out of love and loyalty, even though they had divorced. Rock star Paul Simon's 1968 hit song "Mrs. Robinson" contained the iconic lyric "Where have you gone, Joe DiMaggio? . . . / 'Joltin Joe' has left and gone away." Simon was signaling that he believed genuine heroes no longer existed.

In the mid-1930s, at the outset of his major league career, DiMaggio had played four full seasons and part of a fifth with Lou Gehrig. As Ripken's record-setting night approached in 1995, the Orioles contacted him to see if he wanted to attend the game at Camden Yards and represent his late teammate. Peter Angelos, the Baltimore attorney who owned the Orioles, called DiMaggio himself and extended the offer. "At my age, he was my baseball hero," Angelos explained.

The Orioles had not expected DiMaggio to accept Angelos's invitation. Now 80 years old, he was famously private, seldom socializing beyond a small circle of friends in Florida. But to the Orioles' delight, he accepted. "I wanted to be there and see it because Gehrig was my teammate," DiMaggio said later.

The Orioles asked only that he attend; his presence alone elevated the occasion. But DiMaggio had shown up full of enthusiasm, attending a pregame party and asking if he could speak at the postgame ceremony the Orioles had carefully planned — a request the Orioles excitedly accepted.

Later that night, during the ceremony that followed the game, the crowd greeted his introduction with a roar, an audible buzz ripping through the ballpark as he strode toward the dais that had been set up on the diamond: *DiMaggio is here!*

"There's a beautiful monument to Lou Gehrig at Yankee Stadium that says 'A man, a gentleman, and a great ball player whose amazing record of 2130 consecutive games should stand for all time,'" DiMaggio told the crowd. "That goes to prove that even the greatest records are made to be broken. And wherever my former teammate Lou Gehrig is today, I'm sure he's tipping his cap to you, Cal Ripken."

It was more than just a nice touch. Ripken's record-setting night would have been incomplete without Gehrig also being acknowledged. A combination of ingredients had helped make Ripken's streak a larger-than-life achievement — fans could relate to it, Ripken seemed so deserving of acclaim, and it had taken him more than 13 years — but no ingredient was more important than the fact that it was Gehrig's record he was breaking. Gehrig's legend, like DiMaggio's, extended well beyond baseball's normal boundaries of renown.

After growing up shy and clumsy, almost bumbling, as the only child of struggling German-immigrant parents in New York City in the early 1900s, Gehrig had matured into a slugging first baseman standing six feet one and weighing 230 pounds. With thick hands, a square jaw, a thick chest, and massive thighs stretching the fabric of his uniform, he joined the Yankees and became a fixture in their lineup, conveying the classic image of invulnerable strength in the years before weight training became fashionable and performance-enhancing drugs sculpted inhuman physiques. Like Ripken, he played through injuries, illnesses, and slumps for more than a decade, never succumbing to the temptation to rest, even for a day. Sportswriters dubbed him "the Iron Horse," the perfect nickname for a seemingly indestructible human concrete block.

Shortly before he debuted with the Yankees in 1923, their shortstop, Everett Scott, became the first major leaguer to play in a thousand straight games. Gehrig eventually went more than twice as far. In 1931, he reached a thousand. In 1933, he broke Scott's major league record of 1,307 consecutive games. In 1935, he completed a full decade of continuous play.

DiMaggio, who joined the Yankees as a rookie in 1936, was in center field on August 3, 1937, when the club celebrated "Lou Gehrig Appreciation Day" in honor of his pushing his streak to 1,900 consecutive games. Gehrig had always ceded the spotlight to more luminous players such as Babe Ruth and DiMaggio, but this was his day. When he strode to the plate in the bottom of the first before 66,000 fans, the crowd gave him an ovation. A pitcher for the Chicago White Sox hurled a fastball. Gehrig twisted his thick lower torso, unleashed a vicious swing, and made contact. The ball soared off his bat in a high arc, headed for right field. Gehrig tossed his bat and sprinted for first base, then eased up as the ball soared into the distant bleachers. With his first swing on Lou Gehrig Appreciation Day, he had pounded a long home run, leaving no doubt that he remained a force at the plate even though he was 34, with gray flecks dotting his dark scalp.

Later, sportswriters crowded around him in the clubhouse and asked about his playing streak. Several New York columnists had suggested he should rest now that he was older. He disagreed, saying he wanted to reach 2,000 straight games and keep going. But soon after he reached that threshold, his life took a devastating turn. He played so wretchedly early in the 1939 season, failing to hit and botching routine fielding plays, that he took himself out of the lineup, ending his streak at 2,130 straight games. Seeking an explanation, he visited the Mayo Clinic in Rochester, Minnesota, where tests produced a stunning diagnosis: Gehrig had amyotrophic lateral sclerosis (ALS), an obscure, debilitating neurological disease marked by rapidly developing weakness and muscle atrophy. His baseball career was over, and his prospects for a long life had dimmed.

On July 4, 1939, the Yankees staged a second Lou Gehrig Appreciation Day, this one far more melancholy than the one in 1937. Ruth and others lauded the Iron Horse in a ceremony between games of a doubleheader before a teeming crowd at Yankee Stadium. Finally, Gehrig stepped to the microphone, his uniform belt cinched tight around his gaunt waist.

"For the past two weeks, you've been reading about a bad break," he said, his voice thick with emotion. "Today, I consider myself the luckiest man on the face of the earth."

The crowd roared. Gehrig continued, explaining how fortunate he felt to have played on so many great Yankees teams. He thanked his teammates, the fans, even the men in the press box. His grace left many in the crowd in tears.

Within two years, he was dead.

To millions of Americans, it was almost as if Superman, the insurmountable comic-book hero, had succumbed.

No matter how Gehrig's career ended, he was assured of a prominent place in baseball's annals. Although he paled next to Ruth as a charismatic star, he had played on six World Series–winning teams, compiled a .340 lifetime batting average, and bashed 493 home runs. Those numbers did not lie. Few players, if any, had accomplished more.

But Gehrig's career did not end typically — that is, with his skills simply ebbing until it became clear he needed to retire. To the contrary, Gehrig's career ended in such a unique, heartbreaking fashion that in death he became far more than just another revered former ballplayer. As Cal Ripken bore down on Gehrig's consecutive-game record in the 1990s, he chased one of the twentieth century's most tragic figures. Even before Gehrig died in his sleep on June 2, 1941, a movie about his life was being filmed, destined to become a poignant classic. And the rare disease that claimed his life eventually bore his name because, though not the first person to succumb to it, he was by far its best-known victim.

Ripken chased not only a famous number but also a famously doomed legend, literally the stuff of Hollywood, America's mythmaking factory, where the movie about Gehrig, *The Pride of the Yankees*, was hatched as World War II began. Samuel Goldwyn, a producer famous for his bald scalp, temper, and knack for knowing the public's tastes, concocted the idea.

Born Schmuel Gelbfisz in Warsaw, Poland, in 1879, Goldwyn had fled anti-Semitism in his homeland as a teenager, arriving in the United States with a new name and palpable ambition. He first became a successful salesman of fine leather gloves, then married the sister of a New York theater producer and started a partnership that produced one of Hollywood's first full-length movies. As the film industry soared in the 1920s and 1930s, Goldwyn ran studios and owned production companies.

He needed a subject for a new film in 1939, when one of his house writers, Niven Busch, suggested Gehrig, who at that point had recently ended his playing streak. A decade earlier, while working as a magazine journalist, Busch had authored a profile of Gehrig for *The New Yorker*. The ballplayer's rise-and-fall story was rich in cinematic potential, Busch believed.

Goldwyn was unmoved at first. Now 60, he had been in America for more than four decades but did not follow baseball. "That game is box office poison," he told Busch with a dismissive wave. "If a man wants to watch baseball, he goes to a ballpark, not a movie theater."

Busch persisted, ushering Goldwyn to a screening room, where a film of Gehrig's retirement speech was shown. Now Goldwyn was moved. When Busch recounted Gehrig's background, Goldwyn related to a son of European immigrants living modestly in New York before rising up and making a mark in the world.

Goldwyn decided to make the movie. Even though he knew little about baseball, he recognized a compelling narrative.

His first move was announcing a search for an actor to play Gehrig, knowing all along the job would go to lean, craggy-faced Gary Cooper, best known for portraying cowboys in Westerns. Cooper had doubts about depicting one of baseball's greats; he batted and threw right-handed, unlike the left-handed Gehrig, and he was 40 years old. But a dash of movie-making magic could take care of all that. And Cooper was under contract to Goldwyn, so he had to take the role.

Besides Cooper, Goldwyn hired a top director, Sam Wood, and an Oscar-nominated actress, Teresa Wright, a dark-haired beauty who would portray Gehrig's wife, Eleanor, even though Teresa was much younger, just two years out of high school. (Wright would later marry and divorce Niven Busch.) Babe Ruth signed on for a speaking role because, of course, no one else could play Babe Ruth. Now 43 and recovering from a heart attack, he dieted so vigorously for the job that he wound up in the hospital, suffering from exhaustion. But he recovered in time to film his scenes.

At Goldwyn's urging, the screenwriters (Busch was not one) focused on Gehrig's relationships with his strong-willed mother and Eleanor more than on his baseball career. The idea was to attract female movie-goers to his emotional tale along with the millions of male baseball fans who admired Gehrig. The movie depicts his mother seeking to convince young Lou to become an engineer until his talent all but demands that he play baseball. He becomes a star, falls in love, and marries Eleanor shortly before his illness overtakes him, with his consecutive-game streak cited in numerous scenes.

Gehrig died while the movie was being filmed, adding to the tragedy. When Japanese planes bombed Pearl Harbor months later and the United

States went to war, Goldwyn saw Cooper's portrayal of an unpretentious, determined, brave Gehrig as reflective of America's war effort. Those similarities were noted in the text that rolled on-screen as the film opened. *The Pride of the Yankees* premiered on July 14, 1942, with an evening gala and Ruth in the audience at the Astor Theatre in New York. The next day, 100,000 people saw it in theaters across the country.

Several important moments in Gehrig's life were altered for cinematic effect, making it difficult for filmgoers to distinguish what was real from what was enhanced. Did Gehrig really hit two home runs in a World Series game? (Yes.) Did Eleanor really try to talk him into ending his streak at 1,999 straight games? (Yes.) Did he really strike out three times in his 2,000th straight game? (No.) Did he really end his streak by telling his manager on the field, "I can't go anymore"? (No.)

But the public did not mind that license had been taken. The film packed an emotional wallop, ending with a rendering of the Yankee Stadium speech that brought audiences to tears. "In a simple, tender, meticulous, and explicitly narrative film, Mr. Goldwyn and his associates have told the story of Buster Lou with sincere and lingering affection," the *New York Times* wrote in a glowing review. "It is, without being pretentious, a real saga of American life."

The Pride of the Yankees received 11 Academy Award nominations, including Cooper's for Best Actor and Wright's for Best Actress. The story was adapted twice for national radio broadcasts, with Cooper reprising his role. In the 1950s, it became a late-night television staple, introducing Gehrig's story to generations who never saw him play. Decades later, the American Film Institute ranked it the third-greatest sports film ever and rated its final line ("Today, I consider myself the luckiest man on the face of the earth") at No. 38 on a list of greatest movie quotes.

Eventually, the line blurred between Gehrig's real life and Goldwyn's version sprinkled with Hollywood fairy dust. Goldwyn's mythologized tale became familiar and was widely accepted as accurate. Eleanor admitted she could barely distinguish Cooper from her late husband.

"Gary and Lou have the same expressions. They are the same type of man," she told a journalist. "Gary had every one of his mannerisms down to a science and he is so like my husband in the picture that there were times when I felt I couldn't bear it."

In death, Gehrig earned a prime place in America's broader culture.

Between *The Pride of the Yankees* and his association with ALS, he became known for his sad fate as much as for his baseball talents, and his consecutive-game record inevitably became his most famous achievement. Some of his fans could not bear that a player so magnificent was now best remembered just for his perfect attendance, but as DiMaggio would point out in his speech at Camden Yards in 1995, Gehrig's testimonial plaque at Yankee Stadium includes the observation that his "amazing" consecutive-game record "should stand for all time." Although it did not, Gehrig's indelible legend was that of a baseball Hercules whose demise had shocked millions *because* he had seemed so strong, and his record of playing in so many games in a row was the ultimate measure of that strength.

As Ripken closed in on Gehrig's record in 1995, reporters asked what he knew about the Iron Horse. It was a sensitive subject for Ripken. A career .270 hitter, he was almost embarrassed by comparisons to Gehrig.

"Lou was like Babe Ruth. How was it possible for me to compare myself to him?" Ripken said years later. "I realized what we did share was playing in consecutive games. It was still uncomfortable for me."

He spent little time contemplating Gehrig during the 1995 season. "I didn't want to talk about Lou. I didn't want to hear about his streak," Ripken recalled. He believed if he focused on Gehrig, it would appear his motivation for playing every day was setting the record, and that was not the impression he wanted to give.

But Ripken knew on September 6, 1995, that he needed to salute the man who had elevated the consecutive-game record from a statistical footnote to the highest level of acclaim. Though Gehrig had been dead for nearly two decades when Ripken was born, they were inextricably linked. More than 17,000 men had played major league baseball since 1876. Only two had played in more than 2,000 straight games.

After the final out of the Orioles' 4–2 victory, a dais was quickly erected in the infield at Camden Yards. Orioles broadcasters Chuck Thompson and Jon Miller introduced the team's starting lineup from the first game of the streak. Ripken came onto the field with his arms around his parents. Orioles pitcher Mike Mussina presented him with gifts from the team: a pool table and decorative landscape rock with "2,131" chiseled into it. Outfielder Brady Anderson, Ripken's best friend, offered laudatory remarks, as did Mark Belanger, Ripken's predecessor as Baltimore's shortstop.

When DiMaggio spoke, Ripken stood near the podium with his hands clasped respectfully behind his back, then shook hands with the white-haired former Yankee, whose speech elicited a roar. Angelos followed with a speech so long some fans booed. It was after midnight. They wanted Ripken.

Finally, Ripken stepped to the microphone. Ever the planner, he had started working on his speech a month earlier, bouncing ideas off his agent, Ron Shapiro, in what Shapiro later called "wordsmithing sessions." He was still tinkering on the afternoon of his record-setting game. He started by thanking four people for making his success possible: his parents, former Orioles teammate Eddie Murray, and his wife. His voice almost cracked when he turned to Kelly and said, "You, Rachel, and Ryan, you are my life."

But with DiMaggio standing by him, he concluded his remarks, appropriately, with a nod to Gehrig:

> Tonight I stand here, overwhelmed, as my name is linked with the great and courageous Lou Gehrig. I'm truly humbled to have our names spoken in the same breath. Some may think our strongest connection is because we both played many consecutive games. Yet I believe in my heart that our true link is a common motivation — a love of the game of baseball, a passion for our team, and a desire to compete on the very highest level.
>
> I know that if Lou Gehrig is looking down on tonight's activities, he isn't concerned about someone playing one more consecutive game than he did. Instead, he's viewing tonight as just another example of what is good and right about the great American game. Whether your name is Gehrig or Ripken; DiMaggio or Robinson; or that of some youngster who picks up his bat or puts on his glove: You are challenged by the game of baseball to do your very best day in and day out. And that's all I've ever tried to do.

3

Ironmen

FIRST OF THEIR KIND

He lived centuries ago on another continent, but Pheidippides, a lithe, dark-haired warrior in ancient Greece, inspired America's fascination with sports endurance.

In 490 BC, during the long war between Persia and Greece, a large Persian army mustered at Marathon, prompting a Greek general to order Pheidippides to run to Sparta and return with reinforcements. Pheidippides, who was known for being able to traverse long distances, covered 150 miles in two days, brought back soldiers, donned armor, and helped the Greek battalion prevail despite its being badly outnumbered. The general then ordered Pheidippides to run to Athens, 25 miles away, and herald the surprising victory. Pheidippides raced to Athens and shouted, "Rejoice! We conquer!" Then he dropped dead.

Some historians doubt the tale, attributing it to mythmakers. But it has endured. In 1879, Robert Browning, the English poet, put it to verse, writing that Pheidippides "ran like fire" and succumbed to "joy in his blood bursting his heart." Browning's poem inspired France's Baron Pierre de Coubertin and other founders of the modern Olympics, who conceived a running event roughly retracing Pheidippides's path from Marathon to Athens — a distance of some 25 miles. They called the race the marathon.

At the inaugural modern games in Greece in 1896, the marathon was widely anticipated. Spectators packed a stadium in Athens, where the finish line was located. When Greece's Spyridon Louis entered the stadium in the lead after running for nearly three hours, two Greek princes were so excited that they jumped from their seats and accompanied Louis on his final lap around the track. Louis, a lowly water carrier by trade, became a national hero.

A U.S. Olympic team manager, John Graham, witnessed the dramatic scene, and upon returning home he convinced his fellow members of the Boston Athletic Association to stage a similar race. A route of 24.5 miles, starting at Metcalf's Mill in Ashland, Massachusetts, and ending at the Oval on Irvington Street in Boston, was selected, and on April 19, 1897, a New Yorker named John McDermott captured the inaugural Boston Marathon.

The race was a hit with the public. Spectators lined the course to witness what was deemed a grueling test of man's physical limits. One-third of the field stopped short of the finish, and McDermott, exhausted, had to walk several times in the final miles to reach the end upright. The second Boston Marathon took place on April 19, 1898, with a Boston-area college student finishing first, and the race soon became an annual staple of America's developing spectator sports scene. Thus was introduced the idea of endurance as a fundamental athletic quality along with strength, agility, and hand-eye coordination — traits that mattered in baseball, boxing, tennis, golf, and Olympic sports such as weightlifting, wrestling, and shooting. (The marathon distance was changed in 1908 to 26 miles and 385 yards, reflecting a new Olympic standard.)

America's fascination with endurance tales was not new. Although early settlers and Native Americans did not contest in well-known races, some were famous for their durability. In 1835, *The Spirit of the Times* newspaper wrote of a Native American who ran 100 miles in a day while carrying a 60-pound bar of lead. The paper's editors rightfully assumed the public wanted to read about individuals possessing the strength, determination, and will to accomplish what few could.

On August 25, 1875, a British steamship captain, Matthew Webb, made headlines on both sides of the Atlantic Ocean by becoming the first person to swim across the English Channel from England to France — a distance of 21 miles. Webb had previously gained fame for diving into ocean waters to rescue a passenger, and when he read of another man's failed attempt to swim across the Channel, he decided to try. After failing once, he made it in 21 hours and 45 minutes, battling a jellyfish sting and strong currents to reach shore at Calais, in northern France.

Taking advantage of his celebrity, Webb became his century's version of a professional extreme athlete, performing swimming challenges and other outlandish stunts for pay. His act was popular in the United States, where he once floated in a tank of water for 128 hours. After he died trying to swim through rapids in the Niagara River, below Niagara Falls, a memorial erected in his English hometown included this inscription: NOTHING GREAT IS EASY.

Webb's successful Channel crossing spawned numerous imitators, but 36 years passed before a British-born French water polo player, Thomas Burgess, finally became the second person to make it across. Henry Sullivan, a stocky businessman's son from Lowell, Massachusetts, sought to become the first American to achieve the feat in 1913. Rough waters forced him to abandon his attempt well short of Calais, but he kept trying over the years while also undertaking other swimming challenges, such as a race from Provincetown to Nantucket in his home state, which he won in 20 hours and 28 minutes after a shark attack forced a rival to stop. Sullivan finally successfully crossed the English Channel on his eighth try, in 1923.

In its first decades, baseball seemed incapable of producing staggering endurance tales. Boxing could: on April 6, 1893, two fighters in New Orleans battled for 110 rounds over 7 hours and 19 minutes before the match was deemed a draw because neither could lift his arms, much less knock the other out. But baseball did not test man's physical limits. In the 1800s and early 1900s, most games were over in less than two hours, and many players were at a local bar within minutes of the final out. And even though the season lasted months, the players sat on benches when not batting or playing the field. How tough was that?

The notion of durability finally entered the baseball conversation in the early 1900s. Joe McGinnity, a chubby right-hander for the New York Giants, pitched an astounding 434 innings while winning 31 games in 1903. Such hardiness was common in those years, before it became clear that heavy workloads could ruin arms, but McGinnity, a feisty former bartender from Peoria, Illinois, who once spat tobacco juice in an umpire's face, was the ultimate example. Sportswriters called him "Ironman."

According to Lee Allen's book *The National League Story,* McGinnity's nickname initially came from an interview early in his career. When a journalist asked what he did in the off-season, he replied, "I'm an iron man. I work in a foundry." Indeed, his wife's family operated a foundry, or iron factory, in McAlester, Oklahoma. But the nickname proved just as appropriate on the diamond when McGinnity made a habit of pitching both ends of a doubleheader, as if his arm were made of iron.

The Ironman nickname was not attached to position players on consecutive-game streaks until after World War I. Statisticians were just getting around to clarifying the game's early history, poring over old box scores like archaeologists searching for dinosaur bones at a dig. The challenge of playing every day was not new, but it was beginning to draw attention. On August 3, 1919, when Fred Luderus, a first baseman for the Philadelphia Phillies, ran his streak to 479 consecutive games, surpassing Eddie Collins, a White Sox second baseman whose streak had ended not long before, the *Philadelphia Inquirer* labeled Luderus "the new 'Iron Man' of the majors."

Patterned after English and Gaelic "field games" such as cricket and rounders, baseball had first gained footing in and around New York City in the 1850s, and then emerged from the bloody ruin of the Civil War as one thing most Americans agreed on. The first professional club, Cincinnati's Red Stockings, toured the country in 1869, drawing crowds on both coasts. Eight clubs formed the National League in 1876, and a rival "major" league, the American Association, opened for business in 1882.

At first, pitchers stood 50 feet from home plate, on flat ground, lobbing underhand tosses at batters who could declare whether they wanted the pitch thrown high or low. As many as seven balls and four strikes comprised an at-bat at different times as organizers experimented with the rules. Finally, the distance between the mound and home plate was established at 60 feet and 6 inches, and four balls and three strikes per at-bat became the norm.

In 1876, the National League's inaugural season, teams carried only a few players more than the nine-man minimum, in part because their owners could not fathom paying reserves to sit and watch. Managers had no choice but to use mostly "set" lineups, featuring the same players at the same positions day after day. The schedule was short and unorganized, with teams playing anywhere from 56 to 70 league games. Six Chicago White Stockings, four St. Louis Brown Stockings, and four Boston Red Caps played in every game for their teams.

The set-lineup tradition continued in the coming years. It was not always easy to play every day for months, especially as the players' bruises and aches mounted during the season. (Many played defense without a glove until the late 1880s.) But rosters remained small, and no substitutions were permitted during a game unless a player suffered an injury so severe he could not continue. Pinch hitters, defensive replacements, and designated hitters belonged to the sport's distant future.

In 1882, four of the National League pennant–winning Chicago White Stockings played in every game, as did four Buffalo Bisons, four Cleveland Blues, and three Providence Grays. In all, 28 players among the league's eight teams — 38.8 percent of the starters — contested the entire season without taking a day off.

For Joe Hornung, a speedy, peculiar left fielder for the Boston Beaneaters, the 1882 season marked his third straight without a day off. One of the league's finest fielders, he shouted a nonsensical phrase, "Ubbo, ubbo," whenever he made a nice grab or collected a base hit. Proudly rugged, Hornung continued to play barehanded even as gloves came into vogue, and eventually played in 464 straight games until he sat one out on September 13, 1884.

By then, baseball was "the established favorite game of ball of the American people," according to *Spalding's Base Ball Guide,* a volume published annually by A. G. Spalding and Bros., a sporting goods company owned by an entrepreneurial former pitcher, Albert Spalding. Horse races and boxing matches also drew crowds of spectators, but in the years before football and basketball became popular, baseball was easily the top attraction. Newspapers across the country covered their local teams, publishing long articles about games and features on players. Magazines such as the *Sporting News,* published in St. Louis, and the *Sporting Life,* published in Philadelphia, circulated nationally with detailed reporting on players, rules, and games.

Club owners recognized that, given the public's growing appetite for games, they could lengthen their season, sell more tickets, and make more money. When the Detroit Wolverines won the National League pennant in 1887, they played 127 games — 43 more than they had played six years earlier. The longer season intensified the challenge of playing every day. Many players still did not wear gloves or protective gear and accumulated cuts, bruises, scrapes, and more. Travel was not easy, composed of long hours on lurching, crowded trains and nights in stifling-hot hotels. And instead of resting when the schedule provided a rare day off, teams played exhibitions, arranged by their owners, to generate more revenue. Most players took an occasional day off. In 1886, just two National League players, representing 2.7 percent of the league, contested every game for their teams, constituting a precipitous decline from just a few years earlier.

That year, five players in the eight-team American Association also played in every game, including George Pinkney, a third baseman for Brooklyn. Encountering him out of uniform, few strangers would have guessed Pinkney was a ballplayer, especially one noted for his durability. Standing five feet seven and weighing 160 pounds, he was shaped like an egg, with the bulk of his weight seemingly bunched at his wide hips. His narrow, patrician nose pointed straight out in what seemed a permanent sniff. A manicured layer of thin blond hair fell daintily across the top of his head.

Without a uniform on, Pinkney resembled a deskbound white-collar professional, and in fact he was from a prominent Illinois legal family, his father a judge on the state supreme court, his brother the district attorney in Peoria, their hometown. Had their profession also interested him, he surely would have spent his working years in courtrooms. But he preferred baseball's dirt diamonds instead.

Playing third base without a glove, Pinkney was agile and sure-handed. "Some of his stops of hot-hit balls are simply marvelous," reported the *New York Clipper*, a newspaper that focused on sports and the theater. At the plate, he walked or made contact almost every time he batted, exhibiting a sharp eye and consistent left-handed swing. Though not a slugger, Pinkney consistently drove balls between fielders and then ran the bases with a horse jockey's daring, his thick thighs blurring. "One of the greatest third basemen in the profession," the *Clipper* called him.

Though popular, baseball was still a raw entertainment in the late 1800s, populated by drunks and gamblers both in the stands and on the field. Originally intended as a lighthearted pastime for the wealthy, it had degenerated into something darker. A hostile, unseemly atmosphere prevailed at many games. Incessant bickering among players, umpires, and "cranks," as fans were called, was routine. "Many games featured fist fights, and almost every team has its 'lushers,'" Albert Spalding wrote. "A game characterized by such scenes, whose spectators consisted for the most part of gamblers, rowdies, and their associates, could not possibly attract honest men or decent women."

Conditions were slightly better in the National League, the older, more sober circuit, which sought a higher class of fan by charging 50 cents per ticket, banning alcohol sales at games, and taking Sundays off, distinguishing it from the rowdier American Association, which was run by beer-baron club owners who plainly sought to lure a more common crowd by charging half as much for tickets, selling alcohol, and playing on Sundays.

Charles Byrne, a sharp-talking realtor who owned Brooklyn's club, had strong feelings about the sport's general character. An opera and theater buff who had studied law and worked as a journalist before making his money in real estate, Byrne thought the sport needed cleaning up. When he founded his club with a partner in 1883, he tried to join the National League, found its ranks closed, and settled for playing in a minor league for a year before the American Association let him in. He pointedly sought players of "superior" character, hoping they would attract a higher class of fan.

"Brooklyn's management will under no circumstances employ any player where integrity of character is not a feature of his recommendations, nor anyone who has not a clean record of temperate habits," the *New York Clipper* reported. "They want men of intelligence and not corner-lot toughs who happen to possess some skill as a player but whose habits and ways make them unfit for thorough team work."

Pinkney was exactly the kind of player Byrne wanted. Some fans called him "Gentleman George." Henry Chadwick, the legendary baseball writer, described him in the *Brooklyn Daily Eagle* as "tender and high bred." Pinkney brought dignity, almost delicacy, to the baseball scene, exuding class as he crouched at third base and waited for balls to come his way.

A product of Peoria's sandlot leagues, he had played in the minors for several years before breaking into the majors in 1884 with the Cleveland Blues, a National League club that folded. Picked up by Byrne, he split time between second base and third base in 1885 as Brooklyn, known as the Grays, finished under .500 in the American Association, behind such foes as the St. Louis Browns, Cincinnati Red Stockings, and Pittsburgh Alleghenys.

Near the end of that season, on September 19, Pinkney sat out an 8–2 loss to Pittsburgh. It was the last game he would miss for more than four years. In 1886, he became Brooklyn's regular third baseman and was on the field for every inning of the team's 139 league games. He repeated the feat in 1887, playing every inning of 134 games. It was an especially long, hot, difficult campaign. The Grays trudged through a 16-game road trip early in the season and later played 15 straight on the road. Byrne tried to manage the club himself but had no aptitude for the job. Brooklyn finished 34½ games out of first.

Byrne took drastic action after the season, firing himself as manager and spending $19,000, a huge sum, to wrest three stars from the pennant-winning Browns. Suddenly, Brooklyn had a new catcher, new right side of the infield, entirely new outfield, and new manager, William "Gunner" McGunnigle, a dapper New Englander who wore dark patent-leather shoes, lavender trousers, and a suit coat, silk tie, and derby hat during games. The club even adopted a new unofficial nickname, the Bride-grooms, when several players, including Pinkney, were married during the off-season.

Pinkney survived the sweep of change, keeping his job at third base. He could not match the prodigious slugging of Dave Orr, a mountainous teammate who had bashed 31 triples while hitting .338 for the New York Metropolitans in 1886, but his defense was superb, and by playing every day, he piled up enough hits, walks, and runs to rank among the league leaders despite a relatively modest batting average.

After Byrne's reshuffling, Brooklyn nearly captured the American Association pennant in 1888. Attendance swelled at Washington Park, the team's home ground in Brooklyn's Park Slope neighborhood. Pinkney played a vital role in the success. Although he hit just .271, he led the league in runs scored, helped by the fact that he was the only player in the league to play in every game. By the end of the season, he had played in 432 straight.

On May 27, 1889, Pinkney passed Joe Hornung and now owned the sport's longest consecutive-game streak — 465. But his achievement did not receive mention in newspapers or magazines. Baseball's infatuation with statistics and records would not intensify until the 1900s.

McGunnigle had told reporters before the 1889 season that he would "make a headlong plunge from the top of one of the towers of the Brooklyn Bridge into the East River" if his Bridegrooms did not capture the American Association pennant. After starting slowly, they reeled off a winning streak, gained a grip on first place, and maintained it, finishing ahead of St. Louis. McGunnigle was spared a dive off the majestic bridge connecting Brooklyn and Manhattan, which had opened six years earlier.

That season, Pinkney's batting average dropped below .250 as he again played in every inning of every game. Was he feeling the effects of having not taken a day off for more than four years? The question surely would have circulated if he had played a century later before a more questioning media, but Henry Chadwick never brought it up in print. Pinkney was above reproach, it seemed. His dependability, character, and unflinching work ethic made him a fan favorite. A typical workweek in Brooklyn in those years consisted of 60 hours over six days at a dockyard or sugar refinery. Fans worked hard, often in unsafe conditions, and had little leisure time or tolerance for slackers. They envisioned Pinkney as one of their fraternity, punching a clock every day. When the *Sporting Life* published scandalous gossip about him, suggesting he enjoyed "killing two bottles of beers per day at a hostelry near the ball field," his fans flooded the magazine with complaints, clamoring for the record to be set straight. *Sporting Life* printed a correction, admitting it was wrong to have suggested Pinkney "may degenerate and be known as a member of the rosy nose circle." The suggestion that he was "smuggling a too good will for the amber fluid" was groundless, the paper admitted.

Every team, including Brooklyn, featured players who drank, fought, and gambled through the season. "The evil of drunkenness among pro teams has grown until it has become too costly an abuse to be longer tolerated," the Spalding guide reported. But Pinkney floated above it all. Decades before Lou Gehrig and Cal Ripken Jr. personified the consecutive-game record's golden-boy hue, Pinkney established the prototype. Chadwick proudly reported that he "has not asked the club for an advance on his salary in three years," apparently distinguishing him from teammates who forever knocked on Byrne's door and asked for his help covering their gambling debts and bar tabs.

After enduring a cold winter that had lingered too long for anyone's taste, fans of Byrne's club emerged from hibernation when warm sunshine bathed Brooklyn on the afternoon of May 1, 1890. Flocking to a game against the Boston Beaneaters, they either took advantage of the weather and walked to Washington Park or rode one of the Brooklyn City Railroad Company's horse-drawn streetcars to a nearby stop.

Approaching the park's entrance, they traversed a sidewalk with the words BROOKLYN BASE BALL CLUB etched ornately into the pavement. The crowd was mostly male, although a "Ladies' Day" promotion had brought out more women than usual. The purchase of a 50-cent ticket got them through the wooden turnstiles Byrne had installed so he could determine the size of his crowds more accurately. Few in that day's crowd paid attention to dark clouds gathering in the sky to the west.

Washington Park was named for the first president of the United States, who had headquartered in the spot during the Battle of Long Island in the Revolutionary War. The manicured playing diamond was laid out beside a stone house that had been used to store munitions a century earlier; now female fans sought shade there during games. Men filled the wooden grandstand that hugged the diamond, making it easy for them to shout at players and umpires.

After winning the American Association in 1889, Byrne had finally jumped to his long-sought destination, the National League, over the winter. Another winning season was anticipated. The team's core was back, featuring familiar faces such as William "Adonis" Terry, a tall, handsome pitcher who made the ladies swoon; Thomas "Oyster" Burns, a loudmouth outfielder who continually bitched at umpires; Dave Foutz, a slugger who seldom passed a bar without stopping and buying everyone a round; and Darby O'Brien, a goofy outfielder who carried snakes in his pockets and enjoyed pulling them out to startle strangers.

Then there was Pinkney, so entrenched at third base that no one could remember when anyone else played the position even for an inning. He assumed his familiar pose, crouching in anticipation, as the game began, with Boston's leadoff hitter, James "Chippy" McGarr, stepping to the plate. The umpire, sporting a dark blue coat and green cap, shouted, "Play ball!" Clouds scudded overhead, but the crowd settled in for nine innings of slap hitting, daring baserunning, flashy fielding, and incessant bickering with the ump — the elements that had helped make baseball so popular.

McGarr lined a single to right field, darted for second when the next batter put a ground ball in play, and churned for third when an errant throw bounced against the grandstand. Pinkney sprinted to his base, hoping to catch a throw and tag out the aggressive runner. When the throw came, Pinkney grabbed the ball, bent over, and applied a tag as McGarr slid in with his spikes turned up.

Even before the umpire could rule on the play, Pinkney straightened abruptly, as if jolted by a lightning strike, and hopped away on one foot, pain contorting his face. A spike on McGarr's cleats had gashed his left foot.

As blood stained his sock, Pinkney saw he could not continue and hobbled to the bench, disappointment etched on his round face. Fans stood and cursed McGarr for daring to put Gentleman George out of the game, and adding insult to the injury, Pinkney had missed the tag, the umpire ruled, so McGarr was safe at third. He stood on the base while manager Gunner McGunnigle, dressed in his usual finery, orchestrated changes in his team's defense, sending the second baseman to third and putting a new man at second.

When play resumed, Boston's next three batters made outs, stranding McGarr. As Brooklyn batted in the bottom of the inning, the sky darkened, the wind gusted, and trash blew across the field. Rain began to fall and quickly accelerated into a downpour. The ideal spring afternoon had vanished. The game would not continue.

Fans fled for cover, relieved that Byrne's "rain check" policy meant they could use their tickets to attend another game; their 50 cents was not wasted. Henry Chadwick, dressed in a high-collared suit, with his long white beard protruding from his chin, also ducked out of the ballpark and headed for his newspaper's office. Though nearly 70 years old, the sportswriter was as immersed as ever in his beloved game.

Born in England in 1824, he had immigrated to New York not long before Americans began playing baseball. As the sport grew, Chadwick, equally adept with numbers and words, wrote about it for several newspapers while also developing statistics that helped identify who played well. Now in his eminence, he carried strong opinions about how the game should be played, preferring the "science" of steals, sacrifices, and speed to "brutish" displays of batting power, which increasingly thrilled fans.

Still cranking out daily stories, Chadwick had no game to report on today, but there was news: Pinkney was out. "His bleeding foot will disable him for the remainder of the week, thereby breaking his famous record of four years of continuous play without missing a game," Chadwick wrote.

He did not specify how many games in a row Pinkney had played in. It is likely no one knew, not even Pinkney.

When Brooklyn and Boston played the next day at Washington Park, Pinkney was on the bench. Years later, his absence from the field would give historical importance to an otherwise forgettable game, but Chadwick's account of the contest, which Boston won, 11–0, did not mention that baseball's greatest endurance streak had ended at 578 straight games.

Pinkney sat out two games as his gash healed, then picked right back up where he left off, playing in every game for the rest of the 1890 season. His durability was never more valued as Brooklyn battled the Chicago Colts and Philadelphia Phillies for the National League pennant. Adonis Terry missed time due to heat exhaustion. Pop Corkhill, the center fielder, had a sore arm. Darby O'Brien put his hand through a glass case late one night, severing an artery. At one point, the club had just two healthy pitchers. But with Pinkney batting .309, his career high, Brooklyn captured the pennant with a strong finish.

Pinkney, now 31, was battered with nicks and bruises, and plainly worn down by the end of the season. His daily playing habit had exacted a toll. When Brooklyn played Louisville in a postseason "World Series" matching the champions of the National League and American Association, Pinkney sat out several games before the Series was called off due to bad weather and poor attendance, with the teams deadlocked after seven games. (One had ended in a tie.)

A year later, Byrne let Pinkney go after his seventh season in Brooklyn. It was an amicable parting; Pinkney would later work for the team as a scout. Catching on as a part-time player with the St. Louis Browns, he made it through two more major league seasons before retiring in 1893.

The end of his career was unremarkable. There was no great public farewell for the holder of a record that would later reflect one of baseball's most revered achievements. Pinkney just slipped away, returning to Peoria. It would have stunned him to know his name would still reverberate among fans a century later not because of his handy fielding or the consistency he exhibited at bat, but for the simple fact that he always wanted to play.

When he reflected back on his career, Pinkney was proud of his durability. In 1896, a sportswriter using the byline "Hurley" in the *Sporting Life* mistakenly wrote that Bill Everett, the Chicago Cubs' second baseman, "had not missed a game in two seasons, which was the record for consecutive playing." Pinkney wrote to Hurley, who printed a correction.

"George says one is soon forgotten when he is out of the game, as he holds the record in that particular," Hurley wrote. "During the seasons of '86, '87, '88, and '89, George never missed a game, neither championship nor exhibition, and since each team played 152 championship games then instead of the number played now, it is easy to see the record belongs to Pinkney by a long lead. President Byrne of the Brooklyn club can verify the above."

Pinkney actually never played more than 143 games in a season, so the *Sporting Life* needed to correct its correction. But it did not. And the topic of "consecutive playing" faded away for more than two decades while Pinkney continued to work in baseball as a scout, reporting first to Byrne and then, after Byrne died, to Charles Ebbets, Byrne's successor as Brooklyn's owner. In fact, it was Pinkney who discovered Joe McGinnity pitching on a semipro team in Peoria in the late 1800s, surely the only instance in baseball's long history when an Ironman discovered an "Ironman."

4

Ripken

BLUE-COLLAR STOCK

The first Ripkens in America were German immigrants who worked as farmers, blacksmiths, and millers in Harford County, Maryland, in the mid-nineteenth century. Then they opened a general store at a crossroads just south of Aberdeen, one of those little institutions a rural community could not live without. You could buy groceries, drink coffee on the way to the train station, sit and eat a meal. Travelers could rent a room for the night on the second floor. When cars came along, drivers could fill their tanks at the Sunoco gas pump out front.

The general store supported several generations and by the 1920s was in the hands of Arend and Clara Ripken, a young couple not yet 30. Clara, a brunette of Irish descent, ran the restaurant, serving meals on linen tablecloths. Arend kept the rest of the place going. The couple had two sons, Oliver, born in 1918, and William, born in 1925, and it seemed they would have no more children, until Clara became pregnant in 1935, a surprise that was welcomed but not timely. The Great Depression had cut so deeply into the general store's business that Arend had taken a second job at a lumberyard to help make ends meet.

On December 17, 1935, in one of the tiny guest rooms above the general store, Clara delivered another son, Calvin Edwin Ripken. Her older boys were 17 and 10. When Arend was killed in an automobile accident shortly before Cal's ninth birthday, in 1944, Oliver interrupted his military service to come home for the funeral. The older boys split up their father's chores, mowing the lawn, running the Sunoco pump, tending their mother's beloved rock garden.

When World War II ended, the Ripken boys played baseball on Sundays for the Aberdeen Canners, a semipro team in the Susquehanna League. Their father had played some baseball, but "I got involved . . . because of my brothers," Cal later wrote in his book, *The Ripken Way: A Manual for Baseball and Life.* Oliver was a catcher, Bill a talented outfielder. Cal wore the team's uniform for the first time as an 11-year-old batboy, in 1946, and even at that age, in that role, he displayed savvy. The Canners' manager feared opponents were stealing signs, so he gave them to Cal, who relayed them to players in the field.

A scout for the Brooklyn Dodgers noticed Bill could hit, throw, and run, and signed him. Bill left the Canners and played in the minors, hitting .318 over three seasons to reach Brooklyn's Triple A farm team in Montreal, one level from the major leagues. But Canada was cold, and Bill believed he would never be more than a utility player in the majors, so he quit playing in 1949, came home to Harford County, and took a job at a bank.

As Cal grew up, he filled out to six feet one and 175 pounds. Nimble and wiry-strong, with fierce blue eyes blazing beneath a blond brush cut, he became the Canners' starting catcher and also played baseball and soccer at Aberdeen High School. Washington and Lee University offered him a scholarship after he graduated in 1953, but he turned it down, intending to follow his brother's example and try professional baseball.

Initially, no scout was impressed enough to sign him. Cal continued to play for a Susquehanna League team in Havre de Grace, Maryland. His odds of becoming a pro improved when the American League's downtrodden St. Louis Browns relocated to Baltimore in 1954 and became the Orioles, and in 1956 an Orioles scout saw enough in Cal to sign him.

His first years as a pro were spent on the game's outermost fringes: the Arizona-Mexico League, the Alabama-Florida League, the Northern League. He played in a dirt bullring in searing heat in Mexico, slept on overnight bus rides, earned $150 a month. Along the way, he married the former Violet Gross, a mechanic's daughter whom he had known in high school. They made Aberdeen their home and had a child, a daughter named Ellen.

Cal recognized that his talents were relatively modest, so he sought to master what he could control, the fundamentals, a professional approach. "Cal was baseball through and through: respect the game, do things the right way on the field, don't show people up, just go out and grind it out day after day," said Pat Gillick, in those days a tall pitching prospect and teammate of Cal's in the Orioles' minor league system.

In 1960, Gillick, destined to become a Hall of Fame baseball executive, played with Cal on the Fox Cities (Wisconsin) Foxes in the Illinois-Indiana-Iowa League, a Class B circuit. Their manager was Earl Weaver, a diminutive former minor league infielder, feisty and foulmouthed at age 29. Weaver was tough, but so was his catcher. In one game, Cal could not find his mask as he headed to the field for an inning, so he grabbed a softball mask, which had a wider space between the safety bars across the front. The barrel of a bat came through the bars and hit Cal in the face. He kept playing. Another time, a foul ball gashed the middle finger on his throwing hand. Weaver trotted out to inspect the injury.

"I'm taking you out," Weaver said.

"Like hell you are," Cal growled. "Just put a bandage on it, rub a little dust on it. It'll be fine. I'm not coming out of this game."

In an interview for this book, Gillick explained his former teammate's mindset: "In those years, and really going back to Gehrig and that era, the thinking at every level was, if you came out of the lineup, you might not get back in. It's different now with so many guaranteed contracts, but before the 1970s and free agency, people didn't want to go on the disabled list or come out of the lineup, because there was a chance someone would take your job. Cal was sort of a journeyman, so a guy like that, if you didn't show up or were injured too much, you were gone. I was the same way. I played five years of minor league ball and went near the trainer's room maybe two times. You didn't want to be there. If you were there too much, there was always the chance you would get released."

Cal's wife, Vi, was with him at Fox Cities that summer until she left in July to return to Maryland to deliver their second child, Calvin Edwin Ripken Jr., who was born on August 24, 1960.

Weaver, the young manager, liked his dogged catcher. Cal was nothing if not resourceful. When the team's bus driver proved unreliable, Weaver fired him and asked Cal to take the wheel on road trips. Cal handled the job while continuing to catch every day. He ended the 1960 season with a .281 average and 74 runs batted in, and at spring training in 1961, he was on the roster of the Orioles' Triple A affiliate — one level from the majors, just like his older brother in the late 1940s.

But in an exhibition game in Daytona, Florida, in 1961, a pair of foul balls struck Cal's right shoulder, one right after the other. He managed to finish the game, even threw out a pair of base runners, but his shoulder was so sore the next day he could barely lift his arm. His playing career nose-dived. The Orioles sent him to their Double A affiliate in Little Rock, Arkansas, thinking the warm weather would help his shoulder, but it continued to throb, and his batting average plummeted.

In June, Harry Dalton, a former sportswriter who now ran Baltimore's minor league operation, asked Cal to become the player-manager of the Orioles' team in the Florida State League, a lowly Class D circuit. Weaver had given Dalton a positive scouting report on Cal, suggesting he might make a good coach because he was smart and responsible, knew the fundamentals, and acted like an adult.

Cal took the job and finished out the season in Florida. The next year, the Orioles sent him back to Fox Cities, this time as a player-manager. The owner of the local bus company refused to rent the team a bus unless Cal agreed to drive it. He started at catcher early in the season, then cut his own playing time when a hotter prospect joined the club.

That was his final year as a player. Beginning in 1963, Cal became a cornerstone of Dalton's player development operation, which would churn out major leaguers for more than a decade, helping fuel a long run of success for the Orioles. Dalton relied on Cal to complete an array of tasks. Cal drove the team's spring training equipment from Baltimore to Florida every winter, barreling south in a wood-paneled station wagon with an Orioles decal on the back. During spring training, Cal worked with a baseball glove on one hand and a hammer in his back pocket, alternately running drills and maintaining the fields.

After spring training, Cal spent the summers managing low-level minor league teams such as the Tri-City (Washington) Atoms and Aberdeen (South Dakota) Pheasants. He drove the bus, threw batting practice, groomed infields, made out lineups, and managed games, all while continually mentoring raw prospects in nuances such as how to run the "wheel play" against a sacrifice bunt or how to organize a rundown. One of his favorite messages was football coach Vince Lombardi's spin on the "practice makes perfect" cliché. "Practice doesn't make perfect. Only *perfect* practice makes perfect," Cal declared.

After a few years, Dalton put him in charge of more polished squads in the high minors. Wherever he went, Vi and their four children (sons Fred and Bill had joined Elly and Cal Jr.) spent the summer with him. He set a tireless example: gone early, home late, always in motion, driving a tractor to prep an infield, throwing batting practice, managing a game.

The kids invented games in cramped clubhouses, sorted socks for pennies, shagged batting practice flies. In Asheville, North Carolina, in the early 1970s, Cal Jr. and Fred ran the visitors' clubhouse, Bill was a batboy, and Elly swept the bases with a broom between innings. Minor league baseball was their world. Watching their father's every step, they became steeped in baseball's rhythms and rituals.

They similarly absorbed lessons when they returned to Maryland for the school year. "There was always something going on, growing up with dad," Bill Ripken recalled. "Even if we were doing the smallest of tasks —cleaning the windows, shoveling snow, working in the garage, or cutting the grass — there was a right way to do it. And then there was that moment when you finished one of these tasks. Dad would poke you in the side and say, 'Looks pretty good, doesn't it?' You'd say, 'Yeah, it does.' It was the pride of doing things right. He instilled that in all of us."

One winter, Senior — as he would become known in baseball circles, differentiating him from his son with the same name, who would be called Junior — pulled out a makeshift plow to drag the neighborhood after a heavy snow. As he tried to get it started, a metal engine crank came loose and hit his head. Blood smeared his face, but when a trip to the emergency room was suggested, Senior snorted, applied a butterfly bandage, went back outside, started the engine, and plowed the neighborhood.

"Anything he did in his life, nothing could stop him," Junior said. "He loved to play soccer. He'd get his big toe stepped on, and the nail would fill with blood. He would come home, take out an electric drill, and drill through the nail. Blood would pop up. Tape it up, go on with his life. You wouldn't hear anything else about it. It was almost like, 'No matter what happens to you, the game goes on and you play.' That was the mindset. That was the example he set."

After more than a decade of minor league managing, Senior worked as a scout for the Orioles in 1975, then joined Weaver's major league staff as the bullpen coach in 1976. Weaver had become a highly successful manager, leading the Orioles to five postseason appearances in seven seasons and a World Series victory in 1970.

One day at Boston's Fenway Park, Senior stood behind a screen while throwing batting practice, attempting to help a young Oriole, Kiko Garcia, polish his swing. He became so absorbed in the job that he drifted out from behind the screen as Garcia whacked a line drive right at him. Senior put his glove up and deflected the ball, but it ricocheted off his face. This time, there was too much blood for him to stanch the wound with a homemade bandage. He went to the emergency room, fussing the whole way, but left as soon as a doctor finished with him. That night, he performed his usual duties during the game.

"That happened before I got there," Junior said, "but you hear stories like that, and there were a lot of them about my dad, and you figured it was your role to play, regardless of what happens."

As the four Ripken children grew up in the 1960s and 1970s, there was never any doubt about which one possessed the burning competitive streak. Cal Jr. was determined to win whatever contest he and his siblings undertook.

"Who could stay quiet the longest in the car? He would provoke the rest of us into making some sort of noise so he would win the penny being offered," Bill Ripken recalled.

As a nine-year-old, Junior became so excited after winning a game of checkers on a park bench in Miami that he jumped up and conked his head on a tree, knocking himself silly.

"It was just the way he was wired. Playing checkers, playing cards, anything, he wanted to win as much as any individual I've ever been around," Bill said. "If you gave him a challenge, he did everything he could to conquer it."

Years later, many of Junior's major league teammates would make similar statements. "It was like a sickness with him," Rex Hudler said. "I had a competitive bug, but geez, not like that. I played in the majors for 11 years and there was only one other guy who wanted that badly to beat you in Ping-Pong or whatever you did, and that was [Atlanta pitcher] John Smoltz."

As an emerging baseball prospect in the 1970s, Junior combined his natural competitiveness with a grasp of the game's fundamentals, which he absorbed from his father. He often tagged along when Senior worked off-season clinics, the car rides presenting Senior with the perfect time to teach.

"Certainly Senior's work ethic and thought processes were transferred to Junior," Pat Gillick said years later. "Junior developed his own character, but a lot of the things that developed his character came from his father."

Fortunately for Junior, he alone among his brothers did not inherit Senior's wiry physique. Bill and Fred closely resembled their father as adults, but Junior sprouted 3 inches taller and 40 pounds heavier by the time he fully matured. He towered over his father even as a youngster. It did not look unusual for him to take infield with his father's Double A team in Asheville in the 1970s. After Senior joined Weaver's Orioles staff, Junior accompanied him to games at Baltimore's Memorial Stadium and took batting practice.

"I think I was 15 when I pulled the ball down the line and reached the seats the first time," Ripken recalled.

Tall and commanding, he pitched and played shortstop for Aberdeen High School in the spring, then competed in a local summer league. On the mound, he dominated as a right-hander mixing 90 mph fastballs with sharp breaking balls. As a hitter, he routinely drove balls over the fences.

"He was a great pitcher, a great player. He'd throw a shutout and hit a home run to win the game," said Fred Tyler, a shortstop for rival Bel Air High School in those days.

Tyler, like Junior, lived in an Orioles household. His father, Ernie, handled the balls at home games, and his older brother, Jimmy, worked as a clubhouse attendant. Junior and Fred were the same age and knew each other from being around the Orioles. When their high school teams played in the spring of 1978, their senior year, Tyler got the best of Junior.

"We won, and I got a couple of hits off him," Tyler recalled. "But they were scared hits. One was a swinging bunt, and the other was a cheap shot over the third baseman's head. I was left-handed, and his curveball was so hard that was all I could do with it. He was so much better than any other pitcher we faced."

(Fred Tyler also eventually worked for the Orioles, running the visitors' clubhouse for many years, and remained friendly with Ripken. On the day of Ripken's final major league game in 2001, Ripken presented signed jerseys to Ernie, Jimmy, and Fred Tyler and two other Orioles officials in a pregame ceremony. "My jersey was inscribed with a message about how well I hit him that day in 1978," Fred said.)

With pro scouts tracking him, Junior went 7-2 on the mound as a high school senior in 1978. There was little doubt he would get selected in baseball's amateur draft that summer, but questions persisted. How early would he go? Which team would take him? Would he pitch or play shortstop as a pro? The scouts lacked a consensus on the latter question. At least one thought he was too big for the infield, writing in a report that a "lack of fluid mobility" limited him as a shortstop prospect.

When the draft unfolded on June 6, 1978, the Orioles selected Robert Boyce, a third baseman from Deer Park High School in Cincinnati, as their first-round pick. They had four selections in the second round. With the first two, they took Larry Sheets, an outfielder from Robert E. Lee High School in Staunton, Virginia, and Eddie Hook, a pitcher from Point Loma High School in San Diego. With their third pick in the second round, the draft's 48th overall selection, they took Ripken.

The next day, he struck out 17 batters in seven innings to lead Aberdeen High School to an easy victory in a state championship game. Off that performance, his future seemed clear. "The Orioles picked me to be a pitcher, no question," Ripken said years later. "I had a good arm, a lot of strikeouts. I was hitting 90, 91 mph on the [radar] gun. I was pretty dynamic. It was clear I was a pitcher. Everyone in the organization wanted that — Hank Peters, the general manager; Tom Giordano, the scouting director."

In giving up only two hits to Thomas Stone High School in the title game, Ripken "left no doubt about his major league potential, as he zipped assorted fastballs, curves and change-ups past the Lions," the *Baltimore Sun* reported. "For the most part, facing Ripken became an exercise in futility, as every Thomas Stone batter fanned at least once and many came back to the dugout shaking their heads in disbelief at Ripken's pitching."

But after the game, Ripken told the *Sun* he wanted to play shortstop, not pitch, as a pro. And Dick Bowie, the Orioles scout who had tracked him, also "had some feeling that maybe I could be a regular player," Ripken recalled. "The issue came up because that's what I wanted."

Peters, Giordano, Bowie, Senior, and Junior met to discuss his future. Senior backed the idea of trying his son at shortstop. You could not start a prospect as a pitcher and then make him a position player later, because he would have missed too much important developmental time, Senior said, but if you started him as a position player and switched him to the mound later, it could work.

In the end, Peters asked Junior what he wanted. He was 17 years old. "A pitcher only gets to play one day out of five," Junior said. "I want to play every day."

That settled it.

Ripken and another well-known Baltimore-area high school player whom the Orioles had drafted, Tim Norris, a right-handed pitcher, signed their contracts in a press conference at Memorial Stadium, then climbed into Norris's car and drove to Bluefield, West Virginia, where the Orioles fielded a team in a rookie circuit, the Appalachian League. Ripken slept for most of the drive, Norris recalled. Their contracts called for them to make $400 a month and $6.50 a day in meal money. "It was enough for either one big meal or two small meals at Hardee's," Norris said.

The Orioles arranged for them to share a rented house with Sheets and Mike Boddicker, a pitcher from the University of Iowa. Away from home for the first time, the two Baltimore-area teenagers spent a lot of time together. "We were always at the ballpark, but if we weren't on the field, it was me against him in basketball, pinball, wrestling, whatever," Norris said. "We both wanted to win, no matter what we were playing."

Typical of teams in a rookie pro league, the Bluefield Orioles played a "short" season of 69 games, beginning in late June. The manager, Junior Miner, gave Ripken the shortstop job.

"He was this tall, skinny kid. Some of the other guys were college players, and a few were a little more polished," said John Shelby, the Orioles' 1977 first-round draft pick, who played in the outfield for Bluefield that season. "You could tell [Ripken] was young; he looked young. The buzz started going around that he was the son of one of the major league coaches."

His performance raised eyebrows. Although he hit a respectable .264, he produced just eight extra-base hits and no home runs. "I remember one time he hit a little flare for a game winner, and I kidded him about this later. He celebrated like it was the biggest hit of his life, this little flare," Shelby said.

His defense was even more alarming. Ripken committed 33 errors in

62 games, mostly on wild throws. "Some balls went through his legs, too. I joked with him about me catching the balls hit to him. It seemed like every time one went to him, I was running in and fielding it," Shelby said.

Ripken sensed the Orioles doubting their decision to let him play shortstop. "I felt they were looking at me every minute, saying, 'He should have pitched, he should have pitched,'" Ripken said.

Determined to prove himself, he fared no better early in the 1979 season. Now playing in Miami for the Orioles' Single A affiliate, he struggled to drive the ball and continued to pile up throwing errors. The team's manager, Lance Nichols, tried him at third base, searching for any spot where he felt comfortable. Every day, Junior came to the park early for extra fielding practice. Nichols hit him hundreds of balls. He made perfect throws in practice, but not in games, and injured his arm in the process, forcing him to sit out a week of games. "My arm was killing me," Ripken recalled.

Then suddenly, in July of that season, everything clicked. He started hitting line drives and even knocked some pitches over the fence. His throwing accuracy improved. Shelby, also now in Miami, recalled it as "one of the biggest transformations I've ever seen in a player. He just developed all of a sudden. He hit his first professional home run, and then he hit another. His defense was so much better. He was stronger. He just seemed more polished and mature than some other guys."

Near the end of the 1979 season, Ripken was promoted to the Orioles' Double A affiliate in Charlotte, North Carolina. He dislocated the little finger on his throwing hand but taped it up and played on, Senior's stories echoing in his mind.

"Pain tolerance is a very subjective thing," said Richie Bancells, a trainer who worked with Ripken in the Orioles organization for almost a quarter century, starting in Bluefield in 1978. "Some guys are able to minimize it, discern the difference between a truly debilitating injury and something they would call an annoyance. Those annoyances, whether they be contusions, sprains, a lot of guys will say they can't play, but Cal said, 'I can.' He just thought it was part of the job to get himself on the field."

Returning to Charlotte in 1980, Ripken blossomed, hitting 25 home runs, tightening up his defense, and making the Southern League All-Star team. He also played in every game of a season for the first time as a pro, starting 144 games, mostly at third base.

The Southern League split its season into halves, with the teams that won each half then meeting for the league title in early September. Two of Ripken's teammates, Shelby and second baseman Tom Eaton, also played in every game in the first half as their team finished first. The manager, Jimmy Williams, wanted to give all three some rest in the second half so they would be fresh for the championship series. Shelby went first, taking the three days off Williams mandated. Now it was Ripken's turn, and he balked. "I don't want to do that. I don't want to take any days off," he told Williams.

Williams relented. "I wanted to play. I was 19 and strong and wanted to be out there," Ripken recalled. "By August, I was determined to hold on. I slumped pretty badly but held on. My average went from .290 to .276, and I remember thinking how exhausting this was. Then the playoffs started, and that renewed you and I got it going again."

John Shelby recalled: "There wasn't any conversation about playing streaks or anything like that. It was just what you did; you played every day. I was like Cal. We both wanted to play. I enjoyed it. When Jimmy came to me and said he was going to give me a few days off, I had a 21-game hitting streak. I told him, 'I don't want any days off,' but Jimmy was very blunt and said I would take them. I went 0-for-12 when I came back. The time off didn't help. Cal said the same thing I did, and Jimmy let him play."

Ripken's everyday habit continued the next year with the Orioles' Triple A affiliate in Rochester, New York. The manager, Doc Edwards, put him at third base alongside a hot shortstop prospect named Bob Bonner. Ripken played in each of the team's first 114 games, giving him 258 straight over two seasons, an inkling of what lay ahead. He batted .288 with 23 home runs and 75 runs batted in, and his consecutive-game streak ended when the Orioles called him up to the major leagues on August 8, 1981.

His arrival in Baltimore was a proud moment for the family. Ripken's uncle had reached Triple A shortly after World War II. Senior never played above Double A. Junior was the first Ripken to reach the major leagues as a player.

Joining a veteran team in a pennant race, he sat in the clubhouse and on the bus among accomplished Orioles such as Jim Palmer, Ken Singleton, Mark Belanger, Doug DeCinces, and Eddie Murray. Living with his parents and driving to work with his dad, he felt like a kid and sought desperately not to be the reason the team fell short, if it did.

On August 10 in Baltimore, he made his major league debut as a pinch runner, replacing Singleton on second base in an extra-inning game. The Kansas City Royals immediately tried to pick him off. "Just checking, kid," Kansas City second baseman Frank White said as Ripken slid back safely. John Lowenstein promptly doubled him home with the winning run. He crossed the plate wearing a broad smile.

His elation cooled when it became clear there was no spot for him in the lineup. DeCinces and Belanger were entrenched on the left side of the infield. Ripken was part of the Orioles' future, but that future had not arrived. Weaver gave him a few shots at shortstop and third base, but he made three errors, went 5-for-39 at the plate, and mostly just sat on the bench munching on sunflower seeds. As the pressure on the Orioles mounted in September, he did not bat in the team's final 27 games.

"It was a miserable time," he recalled. "Sitting there watching every game from the bench, that was just painful. I had never done that and didn't like it one bit. I made the comment that if I ever got a chance, I'm never coming out."

5

Ironmen

CONFUSION

Seven years after George Pinkney's playing streak ended at 578 straight games, Walter Scott "Steve" Brodie, an outfielder for the Pittsburgh Pirates, was poised to pass him and become the new consecutive-game record holder. Brodie was just three games away after playing in the Pirates' 5–3 victory over the St. Louis Browns on June 25, 1897.

After that game, however, the Pirates left for a weeklong trip to Cleveland and Chicago, and Brodie did not accompany them. His throwing arm ached. The Pirates hoped it would improve if Brodie took a week off. When they played without him on June 28 in Cleveland, losing to the Indians, 12–2, Brodie's consecutive-game streak ended.

Given the acclaim Ripken and Gehrig later received for their streaks, it is hard to reconcile a player giving up when he was so close to the record. But if any player was unpredictable enough to do it, Brodie was. An early version of what would become known in baseball's parlance as a "flake," he talked to balls, caught flies behind his back, and wrestled a muzzled black bear in his backyard to stay fit in the off-season. He went by Steve, not his given name, because someone named Steve Brodie had once jumped off the Brooklyn Bridge. One day, to avoid making a comment to an umpire that he knew would prompt his ejection from a game, he stuffed a sock in his mouth and kept it there while continuing to play.

It was entirely possible Brodie would abandon his quest for a record just before he reached his goal. What almost surely happened, though, is he did not know that he was close, or even that he had a long streak of consecutive games played. In his day, baseball record keeping was limited in scope, riddled with inaccuracies, and widely regarded as a lark more than the intrinsic aspect of the sport it would become. An achievement as complex as Brodie's, which included games played for three teams over parts of five seasons, was more than record keepers could handle. And in any case, a consecutive-game streak was deemed trivial, a stunt more than a worthwhile achievement. The press ignored Brodie's flirtation with the record.

The fundamentals of a more sophisticated statistical apparatus, which would soon evolve, were already in place. The box score, a numerical summary of an individual game invented and refined by Henry Chadwick, had appeared in newspapers since the game's inception before the Civil War. An "official scorer," usually a local sportswriter, oversaw every game, recorded what happened, and sent a box score to the league, which maintained ledgers for players and teams. Fans anticipated the year-end numerical summaries the leagues released, identifying which players fared well in such categories as hits, doubles, triples, home runs, and runs scored (for hitters) and innings pitched, strikeouts, and runs allowed (for pitchers).

But while this "system" conveyed a general statistical picture, it was flawed. Some official scorers were more enthusiastic than others, often depending on how much they were paid for the job. Some blatantly favored hometown players when making judgments. Printing errors were common, and basic communication was undependable, making inaccuracies likely, not just possible. The accounting of Steve Brodie's consecutive-game streak illustrated these shortcomings.

A stout Virginian with a long neck and dark hair parted down the middle, Brodie had broken into the majors with the Boston Beaneaters in 1890, then joined the St. Louis Browns in 1892 and played in every game until the final day of that season, when a game against Chicago was moved to Kansas City. Brodie did not make the trip, and the fact that the game was played at a neutral site seemingly affected the official reporting of it. Some statistical accounts of the 1892 season failed to note that Brodie had missed the game.

The next year, Brodie played center field for the Browns in every game, hitting .319, until he was traded to the Baltimore Orioles in August. Baltimore's manager, Ned Hanlon, wanted him because he hit for a high average, possessed a strong throwing arm, and was "as fast on his feet as a Kansas grasshopper," one columnist wrote. In 1894, "Wee Willie" Keeler, the Orioles' left fielder, batted .371; Joe Kelley, the right fielder, batted .393; and Brodie, the center fielder, batted .366, and all three played in every game as the Orioles won the first of three straight National League pennants.

After that season, a Baltimore sportswriter hailed Brodie's "everyday playing habit," calling it "a remarkable record any player should be proud of." But the writer erroneously stated that Brodie had not missed a game since shortly after he broke into the majors in 1890. In fact, Brodie had missed the 1892 season finale.

That was not the only statistical mistake about Brodie that circulated that off-season. Because of a typographical error in a popular review of the 1894 season, he was credited with having played in 120 games rather than 129, the actual total. Thus, when Brodie again played in every game for the Orioles in 1895 and 1896, pushing his streak to 524 games, the league's official records indicated that his streak was considerably shorter — not that anyone was looking.

Baltimore traded Brodie to Pittsburgh before the 1897 season, and he was so unhappy about leaving a pennant-winning club that the Pirates held their spring training camp near his Virginia home, seeking to appease him. He proved a disappointment once the season began. After his streak ended in June, he was in and out of the lineup for the rest of the season, missing more than 30 games. The Pirates finished eighth in the 12-team National League.

Confusion about his consecutive-game streak persisted for decades. After he died in 1935, the *Sporting News* investigated his career, discovered that his games-played total for 1894 was wrong, and reported that he had played in 727 straight games, making his streak the longest of the 1800s. "He went to his death not knowing he owned the record," the baseball weekly stated. For more than two decades after that, he was credited with owning the longest streak of the 1800s. But the *Sporting News* had missed that he sat out the 1892 season finale. It took another round of painstaking research, conducted in 1961, decades after he played, to learn definitively that Brodie had, in fact, played in three fewer consecutive games than Pinkney.

Shortly after the turn of the century, the National League's top executive, Harry Pulliam, surveyed his league's reams of statistics and judged them "a tangled mass." Pulliam was a notorious control freak who eventually committed suicide over the stress of serving as the league president, secretary, and treasurer at the same time. But before that, in 1903, he hired John Heydler, a slender, circumspect baseball fanatic from Rochester, New York, to clean up the statistical mess.

Originally a newspaper printer, Heydler had been working as a baseball writer, covering the Washington Senators, a National League club, for the *Washington Star.* He kept detailed statistical ledgers for players and dressed up his coverage with numbers, a tactic few of his press box colleagues used. Pulliam liked his work and hired him to improve the league's efforts to keep accurate statistics for players and teams. Upon moving to New York, Heydler set up shop at the National League office in the Metropolitan Life Insurance Company Tower, high above Madison Square Park. According to *The Numbers Game,* a history of baseball statistics by Alan Schwarz, he charted 18 categories for hitters and 17 for pitchers, signaling the beginning of a more purposeful commitment to statistics throughout the sport.

Heydler, who would work for the National League for the next half century in roles of ascending importance — secretary-treasurer, president, chairman — belonged to the first generation of serious baseball statisticians, along with Al Munro Elias, founder of the Elias Sports Bureau, and sportswriters Ernest "Ernie" Lanigan and George Moreland. In the early 1900s, they all endeavored to keep more accurate current numbers and also delved into the game's history, seeking to clarify what happened before their time.

In 1914, Moreland, who wrote for the *Pittsburgh Press,* published a groundbreaking baseball encyclopedia, the first of its kind. His 300-page volume, titled *Balldom,* detailed the histories of leagues and teams and identified yearly statistical leaders going back to the 1870s. It included a section subtitled "Hundreds of Records Never Before Published." These were "facts that will interest fans," Moreland wrote, and "if the reader wants to know what-is-what in baseball, he will find it here."

The book represented the first attempt to identify and organize important statistics and records. It listed hundreds of achievements, but not George Pinkney's 578-game playing streak. Pinkney's name appeared only on a year-by-year list of who played for Brooklyn.

Lanigan, a frail nephew of the founders of the *Sporting News,* worked for newspapers in New York and Cleveland and doggedly delved into the game's history. A statistical purist, he preferred studying his charts to actually watching games. In 1922, he published *The Baseball Cyclopedia*, another attempt to organize records and statistics. Again, Pinkney's consecutive-game streak went unmentioned.

Lanigan admitted that his book, while admirable, was hardly definitive or complete. "Gallant work on the part of certain archaeologists in the last 15 years has brought to light a mass of valuable information," he wrote in 1922, "but much more remains to be turned up before the statistical side of the game can be deemed near perfect."

That was certainly true. Statistical focus was almost a matter of personal taste, it seemed. While Moreland and Lanigan ignored Pinkney and feats of endurance, the consecutive-game record intrigued Al Munro Elias. Although it did not require hitting, pitching, or fielding prowess, it did reflect determination and consistency. Few players stayed healthy enough and performed well enough to play in every game for several seasons in a row. It was actually quite remarkable, Elias thought.

A native of Charleston, South Carolina, Elias had moved to New York around the turn of the century because he enjoyed baseball and wanted to be nearer the game. He believed statistics helped fans understand what they saw. With an accountant's resolve, he meticulously tracked the performances of players and teams, peering through round tortoiseshell glasses while maintaining elaborate ledgers for hitters and pitchers. Diminutive and formal, he started out peddling his findings to fans in bars and pool halls, charging pennies. Not earning nearly enough to live on, Elias and his brother, Walter, sold shoes, shirts, and salad oil on the side. But Elias built enough of a following to form what he called the Elias Statistical Bureau in 1913.

After the *New York Evening Telegram* began using his material in 1916, more freelance opportunities came his way, including a weekly column in the *New York Journal-American*. In March 1918, Elias devoted his column to the history of consecutive-game streaks. It was newsworthy, he wrote, because Eddie Collins, a second baseman for the Chicago White Sox, was about to set a record. The longest streak in major league history, Elias wrote, belonged to Sam Crawford, an outfielder for the Detroit Tigers who had played in 472 straight games before being sidelined by a cold in 1916. Collins had played in just three fewer consecutive games, Elias wrote, and would set a new record by playing in the first four games of the upcoming 1918 season.

Other players who had fashioned long streaks, Elias wrote, included George Burns, a New York Giants outfielder who played in 459 straight games between 1914 and 1917; Lave Cross, an infielder for the Philadelphia Athletics who played in 447 straight between 1902 and 1905; and Frank Isbell, a first baseman for the White Sox who played in 412 straight in the early 1900s. But it was "indisputable," Elias concluded, "that Sam Crawford reigns supreme" as the major league consecutive-game record holder.

Elias's conviction was admirable, but his research was incomplete. He had missed Pinkney's streak of 578 straight and several others of more than 500. George LaChance, a muscular first baseman nicknamed "Candy" because he preferred sucking peppermints to chewing tobacco while he played, had appeared in 539 straight games for Boston's American League club in the early 1900s. His teammate John "Buck" Freeman, a slugging first baseman, played in 536 straight. Clyde Milan, a speedy center fielder for the Washington Senators, appeared in 511 straight between 1910 and 1913. Elias had overlooked them all.

Elias experienced his big break at age 46 in 1919 when Heydler, now president of the National League, hired him to keep accurate statistics for teams and players, track weekly leaders, uncover interesting tidbits, and promote his work to sportswriters. Already known in the press boxes at the Polo Grounds and Ebbets Field, Elias became even more of a regular.

On June 3, 1919, shortly before the start of a game between the Giants and Phillies at the Polo Grounds, he took a seat in the press box and checked the lineups. He was surprised to see George Whitted, a toothy reserve known as "Possum," playing first base for Philadelphia. Fred Luderus, a dependable veteran, had manned first base for the Phillies for most of the past decade.

Elias asked around, wondering why Luderus was out. A Philadelphia sportswriter explained that he had a "charley horse," a sore thigh muscle. He had played with it the day before as the Phillies were swept in a doubleheader at the Polo Grounds, going hitless in the first game before leaving the second game early due to the injury. Jack Coombs, the Phillies' manager, felt he needed a rest.

As the game began in bright sunshine before several thousand fans, Possum Whitted, aptly nicknamed for his buck teeth and big eyes, made Coombs look smart, singling to lead off the top of the first and coming around to score. In the fourth, he bashed a drive to deep center that was misplayed, enabling him to circle the bases for a three-run inside-the-park homer.

Elias watched with growing unease. He was looking for statistical material and knew Luderus had a lengthy consecutive-game streak: 446 straight, it turned out. In the sixth inning, Elias left the press box, descended to the stands, stopped by the Phillies' dugout, leaned in, and signaled to Coombs. Gaining the manager's attention, he shouted that "Luddy" should get into the game to keep his consecutive-game streak going.

Coombs squinted up at Elias as if he were a visitor from another planet. Elias had breached basic protocol by invading the sanctity of the dugout during a game. Coombs growled that he did not care about some damn streak; Luderus was injured.

Elias persisted, pointing out that Luderus only needed to bat once to keep his streak going. Coombs did not appreciate a denizen of the press box telling him what to do. The manager was a bona fide baseball man, a former pitcher who had once won 31 games in a season. The Phillies had put him in charge partly because he had a chemistry degree from Colby College in Maine; he was a smart guy. But while he was not anxious to accede to Elias's suggestion, Coombs did not see the harm in letting Luderus bat, especially since the Phillies were well ahead. He gave in. When Whitted was due up in the ninth, Luderus pinch-hit for him.

A thick-bodied, square-jawed German American from Wisconsin, Luderus walked gingerly to the plate, clearly favoring his injured thigh. But after taking two pitches, he swung hard at a fastball and lined a single up the middle. Then he manned first base in the bottom of the ninth as the downtrodden Phillies wrapped up a rare victory.

Though it was not a long workday, Luderus received credit for playing in the game, extending his streak. Seven years earlier, the National League had adopted guidelines for what counted as an official game appearance. Before 1912, the league had not credited most pinch runners, pinch hitters, or defensive substitutes with playing; only starters received that recognition. But as of 1912, "all appearances by a player in a championship game count as a game played," according to the modern encyclopedia *Total Baseball*. The American League had adopted the same guidelines in 1907.

Back in the press box, Elias positively beamed as the ninth inning unfolded. Due strictly to his persistence, Luderus had now played in 447 straight games. It was one of the longest streaks the major leagues had witnessed. Elias could provide sportswriters with numbers and facts extolling the achievement. There would be articles in the papers. Elias had done his job.

His involvement illustrated an unusual fact about consecutive-game streaks that soon became evident as they emerged from history's mists as a viable achievement and, for some players, a goal. Unlike most other feats and records, a playing streak could be manipulated. Several players, including Lou Gehrig, would take considerable advantage of that in the coming decades.

On August 3, when Luderus ran his streak to 479 straight games, breaking Eddie Collins's record and becoming "the new 'Iron Man' of the majors," according to the *Philadelphia Inquirer,* the paper did not report that Pinkney actually had a streak that was 99 games longer; that fact was still buried in the game's annals. But the paper did note that Luderus had made it this far only because Elias had convinced Coombs to use him as a pinch hitter in the ninth inning on June 3.

Luderus ended up playing in every game of the 1919 season for the Phillies, who endured two 13-game losing streaks and finished 47½ games out of first place. Luderus generated what little positive publicity they received, and near the end of the season, the Phillies honored their first baseman in a ceremony at the Baker Bowl in Philadelphia. Heydler, the league president, and the Phillies' owner, William Baker, brought Luderus to home plate between games of a doubleheader. Heydler gave a speech and presented Luderus with a gold stickpin from the league. Baker also spoke and gave Luderus a gold watch.

It was "the first occasion in which a big league president has appeared at home plate to present a testimonial from the league to one of its players, and no more deserving player than Luderus could have been selected for this honor," the *Philadelphia Inquirer* wrote. Although he was being honored for his years of solid play and not his consecutive-game streak, his streak embodied the dependability that made him valuable. The few fans at the park gave him an ovation.

With so many statisticians digging around, Pinkney inevitably received recognition for his achievement, now three decades old, of playing in so many games in a row. On January 4, 1920, Pittsburgh sportswriter Mac-Lean Kennedy identified him as the true holder of the consecutive-game record.

"A statistician informs us that Fred Luderus holds the record for playing the greatest number of games consecutively, and his mark of 533 is by all odds the true record of all modern day players," Kennedy wrote in the *Pittsburgh Press*. "However, someone is always taking the joy out of life by digging up old-time records and here is one which is genuine and the player deserves credit for his wonderful steadiness."

Kennedy did not identify his sources, so it was not clear whether he had made the discovery himself or "borrowed" it from a statistician or sportswriter colleague. Either way, he accurately detailed Pinkney's Illinois background, playing career, and record of playing in 578 straight games. The record "is the best ever made and stands for all the reliables to shoot at," Kennedy wrote. "Eddie Collins had a mark of 478 in a row, which was the mark Luderus overcame. Now this old one which had slipped the memories of present-day [statisticians] was dug up."

The Associated Press picked up on the discovery and circulated a story about Pinkney. Now 60 years old, Gentleman George experienced a brief burst of limited fame. A sportswriter for the *Peoria Journal* came to his house to discuss his record.

"I paid little attention to it at the time I played," Pinkney said. "But I knew, of course, that I had established a mark for others to shoot for."

And here they came.

6

Ironmen

DEACON

Though they played decades apart, Everett Scott and George Pinkney shared many qualities. Both were infielders with Midwestern roots, Pinkney from Peoria, Illinois, Scott from Bluffton, Indiana. Both were known for their defense more than for their hitting; Scott often led all American League shortstops in fielding during his heyday with the Boston Red Sox and New York Yankees. Both earned respect for their off-field habits; Scott's teammates nicknamed him "Deacon" after watching him rise early on Sundays to attend church while they slept off their Saturday nights.

Also, Scott, like the egg-shaped Pinkney, did not seem a likely exemplar of toughness and determination. He stood five feet eight and never weighed more than 145 pounds during his 13-year major league career. His flannel jersey fit loosely on his bony body, the excess cloth flapping when breezes swept through the infield. With his bugged-out eyes and broad ears jutting from his football-shaped head, Scott was an adult version of what kids call a pipsqueak.

But as with Pinkney, those initial impressions did not paint an accurate picture. Scott had sure hands and a knack for knowing where to position himself against different batters, enabling him to get to more ground balls before they reached the outfield. Once he had the ball, he threw it across the diamond on such a taut line that Brooklyn manager Wilbert Robinson nicknamed him "Trolley Wire" during the 1916 World Series. He also had an "uncanny" ability to hit his first baseman in the chest no matter where he threw from, according to *Baseball Magazine*.

Most of all, Scott shared Pinkney's burning desire to play in every game, even when dealing with injuries and ailments that would have sidelined others. "I just thought I was supposed to play ball as long I was needed and able to," Scott told the *New York Times* in 1922, when he was just gaining a measure of fame for fashioning the longest consecutive-game streak in major league history.

A star pitcher in high school, Scott was a slender 19-year-old infield prospect on a minor league team in Youngstown, Ohio, in 1912 when the Red Sox, Boston Braves, and Washington Senators all noticed him. The Senators declined to pursue him, deciding his slight frame would not allow him "to keep up the strenuous pace demanded in the big show," their scout wrote. Scott weighed all of 120 pounds. He signed with the Red Sox, who had won three pennants and two World Series titles since their inception in 1901.

As a rookie in 1914, Scott hit .239 while playing in most of the games that year. Boston's player-manager, Bill Carrigan, who was part of the team's catching platoon, liked having Scott anchoring the defense; he could win a game without reaching base, Carrigan thought. Even when Scott really struggled at the plate and hit just .201 the next year, Carrigan still played him in roughly two of every three games as the Red Sox won another pennant. Decades later, when baseball mathematicians developed advanced statistical analytics and applied them to prior seasons, Scott ranked in the top 10 in the American League in 1915 in "defensive wins above replacement"—a calculation assessing a player's value as a defender. He would later lead the league in that metric four times.

Still, in 1915 he was one of Boston's younger, least heralded players, overshadowed not only by veteran teammates Tris Speaker, Harry Hooper, and Duffy Lewis but also by another youngster, George Herman "Babe" Ruth, a barrel-chested 20-year-old left-handed pitcher who won 15 games for the Sox that season. At six feet two and more than 200 pounds, Ruth commanded attention with his bearish physique and broad face dominated by a bulbous nose and wide, flaring nostrils. A prodigious talent, he not only cleverly mixed the speeds and locations of his tosses but also could play the outfield and hit—really hit. Ruth smacked four home runs in 1915, including one that traveled so far it broke a window at a Chevrolet dealership next to Sportsman's Park in St. Louis.

But though Ruth generated more headlines than Scott, he barely left the bench during the 1915 World Series, while Scott played every inning, a measure of Carrigan's growing confidence in him. Scott collected just one hit in 18 at-bats, but he did not commit an error as the Red Sox defeated the Philadelphia Phillies in five games. Afterward, Carrigan noted his key contribution.

The next year, Detroit's Ty Cobb spiked Scott on a play at second base early in the season, prompting Scott to borrow longer spikes from a teammate to better fight such battles. Unaccustomed to the new footwear, he tripped and turned an ankle, forcing him to miss several games. After returning as a defensive replacement late in a loss to the Yankees on June 20, he reclaimed his starting spot on June 21 and did not miss another start all season.

The Red Sox were in fifth place when he returned, and his steadying presence helped them. In the end, they won their second straight pennant, and Scott led the league's shortstops with a .967 fielding percentage, committing just 19 errors in almost 600 chances. It was the first of eight straight seasons in which he would lead the league's shortstops in that statistic.

In Game 2 of the 1916 World Series, the Red Sox defeated Brooklyn, 2–1, in a 14-inning affair that lasted just 2 hours and 37 minutes. Ruth threw every pitch. He had won 23 games and compiled the league's lowest earned run average during the season, but this was his finest hour. The victory gave the Red Sox a 2–0 lead in the series, and they went on to win in five games.

But though Ruth's play on the field drew ovations, his behavior off the field was becoming alarming. A Baltimore saloonkeeper's son, he had spent his youth at St. Mary's Industrial School for Boys, a strict Roman Catholic orphanage, and now that he was on his own, he acted as if he had just been released from prison. He ate and drank excessively and chased women until sunrise. It was rumored he had enough sex to satisfy the whole pitching staff. Although his broad smile and guileless nature made his behavior easier to take, some teammates considered him a selfish distraction.

Scott was a milquetoast by comparison, quiet and watchful, married to his high school sweetheart. His idea of fun was a night of bowling. (After his baseball career, he would own an alley and participate in national tournaments.) Unlike the self-centered Ruth, Scott exhibited adult priorities. When his wife became ill and needed surgery before the 1917 season, Scott left the team and missed a week of exhibition games to help her convalesce in Indiana. But he was back on Opening Day and played in every game of the season for the first time as the Sox finished third.

The next year, with the country's involvement in World War I at a peak, the major league season was shortened by a month as more than 200 players left their teams to comply with a federal "work or fight" directive requiring draft-eligible men to enlist in the armed services or work in a war-related industry. The Red Sox lost 11 players, and as minor leaguers filled in, Ruth campaigned to play the outfield as well as pitch. Given a chance, he hit eight home runs in a month, a startling total; only one other American League player hit more than six home runs all season. Never again would Ruth just pitch for his team.

Scott played in every game of the abbreviated season as the Red Sox won another pennant and defeated the Chicago Cubs in the World Series. His .221 average illustrated his ongoing offensive struggles, but he was now a three-time World Series winner and emerging team leader whose opinions were valued. When the Red Sox and Cubs almost went on strike before the World Series after discovering their postseason bonuses had been slashed, ostensibly as a necessary wartime restriction, Scott was among the players who negotiated with the sport's leaders, to no avail.

On May 16, 1919, Scott played in his 400th straight game, going hitless in four at-bats in a loss to the Chicago White Sox. His daily presence in the lineup was assured, regardless of how low his batting average sank. Boston's manager, Ed Barrow, who had replaced Carrigan the year before, valued his defense. Baseball was at the end of its "dead-ball era," marked by the dominance of pitching, defense, and "small-ball" offensive strategy over the raw power of home run hitting, a set of priorities Ruth would soon invert, leading to sweeping changes in the game's very nature. But those changes were just beginning to percolate in 1919, so a shortstop's offensive shortcomings were tolerated if his defense was as strong as Scott's.

Scott still encountered challenges to his consecutive-game streak. One day in Philadelphia, a rookie pitcher for Boston, Waite Hoyt, uncorked a wild throw that plunked Scott in the back of the head during warm-ups. Knocked out cold, the shortstop lay facedown in the grass for 10 minutes as concerned teammates stood in a circle around him, watching a trainer work to revive him. But then he abruptly stood up and, head clearing, played all nine innings that day, later telling reporters, "I was out but recovered in time; can't beat that for luck, can you?"

He also was beset by small, painful skin infections, known as boils, which would trouble him for the rest of his career. They cropped up on his arms, legs, both feet, scalp . . . just about everywhere. "Boils of all shapes and sizes; I had it bad," he later told the *New York Times*. The infections oozed pus and often throbbed, but he could play with them, he discovered, if he wrapped bandages around them so tightly that he lost feeling in the afflicted areas. Thus began a pregame ritual he would follow for the rest of his career: while his teammates put on their uniforms and sharpened their spikes, Scott sat by his locker patiently wrapping bandages around his boils, a process that could take an hour.

Years later, when asked to reflect on Scott, his teammates usually started with stories about his boils and the thick bandages he painstakingly applied that enabled him to play. A *New York Times* sportswriter, John Kieran, compared him to Job, the biblical figure also beset by boils. Scott, Kieran wrote, played at times "when he was suffering from an attack of boils that would have made Job look like an advertisement for skin food. The shortstop won out by sheer persistency. He simply refused to quit, even when he appeared on the ball field with bandages enough to justify the suspicion that he had just lost an argument with a threshing machine."

On August 28, 1919, Scott played in his 500th straight game. The press paid no attention. The once-mighty Red Sox were experiencing a surprising decline, with the focus on Ruth, who was losing interest in pitching as he hit more home runs. Fans across the league flocked to ballparks hoping to see him uncoil his all-or-nothing swing and swat a majestic fly over the fence. They screeched with delight when he hit one, and Ruth loved the attention. As his star rose, he ran wilder at night, ignored Barrow's attempts at discipline, and held out for a raise in the middle of the season. The nonstop controversies sank the Red Sox, who wound up in fifth place.

Ruth would end the year with 29 home runs, an all-time major league record, after skipping the last game of the season to grab a paycheck for appearing in an exhibition game in Baltimore, his hometown. Scott, playing in his teammate's expanding shadow, quietly churned on. By the end of the 1919 season, he had appeared in 524 straight games. The Phillies' Fred Luderus had a longer streak by nine games, but Luderus sat out the first game of the 1920 season with a sore back, and Scott kept going. He passed Luderus on April 26, 1920, hitting a home run in a Red Sox victory in Philadelphia. He now had the longest active streak in the major leagues, having played in 534 straight games.

"Few of the 4,000-odd fans knew the modest little shortstop was setting a record," the *Boston Globe* wrote, "but the rest of the Red Sox did and gave him a rousing reception in the dugout after he had taken his first stand at the bat."

The *Philadelphia Inquirer* erroneously added that Scott had broken "all major league records for consecutive games," apparently having missed the Associated Press's dispatch about Pinkney's streak that circulated before the season. But when Scott went by Pinkney on June 21, 1920, and definitively established the all-time record, the Associated Press sent another story across its wires, setting readers straight about the consecutive-game record.

Several weeks after that, when Scott reached 600 straight, the Associated Press sent out yet another story, its third in seven months on the subject. Sportswriters around the country chimed in with commentary, many taking note of baseball endurance for the first time. On July 16, 1920, the *Milwaukee Journal*'s unidentified "Sports Insider" columnist wrote:

> Sometimes we baseball fans overlook players like Everett Scott of the Boston Red Sox. Athletes who are more spectacular seem to monopolize the public prints and grab our attention by their home run clouts and circus stunts. So occasionally it may appear that we do not appreciate the steady, unheralded and yet invaluable services of a player like Scott.
>
> He recently established the record for consecutive games played in the major leagues. He completed his 579th game in a row. It was thought that he made the record some time ago when he passed the mark set by Luderus of the Phillies, who played in 533 games without interruption. But always some statistician bobs up to take the wind out of one's sails. In this instance, it was found that way

back in the late 1880s one George Pinkney of Brooklyn played 578 games in six seasons without a break. Therefore Scott had to set out again to surpass Pinkney, and he is quite likely to go right along and establish a record that won't be equaled for a long, long time.

Scott has been playing steady and consistent baseball since 1916 and made his record in five playing seasons. He is a sterling and reliable shortstop and has won a prominent niche in baseball's hall of fame.

The *Milwaukee Journal* column — based entirely on numbers, confusion over them, and the feat they signified — reflected a change under way in baseball and its coverage. There was a developing interest not just in statistics but also in achievements that were years in the making.

Until then, only single-game and single-season statistics received significant attention. In *Balldom,* his 1914 encyclopedia, George Moreland included dozens of pages of such achievements but ignored career statistics and streaks lasting years. Even pitcher Cy Young's astounding lifetime total of 511 wins went unmentioned.

Eight years later, Ernie Lanigan also focused on records and feats from individual games and seasons in *The Baseball Cyclopedia,* while reserving little room for career numbers and streaks. Ty Cobb had established dozens of well-known benchmarks by then, but they were all from single seasons, such as his 248 hits in 1911 or his 96 steals in 1915. Cobb's career totals were seldom publicized.

It seems unfathomable now that players, sportswriters, and fans simply did not consider career totals and streaks lasting years. Today, a century later, such numbers are as integral to baseball as balls and bats. Career statistics and years-long streaks generate attention, determine salaries, and help decide who gets inducted into the Hall of Fame. But baseball was just beginning to note such achievements as Scott's consecutive-game streak grew.

Shortly after his 600th straight game, in 1920, he developed a large boil above his right eye and could barely see when he wrapped his head in a bandage. Barrow, still Boston's manager, told him to stay away from the ballpark one game day, and Scott complied, thinking his streak had ended. But a thunderstorm soaked Boston that afternoon, canceling the game, and Scott's boil "broke" that evening, enabling him to play the next day and continue his streak. The *Boston Globe* reported on his good fortune. It seemed his playing streak had become newsworthy.

Hard as it is to believe now, the New York Yankees were a mediocrity when Jacob Ruppert and a partner bought them before the 1915 season. Previously known as the Americans, Hilltoppers, and Highlanders before adopting the Yankees nickname in 1913, they had never won an American League pennant, and they rented the Polo Grounds from the National League's Giants for their home games, most of which drew few fans.

After they finished more than 40 games out of first place on average in the three years before Ruppert bought them, a *Baseball Magazine* writer asked, "How much longer shall the American League allow this glaring business blunder to exist?" The Red Sox ruled their league, and the popular Giants, managed by John McGraw, New York's preeminent baseball figure, ruled their city.

Ruppert expected better. His family had brewed one of New York's favorite beers for almost a century, amassing great wealth and Tammany Hall political clout. Ruppert, a 47-year-old bachelor who spoke with a thick accent that reflected his German heritage (he would call his most famous player "Root"), favored expensive clothes, slicked-back hair, and a bushy mustache. His favorite possessions included racehorses and show dogs, but he was hardly an idle playboy. Rather than start at the top in the family business, he began as a barrel washer. Once he was in charge, he modernized and expanded the brewery, which occupied an entire block in Manhattan. Along the way, he served four terms in the U.S. Congress, a measure of his family's stature.

A baseball fanatic, he repeatedly tried to buy the Giants, but McGraw's club was not for sale. Finally, McGraw arranged for Ruppert to buy the Yankees with Tillinghast L'Hommedieu Huston, an enterprising former army engineer who had profited during the rebuilding of Cuba after the Spanish-American War. They shared the purchase price of $450,000, a bargain.

From the outset, Ruppert and "Cap" Huston did not get along. They had little in common other than their love of baseball. Huston's fortune was earned; Ruppert's was inherited. Huston was rumpled, impulsive, a risk taker; Ruppert was fastidious and methodical.

Their chances of getting along ended permanently when the Yankees hired a new manager, Miller Huggins, in 1919. Ban Johnson, president of the American League, had recommended Huggins, a diminutive former second baseman for the St. Louis Cardinals who had preached fundamentals as a player-manager in recent years. Huston wanted to hire Wilbert Robinson, who had played and coached for John McGraw and managed Brooklyn to the National League pennant in 1916. When Huston went overseas as part of the war effort, Ruppert hired Huggins.

Furious, Huston would exact revenge in the coming years by steadfastly supporting players who feuded with Huggins. He eventually grew so frustrated that he sold his share of the club to Ruppert. But despite their differences, Ruppert and Huston forever altered the Yankees. With the thoughtful, pipe-smoking Huggins in charge, the club would surpass the Giants and become both New York's favorite team and baseball's premier franchise, playing in America's grandest ballpark.

By 1919, Ruppert had become friendly with the owners of several other American League clubs, including Harry Frazee, a New York theatrical producer who owned the Red Sox. Frazee had an interesting problem. Ruth had become baseball's top box office attraction, but he was also increasingly a pain to both management and the other Red Sox players, who did not care for him. Meanwhile, Frazee needed money to buy Fenway Park, which he rented for games. Ruppert offered to buy Ruth's contract for $100,000, considering it a win-win proposition. The money would enable Frazee to buy Fenway, and the Yankees would get an indisputably exciting player who sold tickets. With Prohibition looming, Ruppert realized he needed to start finding other ways to make money besides selling beer.

They struck the deal, Ruth jumped from the Red Sox to the Yankees, and neither club was ever the same. Ruth was still a pain, but he was worth the trouble, piling up home runs while leading the Yankees to baseball's pinnacle. The Red Sox, meanwhile, would not win another World Series until the twenty-first century.

In 1920, his first season in New York, Ruth slumped early, obviously feeling the pressure to produce. But he knocked a ball completely out of the Polo Grounds on May 1 and wound up hitting 11 home runs that month, setting a major league record for home runs in a month. Then he hit 13 in June. It was an unheard-of pace. Three seasons earlier, the

Yankees' Wally Pipp had led the major leagues with nine home runs. In 1920, Ruth hit 54.

Fans flocked to see him. On May 16, the Yankees drew nearly 39,000 to a game at the Polo Grounds, a record. Although they finished third in the American League that season, they drew 1.2 million fans to their home games, becoming the first major league team to draw more than a million fans in a season. It was time for them to have a ballpark of their own. Ruppert and Huston had scouted prospective locations for several years, having grown weary of their rental arrangement with the Giants. They finally found a suitable location in the Bronx, and construction began on what would be called Yankee Stadium.

Meanwhile, Boston's manager, Ed Barrow, joined the Yankees as general manager and began raiding his former team. The Yankees had already acquired Ruth and pitcher Carl Mays from the Red Sox, and now they acquired pitchers Waite Hoyt and Herb Pennock and catcher Wally Schang. With Ruth hitting 59 home runs to lead the way, the Yankees won their first American League pennant in 1921. After they lost the World Series to the Giants, Barrow vowed to improve the club and targeted Scott, who had hit .262 for the Red Sox in 1921 while exhibiting his usual top-notch defense. In January 1922, the Yankees acquired Scott and pitchers Joe Bush and Sam Jones in exchange for shortstop Roger Peckinpaugh and pitchers Bill Piercy, Rip Collins, and Jack Quinn.

"My transfer to New York was, of course, a very acceptable move," Scott would tell *Baseball Magazine*.

As with many of Frazee's deals, it would prove to be a lopsided transaction favoring the other team.

The challenge of playing an entire season without a day off was easier in Scott's era than when George Pinkney toiled for Brooklyn. Players now wore gloves in the field, so they suffered fewer bruises and cuts. They could come out of a game early if the manager so desired. Off the field, they traveled on faster, more comfortable trains and stayed at nicer hotels. A generation of new steel-and-concrete ballparks featured smoother playing surfaces and spacious clubhouses.

That did not mean it was now easy to play a full season without a break. The same physical dangers existed. Base runners slid in with their spikes up. Pitchers threw at hitters, sometimes breaking bones. Players collided at home plate. And the season itself was longer. Pinkney never played in more than 143 games in a season in the 1800s, but Scott played in at least 152 in every season except those shortened by World War I.

His durability was not an accident. Scott worked at it. In an era when few players exercised in the off-season, he jogged throughout the winter and performed calisthenics. During the season, he wrapped his boils with bandages for an hour before each game and wore special cleats with extra padding to keep opponents' spikes from gashing his feet. "There were days when Deacon's shoes looked like a remnant sale at the ribbon counter, but his little tootsies were safe," a teammate said later.

When pressed to explain his streak after being traded to the Yankees, Scott pointed out that he was not a heavy drinker or eater and went to bed early — hours before Ruth on many nights, no doubt. "I guess the care I take of myself and some good luck have carried me through," he said. "Being in good condition is only a matter of right living. Since regular hours are an important part of good health, I have always made a point to keep them."

He also said there was "no doubt" he had been blessed with good fortune. "I have been spared the kind of injuries that lay up infielders from time to time," he said.

Late in the 1921 season, his last in Boston, Scott reached 800 games in a row. Newspapers noted the milestone, but the sports world was more focused on Ruth's home run barrage and the possibility that gamblers had influenced the 1919 World Series between the Chicago White Sox and Cincinnati Reds. Eight White Sox players were on trial for getting paid to intentionally lose the Series.

Though a jury acquitted the players on August 3, 1921, the sport's new commissioner, Kenesaw Mountain Landis, wielding virtually unlimited powers, banned all eight players from the game for life. "Regardless of the verdict of juries, no player who throws a ball game, no player who undertakes or promises to throw a ball game, no player who sits in confidence with a bunch of crooked ballplayers and gamblers, where the ways and means of throwing a game are discussed and does not promptly tell his club about it, will ever play professional baseball," Landis said.

Baseball had been cast in a dark light before. Players were often lampooned as drunkards in the 1800s, and they were deemed unpatriotic for going to great lengths to avoid frontline military service during World War I. The Red Sox and Phillies did not help matters when they threatened to walk out on the 1918 World Series because of a pay cut while thousands of Americans were fighting and dying overseas.

But the "thrown" World Series represented a new low. The sport suddenly craved positive news, *anything* that cast it in a favorable light. After acquiring Scott before the 1922 season, the Yankees aggressively marketed him to local sportswriters as an upstanding citizen, hoping he could help restore the public's faith in the game. Scott was "in bed early and enjoyed wholesome hobbies such as bridge, whist, poker, fishing, and bowling," one article noted. Grantland Rice, the syndicated columnist whose work was read by millions, praised his durability. "After Everett Scott is dead, we expect to see his ghost out there playing short through force of habit. No such shallow barrier as the grave will ever check the Deacon's tireless pace," Rice wrote.

Having toiled for years in the shadows of more famous teammates, Scott liked the attention. His durability had gone mostly unrecognized and unappreciated in Boston, but on Ruth's Yankees in the early 1920s, he was suddenly at the epicenter of the sports and media worlds, his feats writ large. Eleven daily newspapers assigned beat writers to cover the team. Columnists and feature writers were always hanging around, looking for material. Scott's playing streak was nothing if not unique. He gave several interviews about it before he played a game for his new team, telling some reporters his goal was to reach a thousand straight games. Then, worried that he appeared self-centered for saying that, he told the *New York Times'* John Kieran he actually did not have a numerical goal. Finally, when columnists praised him as "baseball's endurance king," he confessed that, yes, he did want to reach a thousand straight games. No one else in history had come anywhere close to that.

7

Ripken

INFLUENCES

By the time Cal Ripken Jr. put on an Orioles uniform for the first time, in 1981, the Orioles' decision makers were no longer debating whether they should have made him a pitcher. It seemed clear he would become an everyday player in the major leagues; they had made the right call. But after the 1981 season, they were debating a new question: should he play shortstop or third base?

Ripken had mostly played third in the minors, but Weaver envisioned him as a replacement for Mark Belanger, the slick-fielding shortstop who was leaving the Orioles after running the infield for 15 years. (He signed with the Dodgers as a free agent.) Weaver had grown up in St. Louis watching six-foot-four Marty Marion play shortstop for the Cardinals in the 1940s, so he did not believe Ripken's size would hinder him in the middle infield.

Weaver lost the battle. On January 28, 1982, the Orioles traded their third baseman, Doug DeCinces, to the California Angels, clearing the way for Ripken to take over at third. Weaver was against giving up DeCinces, a dependable fielder who hit for power, but the manager felt better about the situation after watching Ripken belt a home run in his first at-bat on Opening Day and then sprint around the bases, his enthusiasm apparent. How could you not love the kid?

After that, though, Ripken fell into a terrible slump, collecting just four hits in 55 at-bats. Weaver called him in for a talk. "Look, we traded DeCinces. There's no one in the minors to come up. We're not sending you back. Just go do what you can do," Weaver said. When Ripken continued to struggle, Weaver pinch-hit for him several times and also hinted that he should consider altering his stance and philosophical approach at the plate. Ripken grudgingly accepted being hit for but did not like the idea of changing his philosophy. Senior quietly told him to stick with what had worked until now.

An on-field conversation with slugger Reggie Jackson helped ease his mind. Jackson, now playing for the Angels, was on third base when several Orioles and Angels began to brawl one night at Memorial Stadium. Instead of joining the fight, Jackson turned and spoke directly to Ripken. They knew each other. Jackson had played for the Orioles in 1976, when Senior was Weaver's bullpen coach and Junior, then in high school, hung around the clubhouse.

"Look, Junior, you've made it to the big leagues; just hit the way you want to hit," Jackson said.

Ripken heeded the advice, calmed down, and eventually began to heat up. His average was near .240 when the Orioles played a doubleheader against the Toronto Blue Jays at Memorial Stadium on May 29. After going 1-for-4 in the first game, he was held out of the second game. Weaver was trying to identify an everyday shortstop, and one of the candidates, Floyd Rayford, needed at-bats, so Weaver let him take Ripken's spot at third for a game. (Lenn Sakata and Bob Bonner were the other shortstop candidates.) Ripken was back in the lineup the next day, May 30, batting eighth and playing third. He went 0-for-2 with a walk as the Orioles lost to Toronto, 6–0. No one could have imagined that a day so forgettable would become such an important historical marker—the beginning of the sport's longest consecutive-game streak.

Less than a week later, on June 4, the Orioles played the Twins in Minnesota and fell behind early, 6–0. It was one of those nights when a lack of hitting became contagious. Weaver paced back and forth in the dugout, cursing and stealing puffs from a cigarette in the tunnel leading to the clubhouse. After Ken Singleton doubled to start the top of the ninth, Weaver hit for Ripken with Jim Dwyer, a veteran who excelled as a pinch hitter. Dwyer struck out. Weaver sent two more pinch hitters to the plate, but a rally did not develop, and second baseman Rich Dauer grounded out to end the game. Ripken had neither batted nor played in the field in the ninth, the last inning he would miss for more than five years.

Weaver continued to shuffle shortstop candidates, but none earned the job, and finally, on July 1, the manager gave Ripken a shot. Weaver had lost the off-season battle to determine Ripken's position, but he had the final say now and had always thought Ripken could replace Belanger.

When Ripken saw a "6" by his name on the lineup card posted in the clubhouse, he thought it was a mistake and went to Weaver. "I'm putting you there to try to get more offense in the lineup. I don't want you to try to do too much," Weaver said. Initially, Ripken felt rusty in the field and struggled to turn double plays, but he soon settled in. Meanwhile, his productivity at the plate soared. Starting the Orioles' final 90 games of the season at shortstop, he finished with a .264 average, 28 home runs, and 93 runs batted in, dwarfing the offense Belanger had provided at the position. He was voted the American League Rookie of the Year, and the "shortstop or third base" dilemma was over.

After falling eight games behind the Milwaukee Brewers in the American League East, the Orioles rallied furiously in September and, in the end, needed to sweep a four-game series with the Brewers at Memorial Stadium to win the division. They won the first three in front of roaring crowds and sent out their longtime ace, Jim Palmer, to pitch the finale. Fans brought out brooms, anticipating a triumph and another trip to the postseason. But the Brewers battered Palmer, wrapped up the division title, and went on to play in the World Series.

"If only I had moved Ripken to shortstop earlier, we'd have won the pennant," Weaver joked years later about a positional decision that would rank as one of his best.

The fiery Weaver, burned-out from years in the dugout, retired after the 1982 season. After 26 years in the organization, Senior was a candidate to replace him, but the job went to Joe Altobelli, who had coached and managed in Baltimore's minor league system for 11 years and more recently managed the San Francisco Giants. Senior was disappointed, but as Ripken later wrote in his autobiography, *The Only Way I Know,* the family was not upset, because Senior was "still young, forty-seven years old. He had plenty of time" to get a shot.

Altobelli inherited a squad of hungry veterans. The Orioles had lost the 1979 World Series after holding a 3–1 lead and had just missed making the playoffs in 1982 and several other times. They knew they had only a few more years together and were determined to leave a mark. Altobelli knew not to disrupt their chemistry. Calm and genial, he was Weaver's opposite in demeanor, but he continued to employ many of Weaver's strategies when making out lineups, using pitchers, and managing games. Like Weaver, he preferred to rely on players hitting three-run homers to win games, as opposed to scratching out single runs with bunts, sacrifices, and steals. "I don't even think we had a hit-and-run sign," said Ken Singleton, adding that the bashing style kept players out of the trainer's room because "you didn't pull muscles or crash into guys running the bases; you just sat back and drove in runs."

Continuing what Weaver had started, Altobelli played Ripken at shortstop in every game in 1983. In fact, Ripken never left the field; he played every inning. When several games became lopsided, Altobelli approached him in the dugout and asked if he wanted to take the rest of the day off. Ripken always said he wanted to keep playing. If anything, he felt stronger as the season progressed, unlike what he had experienced at Double A Charlotte in 1980, when he played an entire season but became worn down at the end. Now, in 1983, he hit .315 in August and .385 in September.

"I finished strong that year and had felt good [at the end] in 1982, too," Ripken recalled. "When you can do that physically, you know you can. It's a mental thing. My experience in Double A, going down [at the end], you kind of learn from that. You didn't really know if it was a good idea to play in all those games or not, because you wore down at the end. To have that change in my first two years in the big leagues, it became a given that I could do it. I could play 162 and finish [with my average] going up. Then it was just a matter of the mental side, how you control it. But it was a big relief to know you could."

He conceded years later that if he had slumped down the stretch of either of his first two seasons in the majors, he never would have played in so many games in a row.

"If you didn't finish well, maybe you should manage your season differently," he said, thinking back. "The thought would be, 'There is no way I should be playing like this at the end of the season, so I should take some days off so I don't get to that point.' But once you finish strong, you know you can, so whether you play in every game is not a factor in how you approach the game."

In 1983, Ripken batted .318, hit 27 home runs, and drove in 102 runs. One year after being voted Rookie of the Year, he won the American League Most Valuable Player award, edging out Eddie Murray in the balloting. The Orioles won 19 of their last 22 games to capture the American League East, then rolled through the postseason, losing just two games as they defeated the Chicago White Sox in the American League Championship Series and the Philadelphia Phillies in the World Series.

At the end of the triumphant season, Altobelli could not believe he had let Ripken play every inning. After the World Series, the manager told his shortstop, "That was great, but I'm not going to let it happen again."

Oh, but he did.

In Ripken's first years with the Orioles, most of his teammates were older and married; they would be met by their wives and children at the Baltimore airport when the team returned from a road trip (having flown commercial before charter-flight travel became the norm throughout the major leagues). Younger and single, Ripken would grab his luggage and take an airport shuttle to the remote parking lot where he had left his car. On many occasions, he shared the shuttle with Eddie Murray, who was also single.

The two players quickly became friends. They had a lot in common. Both had been high Orioles draft picks. Both had come through the team's minor league pipeline and reached the majors with fans expecting a lot from them. Both had naturally reserved personalities and were all business around the ballpark, but were more lighthearted in private than the public knew.

Both also had great respect for Senior, who had coached Murray in the Florida Instructional League in 1973, when some scouts had thought the just-drafted Murray was either lazy or uninterested because he folded his arms at first base between pitches. "That's just how he stands," Senior scoffed, helping defuse the criticism. Later, Senior helped Murray become a switch hitter, a move that set him on the path to being an All-Star.

When Murray reached Baltimore in 1977, he joined a contending Orioles team led by clubhouse elders such as Singleton and 34-year-old first baseman Lee May, whose philosophies had been formed in the 1960s, before more forgiving attitudes about rest and days off became popular.

"Lee always said, 'Unless a bone's hanging out, I'm in the lineup,'" Singleton recalled. "And I think I played in 95 percent of my team's games over my career. Every day when I came to the park, I assumed I was batting third and playing right field. There was no question you were going to be in the lineup. And no one was going to go in and ask Earl for a day off. You just didn't do that. For a lot of guys in my generation, that's just the way it was."

As a 21-year-old rookie in 1977, Murray mimicked May and Singleton, becoming a no-questions-asked everyday player, counted on — by Weaver, his teammates, and the fans — to be in the lineup. He bashed 27 home runs as the team's designated hitter while sitting out just two games. The next year, he switched places with May, becoming the first baseman while May served as the DH, and again hit 27 home runs while sitting out just one game. In 1979, on a team that won the American League and lost a seven-game World Series, he missed just three games. In 1980, he hit .300, drove in 116 runs, and signed a contract making him baseball's first million-dollar-a-year player.

By the time Ripken arrived in 1981, Murray was a key figure in the team's clubhouse calculus, hosting crab feasts and inviting rookies to stay at his house if needed; he had extra rooms and a pinball machine. He was five years older than Ripken, but they bonded on those airport shuttle rides, over road lunches, and in clubhouse conversations before and after games. Senior had molded his son's philosophy, but Murray's influence also became important. Many of Murray's principles became Ripken's, including the importance of playing every day. In his first four seasons in the majors, Murray had sat out just two, one, three, and four games.

"Eddie had a big influence on me," Ripken said. "He understood the value of being in the lineup every day. Even if he wasn't hitting, he batted cleanup as a switch hitter and provided stability for everyone else. If it was first and second, no one out, bunt situation, he could walk out and calm everyone down and say, 'OK, this is the play we're running.' He set the example of what an everyday player was. And he articulated to me that it was important for me to do it, too."

In 1984, Ripken's third full season in Baltimore, the Orioles finished third in their division, well back of the Detroit Tigers, who eventually won the World Series. But Ripken and Murray, their identities now conjoined, played in every game and combined for 56 home runs and 186 runs batted in. Ripken batted third, Murray fourth.

"You're two players, [and] they're counting on you to fill certain roles," Ripken recalled. "You're in the middle of the diamond; he's at first base. You're hitting third; he's hitting fourth. By 1984, I never thought of it as a choice, as in, 'Should I play?' It was, 'I'm an everyday player. I'm counted on. I'm playing.' It was a foregone conclusion. That's what you do. It was valued to be an everyday player, an honorable thing to play through injuries. Whatever it took, you were out there every day, and the team could count on you being there."

Not surprisingly, after earning $180,000 in his Most Valuable Player season in 1983, Ripken saw his salary quickly escalate. He made $700,000 in 1984, and it was clear he would soon join Murray in surpassing the million-dollar-a-year threshold.

Although that was far more than Senior had ever earned in a year, Senior, still parenting, felt compelled to convey his thoughts to his son on the significance of making "big" money.

"I'm pretty sure Dad said, 'You're being paid a lot now to go out there and play, and remember, you owe it to everyone involved to do so,'" Bill Ripken said years later. "It was like, 'OK, you made it, you're making some money; don't forget why you're making some money. You mean something to the Orioles.'"

Assessing that conversation almost three decades later, Bill called it one of the origins of Junior's consecutive-game streak. "I'm sure Junior took what Senior said and understood it was his job to go out there and play every day," Bill said. "He already wanted to do that, but what Senior said really drove it home, reinforced it as a principle. And there was no changing him after that. Junior has always been a person of strong convictions. Once he believes in something, you're not going to get him off it."

The first game of the Orioles' 1985 season almost resembled a science fiction tale. Snow fell on a packed house at Memorial Stadium as Charlie Hough, a knuckleball specialist for the visiting Texas Rangers, baffled the home team's batters with mysterious offerings. The Orioles went hitless for six innings and trailed by one run going into the bottom of the eighth. When Ripken drew a walk from a relief pitcher, the fans stood, anticipating a rally. Murray stepped to the plate and lashed a drive to deep right field that cleared the fence. All was well in Baltimore. After a disappointing 1984 season, the Orioles were off and running.

Their second game, also against Texas, was an afternoon affair before a much smaller crowd. When Ripken played the top of the first at his usual spot in the infield, he ran his consecutive-game streak to 443. He had not missed an inning in more than two years. Altobelli had stopped asking if he wanted to take a break. He never did.

After the Orioles scored an early run, the Rangers loaded the bases with two out in the top of the third. Mike Boddicker, pitching for the Orioles, tried to escape the jam by picking off the runner on second, Gary Ward. Ripken slipped behind Ward, hoping to catch him unaware, as Boddicker turned and threw. Ward slid back to the base ahead of the throw, and as Ripken caught the ball, his left cleat caught on the bag and he fell awkwardly, twisting his ankle.

After Boddicker struck out the batter to end the inning, Ripken limped to the dugout and took off his cleat to inspect the ankle. It had already started swelling. "It was completely blown out, a severe sprain," Ripken recalled. The Orioles' head trainer, Ralph Salvon, quickly wrapped it with tape, enabling Ripken to keep playing. He went 0-for-2 with a walk in his remaining at-bats and handled several fielding chances without difficulty, but after the game, the ankle "was just gigantic," Ripken recalled. Making a trip to the hospital, he listened soberly as a doctor told him to use crutches for a week and not run for two weeks. It appeared his consecutive-game streak would end at 443 games, 40 shy of the Orioles franchise record, held by Brooks Robinson. Heading home from the hospital, Ripken angrily threw his crutches in the backseat of his car. He never used them.

If the Orioles had been scheduled to play a league game the next day, Ripken almost surely could not have played. But they traveled to nearby Annapolis, Maryland, for an exhibition game against the Naval Academy varsity. Salvon accompanied them, leaving his assistant, Richie Bancells, to tend to Ripken in Baltimore. Bancells and Ripken had been friends since they broke into the Orioles system together at Bluefield, West Virginia, in 1978 — Ripken as a young shortstop just out of high school, Bancells as a young trainer just out of college. Like Ripken, Bancells had developed his skills, moved up, and reached the majors. As Salvon's assistant, he taped Ripken's ankles before every game, a routine they would share for years.

As the Orioles played in Annapolis, Bancells went to Ripken's apartment to treat the ankle. "It was a big black-and-blue thing," Bancells recalled years later. Ripken peppered him with questions while Bancells worked. "Even going back to when he was in the minors, he was one of the first players I had that had a true interest in his body and how it functioned," Bancells said. "He always asked a lot of questions about anatomy. When there was treatment, he said, 'Why are we doing this?' I showed him a lot of pictures of body parts, told him, 'This is how we're treating it and why we're treating it.' It gave him a better sense of his body."

After almost two full days of treatment and hobbling around, Ripken drove to Memorial Stadium for the Orioles' next game, against Toronto. His ankle remained swollen and sore, but when he tested it during batting practice and said he could play, Altobelli put him in the lineup.

In the bottom of the third, Ripken came to the plate with Rick Dempsey on third base and two out. He hit a line drive up the middle that Toronto's pitcher, Jimmy Key, deflected and picked up. As Dempsey raced for home plate, Ripken ran toward first, knowing the run would count if he beat the throw. Leaping with his final stride, he landed squarely on the bag, forcing his sore ankle to bear all of his weight.

He beat the throw, enabling the run to score, but would his ankle hold up? Ripken held his breath as he jogged past the base.

It was fine.

"Once I passed that test, I knew I could stop thinking about it," Ripken recalled.

Bancells became the Orioles' head trainer three years later and oversaw Ripken's treatment for the rest of his career. "He did play through some injuries and illnesses," Bancells said. "There were days when he came to the park and had a fever. He had the ankle that day, and several other things. Where it would knock other people down, he felt, 'I can get through it; I'll be all right. Let's get through the game, and we'll deal with it afterward.' The ankle was one of those times where he said, 'Let's just tape it up and go.' He just had this unbelievable ability that, whenever he had a problem, he'd treat it, take care of it, but when the bell rang, all that got put aside and he'd play."

Edward Bennett Williams, the Washington lawyer who owned the Orioles, had high expectations in 1985. During the off-season, he had green-lighted the signings of several big-name free agents, including outfielder Fred Lynn and relief pitcher Don Aase. When the team muddled through April and May, the owner fired Altobelli, who had won a World Series two years earlier, and brought back Weaver, offering a large salary to convince him to come out of retirement. Senior had been passed over again.

Weaver's return did not go well. The Orioles never got untracked in 1985, finishing fourth. In 1986, they were in second place in early August but lost 42 of their last 56 games, a startling collapse. Weaver's magic touch had vanished. He retired again after that season, and Senior soon received word that he would get the job. After three decades with the organization, he would finally manage the Orioles.

His timing was awful. After a long run as one of baseball's shrewdest and most successful organizations, the Orioles were entering a steep decline. Their stars had grown old, and their minor league pipeline had dried up. Their idea of "buying" a contender through free agency had not worked. Quite simply, they were now a bad baseball team.

Senior never had a chance. The Orioles actually got off to a fast start in 1987, thanks largely to Murray and Ripken. In late May, they were in second place in the division, six games over .500. But they crashed hard as summer arrived, losing 4, 10, and 5 games in a row at different times to sink to last place.

For Senior and Junior, the disappointment was mitigated to a degree by the arrival of another member of their clan. Bill, the youngest of Senior's four children, was promoted to the Orioles on July 11 after having percolated in the minor leagues for five years. The move generated feel-good stories that circulated nationally. Never before had a father managed two sons at the same time in the major leagues. *Sports Illustrated* had ruminated on the possibility months earlier in a spring training cover story headlined THE RIPKEN GANG. Now they were all together in Baltimore.

The Orioles had drafted Bill in the 11th round of the 1982 amateur draft. A second baseman built more like his wiry-strong father than his towering brother, Bill had followed Junior's path through the minors, starting in Bluefield and rising to Charlotte before reaching Triple A Rochester. The uncle he was named for — Senior's brother — had also reached Triple A before quitting baseball, but this Bill Ripken persisted. His fielding had been major league caliber for several years, the Orioles believed, and when he collected nine hits in 10 at-bats for Rochester in early July, they brought him to Baltimore.

Senior gave him a job. Bill started on the day he arrived and quickly proved he belonged. After going hitless in his first two games, he doubled off the outfield wall in Kansas City for his first major league hit. Two days later, he homered.

More outgoing than his taciturn father and reserved older brother, Bill brought life to what had been a depressed clubhouse. The Orioles won 11 straight games with the Ripkens manning the middle infield. By early August, Bill was batting second, in front of his brother, with an average over .300.

"I was having as much fun as I ever had playing baseball, swinging the bat well, playing between Junior at shortstop and Eddie at first," Bill recalled.

By early September, Bill had played in 50 games in a row, and Junior had played in 900 straight. "I didn't pay one bit of attention," Bill recalled. "It was just a normal thing for me to see Junior out there every day. It always seemed like the right thing. Even if he struggled at the plate, he brought stability and normalcy. It was just normal to see him there. We never talked about it."

But though the brothers did not discuss his playing streak, Senior was keenly aware of Junior's budding bona fides as an exemplar of extreme baseball endurance. Nine hundred games in a row was a feat, but more re- markably, Junior had not missed an inning in more than five years. Since Jim Dwyer hit for him in the top of the ninth in Minnesota on June 5, 1982, he had played in more than 8,000 straight innings.

Reporters and statisticians had paid little attention to his consecutive- inning streak as it grew. Though baseball's record-keeping apparatus was infinitely more sophisticated than it had been earlier in the century, it had never tracked consecutive innings played. There was no record in the books, no threshold for Junior to surpass, no top 10 list for him to climb.

In 1987, though, the Elias Sports Bureau — founded by Al Munro Elias in 1913 and now baseball's official record keeper — investigated Junior's streak and discovered it was the longest in history. Lou Gehrig had come out of games often enough to prevent him from building a run of consec- utive innings. Everett Scott also missed innings now and then. It turned out George Pinkney had held the record before Ripken, having played in 5,152 straight innings between 1885 and 1890. The record had stood for 95 years until Ripken passed Pinkney on August 31, 1985, without a soul knowing, conjuring the sport's prehistoric statistical era.

When the news broke about Junior owning the all-time record, Senior shrugged. There were no plans to rest him. But by September, Senior was having second thoughts. Junior was mired in the worst slump of his career, his average having plummeted to .258 from a high of .326 in May. Senior wondered if the consecutive-inning streak was part of the problem. Now that it was news, reporters constantly asked Junior about it, and inevitably, with his average declining, they wondered whether he needed a day off. Ripken lashed back at the suggestion.

"I was irritated and it probably showed," he later wrote. "I didn't want an excuse for my slump, especially one as weak and wrong as needing an inning off. When you feel sluggish, you don't feel better sitting on the bench, at least I don't. I perk up when I trot on the field."

His rationale for continuing to play every inning, even as his average dropped, would become familiar. He was not tired, he said, and he believed he could always help the team in some way — with his defense, experience, and sheer presence — even if he did not hit. He believed his slump was attributable to a problem with his stance, approach, or confidence, maybe all three, but certainly not fatigue. Between the six-month off season and nearly two dozen off days during the season, he had plenty of time to rest, he said, even while playing thousands of innings in a row.

Regardless, Senior saw the streak becoming a burden. "I had been watching Cal closely for two weeks in the locker room, and the poor guy could barely get dressed," Senior later wrote. "He was having to hurry to get on the field because he was being hounded by the media so much. I said to myself, 'It's time to give the guy a break.'"

On September 14, 1987, the Orioles played the first-place Blue Jays in Toronto. The surge precipitated by Bill's arrival had given way to a late-season collapse. The Orioles were in the process of losing 17 of 18 games. On this night, Toronto's hitters pulverized Baltimore's pitchers, hitting 10 home runs and building an 18–3 lead in the first seven innings. As the deficit grew, Senior saw an opportunity. After the bottom of the seventh, the manager asked his son in the dugout, "What do you think about taking an inning off?"

Ripken stopped, knowing what was at stake. "What do you think?" he replied cautiously.

Senior said he thought it was a good idea. There was a pause. "OK," Ripken finally said.

Neither mentioned the streak.

Three other Orioles were due to hit before Ripken in the top of the eighth. "If you hit this inning, you're going to come out," Senior said. Ripken ended up batting and grounded into a fielder's choice. He was on first when the inning ended. Bill, performing a routine courtesy, brought his glove out from the dugout, thinking they would play the bottom of the inning alongside each other, as always. But Ripken took the glove and said, "That's all right, I'm out of here," and walked toward the dugout.

"The look on Billy's face was total disbelief, just complete shock — almost like time had stopped or something," Ripken recalled. Seeing his brother almost start to cry, Ripken suddenly felt like crying himself. A teammate, Ron Washington, who would later manage the Texas Rangers, took over at shortstop. It was reported that Ripken had played in 8,243 straight innings. (In 2012, Trent McCotter, vice chairman of the Society for American Baseball Research's records committee, reported that Ripken had actually played in 8,264 straight innings.)

Ripken's teammates offered congratulations and support in the dugout when he left the game. They slapped his back, shook his hand. Ripken was dazed. "I felt out of place, didn't know what to do," he recalled. "I didn't know if I should go in and take a shower or just sit there." Larry Sheets, a teammate who had lost a starting spot, joked, "Here, sit by me. I can tell you about the bench." Ripken sat by Sheets as the game ended. The media peppered Senior afterward. Why had he taken his son out? Did he not want his son to make history? Senior took full responsibility, saying it was his decision; Junior did not have an opinion, and it just was time. "He wasn't going to hit a 20-run homer," Senior groused to reporters.

Junior was emotional. At the team hotel later, he went to see his father and they talked. Senior said he knew Junior was worried about the team and his hitting, and now he would have one less thing to worry about. It did not hurt for him to miss a few innings in a blowout, Senior said. "I thought it was the right decision for Cal and the right decision for the team. It was a team decision and Cal accepted it as one," Senior later wrote.

Junior went back to his room, pulled out a yellow legal pad, and started writing. He filled nine pages that night and two the next day. "I'm not a diary guy, but at that moment, I had some thoughts to get out of my system," he recalled. "Was I happy or sad? Did I give up on a certain principle or approach? Was it weakness or strength? Was it the right thing or the wrong thing? When you play every inning for so long, there's a certain emptiness. I had to figure that out."

Once he expressed his doubts on paper and reflected on them, he concluded that he had not given in — it was not a failure. His manager had simply made a decision. "If I had said, 'I don't want to come out,' and insisted, he would have left me in," Ripken wrote in his autobiography. "But I wouldn't have insisted because I had faith in his judgment. This one time, Senior was dealing with me as my manager AND my father."

On the legal pad, Ripken wrote that he took pride in his ability to play in every game, and that if Senior had wanted to end his consecutive-*game* streak, he would have objected. "I always thought both [the games and innings streaks] would end at the same time," Ripken wrote later. "I do, however, have strong feelings about continuing the games streak & I probably would have objected to ending that."

That was not about to happen.

8

Gehrig

A FAMOUS HEADACHE

Everett Scott was nestled in his sleeper-car bunk when a loud noise reverberated through the train traveling from Fort Wayne, Indiana, to Chicago. The train jerked sharply several times before coming to a stop. Scott threw off his covers and went to investigate. He found the engineer and asked what happened.

"Blown cylinder head," the engineer said.

"How long are we going to be stuck here?" Scott asked.

It would be hours before another train came, the engineer replied. Scott's heart sank. The date was September 14, 1922, just before dawn in the Indiana countryside east of Chicago. In seven hours, Scott was due to play shortstop for the Yankees in a doubleheader against the White Sox at Comiskey Park. In his first season with the Yankees, he had played in every game so far, just as he had in Boston for so long. His playing streak stood at 970 straight games. But now it was in jeopardy.

Scott had been with the Yankees the day before as a train ferried them from the East Coast to Chicago. They were battling the St. Louis Browns for the American League pennant, so every game mattered. Huggins had not given Scott permission to leave the team, but Scott had hopped off the train anyway to spend the night with his wife and son in Fort Wayne, where he lived in the off-season. He had checked the train schedules and knew one departing before dawn would get him to Chicago in plenty of time to play. But now that train was not going to make it.

Scott's mind raced. How could he get from here, basically the middle of nowhere, to Chicago in time to play? Looking across a moonlit field, he spotted a dim light in the distance. He slipped on shoes and jogged through the field toward the light, which hung on the front porch of a small farmhouse.

Scott banged on the door. The farm's animals barked, clucked, and howled. "Who goes there and what do you think you're doing waking us at this hour?" came a voice from inside the house.

Scott identified himself and explained that he was the Yankees' short-stop and needed to get to Chicago. There was a pause. "So you're Everett Scott, are you? I've heard of you," the farmer said. "What do you want?"

Scott asked to use the phone. The farmer let him in. He dialed a nearby garage, hoping it employed a driver who could pick him up and take him to South Bend, Indiana, 60 miles away. From there, he could catch a trolley to Gary, just outside Chicago, and then grab a taxi to the ballpark.

It was a sensible plan, except the garage did not have a driver on call so early. Scott pleaded with the owner and finally got his way. A driver picked him up at the farmhouse and drove him to South Bend. Arriving at the station just in time, Scott handed the driver $25 and jumped on a trolley.

As the trolley rolled toward Chicago, Scott reflected on why he was going to such extremes to get to the game. He was obligated to the Yankees, of course; the last thing he wanted was to let down his teammates in a pennant race. But he also wanted to keep his playing streak going. He was near his goal of a thousand straight games and proud of his record as the sport's all-time leader in consecutive games played. He could not wow crowds like Ruth or Ty Cobb, but he was durable and dependable.

As the trolley rattled toward Gary, the Yankees and White Sox warmed up for their doubleheader at Comiskey Park. Miller Huggins waited to make out his lineup, expecting Scott to come through the clubhouse door at any minute. It was unlike the captain to leave the club hanging.

Finally, with the game about to start, Huggins posted a lineup with Mike McNally, a reserve, playing shortstop. When Red Faber, Chicago's starting pitcher, began the game by tossing a fastball to Whitey Witt, the Yankees' center fielder and leadoff hitter, Scott was still on the trolley, many miles away.

When the trolley reached Gary, Scott hopped off, hailed a taxi, and explained that he was in a desperate rush to get to Comiskey Park. "Go ahead and speed. I'll pay your ticket if you get pulled over," he said. The cabbie drove so fast that, indeed, a policeman stopped them. Scott leaned out of a rear window and explained the situation. The policeman let them go. A few miles down the road, another policeman stopped them. Scott again explained the situation. This policeman agreed to escort the cab to the ballpark, siren wailing.

Scott was running out of time. After the Yankees took a 3–2 lead in the first inning, four scoreless innings quickly rolled by. Many major league games lasted little more than two hours in the 1920s. Would Scott make it?

He arrived at the park as the White Sox were scoring three runs in the bottom of the sixth. Scott hurriedly changed into his uniform in the clubhouse and jogged to the dugout. Huggins gave him a disgusted look. Where had he been? How could he have done this? "Oh, Hug had some serious words for me," Scott recalled with a smile years later.

The fate of his streak lay in the manager's hands. Huggins could punish Scott by keeping him on the bench. But besides this incident, Scott was a pleasure to manage — unlike Ruth, never a headache. His streak was quite a feat, and Huggins was not going to end it.

When the Yankees took the field for the bottom of the seventh, Scott was at shortstop. He never batted but played two innings of defense and recorded a putout on a ground ball. The Sox won, 7–3, but Scott received credit for playing in the game. He had traveled by train, hired car, trolley, and taxi; sweet-talked a farmer, a garage dispatcher, and two policemen into helping; and spent $40 on his wild ride, but his consecutive-game streak was still alive.

After the Yankees lost again to the Giants in the 1922 World Series, sports-writers speculated that Scott might not play every day for much longer. He had turned 30 and committed more errors during the season than in any campaign since he was a rookie. A *Detroit News* columnist wrote that his play during the Series had been "a bitter disappointment." Some fans blamed him for the Yankees' defeat. He simply could not cover as much ground and admitted during the Series that he "felt older." It had been six and a half years since he sat out a game.

But he was determined to press on. If he played in the first 14 games of the 1923 season, he would reach a thousand in a row, his stated goal. Plus, the Yankees were moving into their new ballpark that year, and he did not want to miss that. He spent part of the winter in Hot Springs, Arkansas, taking therapeutic baths and going on long jogs. When the Yankees opened their spring training camp in New Orleans in March 1923, Scott was among the first players to report.

Shortly before the season began, though, he tripped on second base during an exhibition game and needed help leaving the field. The Yankees' doctor said he had suffered a sprained ankle and possibly a torn tendon in his right foot. It seemed he would not make a thousand games in a row after all.

But on Opening Day, Scott wrapped his ankle with tape and convinced Huggins he could play. He hit a double, scored a run, and converted several sharp ground balls into outs as the Yankees defeated the Red Sox, 4–1, in the inaugural game at Yankee Stadium. Seventy-four thousand fans filled the Yankees' majestic new ballpark, and Babe Ruth gave them what they came to see, smacking a home run.

But though Scott made it through the opener unscathed, he told an interviewer later that he "suffered a lot" by playing on his injured ankle and foot early in the 1923 season. Clearly laboring, he bungled easy defensive plays. Huggins pinch-ran and pinch-hit for him several times. It was not unthinkable to suggest that a healthier, presumably more effective teammate should be playing shortstop. Scott, however, did not want to miss a game.

Huggins was ambivalent. The manager appreciated Scott's streak and valued his defense, but truthfully, playing him every day, without fail, was not an absolute must. If Scott had not been so close to his goal, Huggins might have rested him. But Huggins faithfully played him, as much out of loyalty as for any other reason.

On May 2, 1923, Scott's big moment arrived. Ignored until now by most statisticians and previously buried for many years in the game's confusing annals, the consecutive-game record vaulted into the sunlight before 10,000 fans on a cool afternoon at Griffith Stadium in Washington, D.C. Before the Yankees and Senators played, Clark Griffith, the Senators' owner, staged a festive ceremony honoring Scott, with help from the American League office.

Twenty minutes before the first pitch, the teams ended their warm-ups and lined up on the foul lines, the Yankees stretching from third base to home, the Senators from first to home. A line of marines in crisp military dress stretched between them, across the infield. When Griffith gave a signal, a marine brass band struck up a tune, and Scott emerged from the Yankees' dugout with Ban Johnson, president of the American League. They walked together to home plate, where a tall, horseshoe-shaped wreath of roses stood upright against an easel. Scott admired the flowers and shook hands with a bald, husky, jut-jawed man standing by the easel. It was Edwin Denby, U.S. secretary of the navy.

A well-known politician, Denby added gravitas to the occasion. He had played football at the University of Michigan in the late 1800s, worked as a lawyer, and served three terms in the U.S. Congress. Now he commanded the country's naval forces. In a speech, he complimented Scott on "the loyalty and powers of endurance which have enabled you to establish such a remarkable record" and called him "the greatest ballplayer in point of service and achievement that ever trod the diamonds of America, the home of baseball."

When Ban Johnson spoke, he said he was proud to have such a "respected" player in the American League and presented Scott with a solid-gold medal the league had commissioned to commemorate his achievement of playing in a thousand straight games. Dressed in his gray road uniform, Scott smiled and nodded during the speeches. The fans clamored for him to speak, but he declined.

Once the game began, Scott was unable to consecrate his big day with a memorable moment on the diamond. He went hitless in a 3–0 loss to Washington and its ace pitcher, Walter Johnson, still dominant at age 35.

But Scott's achievement generated widespread acclaim. In the edition of the *Sporting News* dated May 3, 1923, a large picture of Scott dominated the front page under the headline A THOUSAND IN A ROW. The paper had gone to press before Scott reached his goal, so the accompanying article noted that he would make it to his goal "providence permitting." In its next edition, the *Sporting News* reported that "in attaining his goal of a thousand straight games, Scott was honored as few players in history have been honored."

Sports columnists around the country praised him. Scott's achievement even received mention in non-sports publications such as the *Christian Science Monitor*. "Perfect attendance, the be-all and end-all for so many school children and church members, is not usually thought of as the chief aim for professional ballplayers, most of whom have their hearts set on reaching new heights of hitting or fielding prowess," the *Monitor* noted in May 1923. "Everett Scott, known as 'the deacon,' was on hand for so many diamond contests, however, that he finally resolved to try to capture the perfect attendance laurels in baseball by participating in one thousand consecutive contests."

Why did people care about his streak? It was a fair question, for as the *Christian Science Monitor* noted, simply playing in games was "not usually" a goal for players. But by playing in so many games in a row, Scott had exhibited dependability, character, and toughness, qualities that transcended sports. Fans could relate to him and his achievement more than to other players and their feats. No, he did not entrance crowds by pounding awe-inducing home runs with mighty swings, but Scott was a stable family man, someone you could count on, more like a neighbor or work colleague than a ballplayer, and he just got up and went to work every day, like millions of Americans. Honestly, what was more admirable than that?

On April 18, 1923, the day Yankee Stadium opened with Everett Scott at shortstop and Babe Ruth in right field, another baseball game, matching collegiate squads, took place nearby. A burly Columbia University sophomore, Lou Gehrig, struck out 17 batters in a loss to Williams College before a sparse crowd that included Paul Krichell, a scout for the Yankees.

A chubby former backup catcher for the St. Louis Browns, Krichell had quietly followed Gehrig for several months. It was not the young man's pitching that intrigued him. Krichell had seen Gehrig wallop a handful of mammoth home runs. Soon after the Williams game, Gehrig hit another blast that traveled more than 400 feet. "This youngster might really be something," Krichell thought. He introduced himself. Soon, they were talking about a contract.

The Yankees offered Gehrig a $1,500 signing bonus and a playing salary of $400 a month, a pittance to the club but a fortune to Gehrig, the son of struggling German immigrants who had lived in a succession of small apartments in Washington Heights, a working-class neighborhood in northernmost Manhattan. Gehrig's father, Heinrich, lacked ambition and seldom held a job for long. Gehrig's mother, Christina, a thick-armed

Frau, was the principal breadwinner and disciplinarian, working as a maid, cook, and laundress—whatever was needed to put food on the table. Of their four children, only Lou had lived past age three.

Though the contract offer from the Yankees was exciting, Gehrig's parents had doubts about their son making baseball his career. They did not care for sports; baseball, in particular, was for the riffraff, they thought. They wanted him to stay at Columbia, graduate, and become an engineer, following in the footsteps of an uncle in Germany. But the signing bonus would pay for an operation Heinrich needed, so Gehrig scrawled his signature on a contract and became the Yankees' hometown kid.

As a youngster, he had attended New York public schools and helped his mother in the afternoons, folding laundry and running errands. Christina lorded fiercely over her only surviving child, telling him how to dress, what to eat, and what to do. When he had free time, he played stickball in the streets and dreamed of playing for John McGraw and the Giants at the nearby Polo Grounds. His prospects seemed faint. He was big and strong, but clumsy.

When Lou was 11, Christina found full-time work at the Sigma Nu fraternity house on Columbia's campus. She cooked extensive meals while Heinrich tended to the furnace and performed other odd jobs. Lou came to the frat house after school and helped his mother serve dinner and wash dishes. Occasionally, the college boys let him into their post-dinner games of catch. "He threw well and liked to play ball," reported journalist (later screenwriter) Niven Busch in a 1929 *New Yorker* profile of Gehrig.

His athletic talent began to develop at Commerce High School. By now weighing over 200 pounds, he played football so adeptly that Columbia offered him a scholarship. In baseball, he threw hard as a left-handed pitcher but lacked control. As a hitter, he flailed at curveballs but also knocked several of the longest home runs ever seen on a high school diamond in New York. He traveled with his team to Chicago to play a championship squad from that city and hit a grand slam completely out of Wrigley Field, generating headlines and comparisons to Babe Ruth.

That summer, before he enrolled at Columbia, a scout for the Giants, Arthur Irwin, invited him to a tryout, telling him McGraw had seen him play, which was not true. During the tryout, Gehrig hit six straight balls over the fence, but he flubbed a ground ball in the field, and McGraw passed on signing him, at least partly because of Gehrig's fleshy physique.

The young man had "beer legs," McGraw reportedly told colleagues, and probably would weigh 250 pounds by the time he was 25.

The insinuation of alcohol consumption was laughable. Christina Gehrig's son was so straight his friends chided him about it. Regardless, McGraw believed the young man was too fat for the major leagues — a projection he would sorely regret.

Still, there was no denying Gehrig had impressive power, and he was so polite that Irwin, the scout, wanted to help him. He recommended that Gehrig hone his skills in a summer pro league, using an assumed name so he could retain his amateur status. "Everyone is doing it," Irwin assured him. Gehrig joined a team in Hartford, Connecticut, and played in a dozen games as Lefty Gehrig or Lou Lewis. But his ruse was discovered, and he was banned from playing college sports for a year.

Regaining his eligibility as a sophomore, he played fullback and kicked field goals for Columbia's football team in the fall of 1922. In the spring of 1923, he pitched and played first base on the baseball team, with Krichell following his every move. After he signed with the Yankees, he finished the semester and began his pro baseball career.

One day in June 1923, he traveled from Morningside Heights to Yankee Stadium. The Yankees were playing Cleveland, and Gehrig would take batting practice so Miller Huggins could see him. Krichell met Gehrig at the stadium and took him to the clubhouse, where he met Ruth, his idol. Huggins escorted him to the field, where the Yankees were warming up for the game, loosening their arms and taking swings at the plate. Huggins told Gehrig to grab a bat. He picked up one of Ruth's 40-ounce weapons.

The story of what happened next has been repeated many times but, as with much about Gehrig, could be exaggerated. With Ruth and the other Yankees watching, Gehrig let several pitches go by, seemingly paralyzed. "Just hit the ball!" one player shouted. Gehrig finally lined a single to left, then used his powerful torso to pound a handful of pitches into the distant bleachers.

"OK, that's enough," Huggins growled.

Gehrig was a naïve 20-year-old, a penny-pinching mama's boy, tongue-tied around girls, a child among men. But he could hit. The Yankees gave him a uniform and a place on the bench, wanting him to soak up the sights and sounds. Four days after his batting practice show, he made his major league debut as a ninth-inning defensive replacement. Three days later, he batted for the first time, striking out as a pinch hitter with the Yankees down by eight runs in the ninth.

There was no spot for him in the lineup of a team rolling toward the 1923 American League pennant, and in any case, he needed seasoning. The Yankees sent him back to Hartford, where, using his real name now, he batted .304 and hit 24 home runs in 63 games, a performance that thrilled the Yankees. They brought him to New York late in the season. Huggins wanted to rest Wally Pipp, his first baseman, before the World Series against the Giants. In one game, Gehrig pinch-hit for Pipp and struck out. In another, he replaced Pipp in the field in the late innings and hit a double.

On the team's final road trip of the season, Pipp twisted an ankle getting off the train in Boston. Gehrig replaced him in the lineup for several days, hit his first major league home run, and batted .423, so impressing Huggins that the Yankees sought to make him eligible for the World Series. But he had joined the team after the cutoff date for postseason eligibility, and the Giants' McGraw refused to grant an exception. "If the Yankees have an injury, that's their problem," McGraw said. Gehrig settled for watching the Yankees defeat the Giants to claim their first world championship, with Ruth leading the way.

Arriving at the Yankees' spring training camp in New Orleans in 1924, Gehrig was in a familiar situation, having little money in his pockets. He tried to land a part-time job as a waiter, but when he went to the restaurant to apply, he noticed teammates Waite Hoyt and Bob Meusel among the diners and did not go inside. When Gehrig told the story to Dan Daniel, a *New York World-Telegram* sportswriter who would cover his entire career, Daniel passed it along to Huggins. The manager called Gehrig in, gave him an advance on his salary, and ordered him to stop hunting for work.

The competition for jobs was fierce throughout the major leagues, with thousands of pro ballplayers seeking roster spots on just 16 American League and National League teams. Veterans guarded their turf tenaciously in spring training, often bullying rookies. Gehrig was an easy mark for the Yankees' established players. His "schoolboyish peculiarities were an inspiration to the team wits," Niven Busch wrote in *The New*

Yorker five years later. "Teammates would remember him as one of the most bewildered recruits that ever joined the club."

Fortunately for Gehrig, Pipp was not into belittling rookies. The veteran had seen Gehrig taking batting practice and guessed the youngster was destined to replace him. But Pipp still adopted Gehrig as a project, teaching him the nuances of playing first base — a gesture Gehrig would always appreciate.

Sure enough, the job was Gehrig's within two years.

During the 1923 season, Huggins had occasionally grumbled, ever so quietly, that Scott was not covering as much ground as in previous seasons. The manager picked up a reserve shortstop in case Scott suffered another injury. Scott's playing streak "had to be near an end," the *Sporting News* speculated in July. But by the end of the season, during which he hit .246, Scott had played in 1,138 straight games.

After the Yankees finally defeated McGraw's Giants in the World Series in 1923, Huggins felt empowered. The soft-spoken manager had spent the season battling with Ruth, whose eating, drinking, and whoring were out of hand. Cap Huston, the Yankees' co-owner, backed Ruth in any dispute, but Huggins somehow kept the club on track, playing well enough to win.

In the heady afterglow of the team's success, Huggins said he might bench Scott for a few games at the start of the 1924 season. It was not hard to see the manager had grown tired of the streak. He had put up with it until now, but he might want to try another player at shortstop occasionally.

Huggins's comment constituted the first inkling that issues could arise when a player forged a playing streak so long it made news. In essence, the manager no longer controlled his lineup, violating one of the game's basic tenets. Years later, Scott admitted his streak put Huggins in an awkward spot. "It handicaps a team when a manager doesn't want to take a man out and spoil his record," Scott said. "Honestly, I don't know why I was so set on playing in all of those games."

After Huggins said he might bench Scott early in 1924, sportswriters thought Scott might get traded. Contacted in Indiana, Scott said he would retire before going to a losing team; he wanted to end his career with his pride intact, he said. In the end, the Yankees retained him, offering him the same salary ($10,000) he had earned in the previous two years. He went through his usual off-season regimen and kept his starting job. Huggins did not bench him. Giving the Yankees his usual blend of modest offense and solid defense, he was near 1,300 straight games by the end of the season.

As the 1925 season opened, the Yankees expected to contend. They had finished a close second to the Senators in 1924, having won three straight pennants before that, and their veteran cast remained intact. Besides Ruth and Scott, it included Whitey Witt, a fleet center fielder who had once been knocked unconscious by a soda bottle thrown from the stands; Aaron Ward, a durable infielder from Arkansas who had considered law school before electing to play baseball after college; Wally Schang, a veteran switch-hitting catcher who had hit .300 in four straight seasons in the early 1920s; Bob Meusel, a taciturn, hard-drinking outfielder who had never batted under .300 in a season; and Wally Pipp, the graceful first baseman who had played for the Yankees for almost a decade.

Tall and bookish, Pipp had studied architecture at Catholic University in Washington, D.C., before becoming a baseball pro. He wrote so expertly that *Sports Illustrated* would hire him as a correspondent years later. Originally signed by Detroit, he had joined the Yankees on a waiver claim in 1915 and become their cleanup hitter, leading the American League in home runs with 9 in 1916 and 12 in 1917.

When Ruth joined the club in 1920, Pipp still batted fourth, and with Ruth in front of him, his production escalated. As the Yankees became a powerhouse, Pipp played solid defense, batted around .300, and drove in close to 100 runs every year. And he was durable. Although he never played a full season of games, he never missed more than several per year.

Shortly before the 1925 season began, Pipp turned 32. He was coming off a season in which he drove in 114 runs, his career high. Big things were expected from him and the rest of the Yankees. From the outset, though, the season was a disaster. During spring training, Ruth suffered stomach pains so excruciating that he could not play. It was front-page news across the country. The source of his ailment was unclear. Some speculated he had eaten too many hot dogs or quaffed too much soda. Insiders quietly wondered if he had contracted a venereal disease.

Ruth sat out the start of the season. In late April, it was determined he had an intestinal abscess and needed an operation that would keep him out until June. The Yankees floundered without him, dropping 11 of their first 15 games, and Scott struggled, his average sinking below .200. He seemed to break out of it with two hits in a win over Philadelphia at Yankee Stadium on May 5, but Huggins had seen enough. The manager was worried about the season slipping away before Ruth returned. Seeking more offense, he put a youngster, Paul Wanninger, at shortstop on May 6.

Scott was stunned to find himself on the bench as the Yankees took on the Philadelphia Athletics in the Bronx. He had played in 1,307 straight games. But Huggins was adamant about ending the streak. Even when the manager pulled Wanninger after two at-bats, he inserted another reserve rather than Scott. For the first time since 1916, Scott sat out a game.

His temper flared after the game, which Philadelphia won. "I was surprised to sit out because I hit so well in Tuesday's game," he told reporters. "If the end had come when the team was losing, I wouldn't have cared. But it seems funny that it should come the day after we win and I get two hits."

He continued: "Not that I care about the record. When I passed the 1,000 mark, I lost interest in the matter. I didn't expect to go on forever. But I'll never sit on the bench."

Following the game, Huggins and the Yankees boarded a train for St. Louis, where they would open a road trip. Scott received permission to take a few days off. He took another train home to Indiana.

"Baseball's greatest record for stamina and consecutive playing came to an end yesterday," the *New York Times* reported. "The iron man of the sport finally came to the end of the road after setting up a mark that will be equaled only through another miracle the equal of his own."

On the train to Indiana, Scott stared at the passing countryside, fearing what lay ahead. Sure enough, when he returned to the Yankees, he made a few token appearances before being released. He caught on with the Senators, played for the White Sox and Reds in 1926, bounced around the minors, and retired.

Meanwhile, Wanninger flopped as his replacement, and the Yankees continued to lose in 1925, even after Ruth returned in June. Suddenly, the Yankees were at a crossroads. Many of their core players had, like Scott, grown old. Ed Barrow, the general manager, wanted Huggins to start breaking in new talent such as Earle Combs, an outfielder who could replace Witt; Mark Koenig, a 20-year-old shortstop ready to assume Scott's spot; Benny Bengough, a 145-pound catcher who was 10 years younger than Wally Schang; and Gehrig, the young slugger stuck behind Pipp.

With Barrow's blessing, Huggins began to make changes. Soon after he ended Scott's streak, he benched Witt for Combs. Pipp, Ward, and Schang would soon lose their jobs, too.

When Ruth made his season debut on June 1, the Yankees were in seventh place. Before a small crowd in the Bronx, he walked once in a loss to the Senators. Wanninger failed to reach base in three at-bats, and when he was due up in the eighth, Huggins sent Gehrig up to hit for him. Washington's Walter Johnson fired a fastball. Gehrig swung late and lofted a soft fly to left that was easily caught. Just 25 days had passed since the end of Scott's consecutive-game streak, widely regarded as a feat never to be repeated. No one could have imagined that Gehrig's eminently forgettable at-bat against Johnson was the start of an even longer streak, destined to become one of baseball's signature achievements.

That same afternoon, Pipp collected one hit in four at-bats against Johnson. Hitting .244 for the season, he had been dropped to sixth in the order. Still, he came to Yankee Stadium the next day expecting to play, as always. But according to the legend of June 2, 1925, when he complained of a headache in the clubhouse and asked a trainer for two aspirin, Huggins overheard him and gave him the day off.

"We'll try the kid today and get you back in there tomorrow," Huggins reportedly said. The kid was Gehrig.

Did that conversation happen? There was no mention in the newspapers about a headache sidelining Pipp. In a 1939 interview with sportswriter Dan Daniel, Pipp said that, indeed, he often experienced headaches stemming from a childhood hockey accident, and a vicious one derailed him that day. But in 1956, he told a different story to the Associated Press, claiming he sat out the game after getting hit in the head by a pitch during batting practice. "The ball hit me on the temple; down I went, and I was much too far gone to reach for any aspirin bottle," Pipp said. But again, no newspaper reported that such an incident occurred.

Regardless, what really happened seems clear in hindsight. Huggins wanted to overhaul an aging team that suddenly had collapsed. On the day he benched Pipp, he also benched Schang and Ward, the catcher and second baseman. Bengough caught; Howie Shanks played second. Combs manned center field. And Gehrig played first base. "Huggins has arrived at the inevitable conclusion that he is carrying too many fading stars and now is the time to lay a new foundation," the *Sporting News* reported.

The Yankees won that day, breaking a five-game losing streak, with Gehrig contributing a double and two singles. Huggins gave him another start the next day, and he went hitless in three at-bats before Pipp pinch-hit for him in the eighth, a move that suggested Gehrig's spot in the lineup was temporary and Pipp might still "get back in there," as Huggins had promised.

But that opportunity never came.

9

Gehrig

PLAYING EVERY DAY

Although Gehrig had batted .405 in his brief time with the Yankees in 1923 and 1924, it was difficult to envision him as a star in the making. He was clumsy in the field. Teammates snickered at his lack of worldliness away from the ballpark. On the day he replaced Pipp as the everyday first baseman, he was batting .167 with no home runs so far in the 1925 season.

To that point, his most memorable contribution to the growing litany of Yankees lore was a brawl with Ty Cobb that he initiated in 1924, a somewhat embarrassing incident later viewed as the first inkling of Gehrig's competitiveness.

Cobb frequently taunted opponents, not because he wanted to fight them but rather to distract them from playing their best. The ultimate proponent of "scientific" baseball, which emphasized bunts and stolen bases over home runs, Cobb saw his game becoming antiquated in the early 1920s. It irritated him, and the plodding Gehrig represented everything Cobb did not like about where his game was going. He taunted Gehrig on the field, reportedly calling him a "thick-headed Dutchman."

Gehrig ignored Cobb until one day in Detroit when he reached base on a single, then got caught in a rundown between first and second. Cobb raced in from center field to complete the play, called for the ball, tagged Gehrig out, and insulted him. Boiling inside, Gehrig waited until the game ended, charged Cobb in the Detroit dugout, took a swing, missed, lost his balance, and hit his head on the concrete dugout roof as he fell, knocking himself out.

Now, less than a year later, Huggins had given him Pipp's job. Plainly nervous, Gehrig hit .208 in his first week as a starter, raising more doubts.

But then he pounded a home run and a triple and drove in three runs on June 8. Two days later, he socked another home run. By early July, he was batting .320 in the heart of the lineup, slotted right behind Ruth and Meusel in Huggins's order.

Huggins was still loyal to Pipp and sought to find a role for the veteran who had played so well for so long. Pipp replaced Gehrig for defensive purposes in the late innings of five games in June. It seemed inevitable he would get another start. But on July 2, Pipp was beaned by a pitch during batting practice, likely the incident he would mistakenly recall as occurring on the day Gehrig replaced him. The newspapers reported the beaning, which put Pipp in the hospital for a week with a skull fracture. He played little the rest of the season.

In case Gehrig faltered, the Yankees acquired 36-year-old Fred Merkle, infamous for a baserunning gaffe that cost the Giants the 1908 National League pennant. He could still hit, and Huggins put him at first base against the Senators in Washington on July 5. After starting 31 straight games, Gehrig was on the bench. Merkle singled twice and scored a run, and it appeared he would finish the game, giving Gehrig the whole day off. But Merkle grew faint in D.C.'s notorious summertime heat, and Gehrig hit for him in the eighth, extending his playing streak.

Two weeks later, at Navin Field in Detroit on July 19, Merkle again started ahead of Gehrig and reached base twice in three at-bats. But when the Tigers rolled to a 12–3 lead through four innings, Huggins replaced Merkle with Gehrig, seeking more power. Gehrig slugged a three-run homer, and although the Yankees lost, Huggins had seen enough. Gehrig did not miss another start all season and ended up hitting .295 with 20 home runs. The Yankees were encouraged enough about his potential to sell Pipp to the Cincinnati Reds after the season.

The Yankees' generational shake-up did not result in a turnaround in 1925. They finished seventh, 28½ games behind the pennant-winning Senators. It was quite a falloff for a team that had won the World Series two years earlier, and Ruth's ailment was deemed the primary culprit. He drove in just 66 runs, barely a third of his 1921 total, leading some sportswriters to speculate he was done as a marquee player.

But big picture, the lineup overhaul was a crucial moment in Yankees history. It set up the club for another run of success. New York would win three straight pennants beginning in 1926 with Combs, Koenig, and

Gehrig as mainstays alongside Ruth and Tony Lazzeri, a slugging second baseman who debuted in 1926.

Paying tribute to Pipp as he departed, the *New York Times* called him "one of the most popular players who ever cavorted locally." Pipp had won two league home run titles with the Yankees, started on three pennant winners, and bashed 121 triples, a club record. And unlike Scott, he showed he was not washed-up after the Yankees gave up on him, batting .291 with 99 runs batted in for the Reds in 1926. By the time he retired two years later, he had driven in nearly a thousand runs. But because of what happened after he lost his job to Gehrig on June 2, 1925, Pipp would only be remembered for a headache that may not even have occurred.

When trying to ascertain what made Gehrig into a player who never wanted to miss a game, it is easy to fall back on convenient psychology: His hardscrabble upbringing taught him to hold on fiercely to whatever he accumulated, be it a dollar, a nice suit of clothes, or a starting job with the Yankees. Once he had that job, he gripped it with all his strength, owing partly to the fear that he could always lose it and wind up back on the bench if he allowed himself to rest and relax, even for a day.

That philosophy likely did inform his approach to some degree. Although no record exists of his domineering mother telling him to "take nothing for granted" as she cooked, cleaned, and folded clothes to support their family while her husband fiddled away the years, it is easy to imagine Christina expressing the thought to her impressionable son in her firm, Teutonic-accented voice.

But while Gehrig's background probably helped carve his determination, other factors played a larger role in what he would one day label his consecutive-game "stunt." There was the era he played in, the team he played on, and, of course, his talent.

Lineup decision making remained relatively unsophisticated in the 1920s, certainly a far cry from what it would become decades later with so many statistical analytics to consider. Although savvy managers had known since the 1870s that left-handed hitters fared better against right-handed pitchers, and vice versa, positional platoons were rare. Although managers benched slumping players and played hunches, they changed their lineups relatively little from day to day. Throughout the 1920s in the American League, almost 12 percent of the starts went to players who did not miss a game all season. (Pitchers and catchers excluded.) In 1926, 10 players in the league, including Gehrig, played in at least 151 games.

"Lou played at a time when there was a huge value placed on being there for your team every day," Cal Ripken Jr. said. "It was important that you were a gamer. The season was long, you faced challenges, and it was a high achievement if you could always play."

Huggins, as the St. Louis Cardinals' player-manager a decade earlier, had believed in giving players an occasional rest, thinking they came back fresh and performed better. In the five years he wrote out lineups in St. Louis, only one Cardinal did not miss any games: Del Pratt, a gritty infielder who had played football at the University of Alabama. Pratt appeared in every game in 1913, 1915, and 1916. The other Cardinals rested now and then.

But Huggins's philosophy changed when he came to New York. He had better players now and let more go entire seasons without resting. Pratt, a personal favorite whom he acquired as soon as he got to New York, kept on going, playing two full seasons of games for the Yankees. Frank "Home Run" Baker and Duffy Lewis also played in every Yankees game in 1919. Pipp did not miss one in 1921, and Everett Scott did not miss one for more than three years after he joined the team in 1922. Ruth played in every game in 1923 and 1924. Aaron Ward played in 567 in a row between 1920 and 1924.

As the 1926 season began, Huggins was still not sure Gehrig warranted such respectful treatment. But with Pipp gone and Fred Merkle now coaching, Gehrig was his only viable option at first base. And once the season began, Gehrig made it impossible for the manager to write out a lineup without him. He hit a triple and double and drove in three runs in the Yankees' opener. The next day, he hit another triple. By early June, Gehrig had driven in more than 30 runs, and the Yankees were in first place.

Few sportswriters had expected Huggins's club to contend after its miserable showing the year before, but the Yankees went on to capture the 1926 pennant with an offensive display that illustrated the passing of the dead-ball era. They scored 5.5 runs per game, almost a run more than the league average, and the whole lineup contributed. Ruth, determined to embarrass the naysayers who had suggested he was finished, cut down on his drinking and viciously battered the league's pitchers, hitting .372 with

47 home runs and 153 runs batted in. Lazzeri, the sloop-shouldered son of a San Francisco boilermaker, had never seen a major league game until he played in one on Opening Day, but he drove in 117 runs. Gehrig hit .313 and scored more runs than any other player in the league except Ruth.

Huggins tinkered little with the lineup. He gave Ruth a day off only after the pennant was secured in the final week. Gehrig and Lazzeri were in every game. When Gehrig slumped late in the season, it appeared he might, in fact, need a break. But the Yankees and Indians were battling for first place, and Huggins kept playing Gehrig in hopes that his bat would reawaken. On September 19, he pounded three doubles and a home run in a crucial win in Cleveland.

Playing the Cardinals in the World Series, the Yankees won the first game as Gehrig drove in the winning run. The Cardinals then won the next two games before Ruth slugged three home runs in Game 4 to even the series. The series came down to Game 7, played on a gray afternoon at Yankee Stadium. The Cardinals led, 3–2, when Ruth drew a walk with two out in the bottom of the ninth. On the first pitch to the next batter, Bob Meusel (Gehrig was batting fifth), Ruth tried to steal second and was thrown out. It was a bizarre end to an otherwise fine season for both the Yankees and their young first baseman.

Home runs had made Ruth one of America's leading celebrities, a larger-than-life figure of great fascination. Every aspect of his life was newspaper fodder — his marriages, his mistresses, his eating and drinking, his hospital visits to sick youngsters. Most men would have crumbled under the scrutiny, but Ruth relished it . . . and profited from it. Aside from playing baseball, he appeared in advertisements, movies, and vaudeville shows; lent his byline to syndicated newspaper columns (actually authored by ghostwriters); and staged elaborate annual salary negotiations. In 1927, when most major league players earned no more than $10,000, Ruth signed for $70,000.

Gehrig was Ruth's polar opposite. He brought his mother to spring training, went to bed early, rarely dated, carefully watched his diet, and seldom drank more than one beer at a sitting. He was excited just to get paid to play baseball. When the Yankees offered him $8,000 in 1927, he quickly signed and sent the contract back, fearing they might change their minds. But Ruppert had taken advantage of him; several backups signed for the same amount.

Watching his famous teammate cavort through life, Gehrig admired how Ruth interacted with reporters and fans; he was so breezy and casual, so adept at conjuring funny lines. But while Gehrig could not match Ruth's off-field persona, he emerged as Ruth's equal on the field in 1927.

Huggins had patiently brought him along, schooling him in nuances such as using his power to hit to all fields, as opposed to just pulling the ball to right. Ruth helped, offering tips about where to aim his swing in certain parks — for instance, right down the right-field line in Cleveland, where the fence was less than 300 feet away. Meanwhile, Gehrig continued to develop physically, his neck and trunk growing thick with muscles. By 1927, he was a man in full at six feet one and 230 pounds.

Batting cleanup on Opening Day at Yankee Stadium, he lined a double and drove in two runs as the Yankees battered Connie Mack's Philadelphia Athletics, a team expected to challenge them for the pennant. The next day, he hit a triple and double and drove in three runs. After two weeks, he was batting .400 with more home runs than Ruth. "This giant of a youth is heading fast for a prominent place among baseball's great players," the *New York Evening World* wrote.

On May 19 in Cleveland, Gehrig hit his ninth home run of the season as the Yankees improved their record to 21-8. That he had played in 300 straight games drew zero attention, but it was becoming clear that Huggins wanted to play him every day. It certainly made sense. Gehrig was young, strong, disciplined, in great shape, and productive. "No one on the team has more of a chance of playing in all 154 games than Gehrig," the *New York Evening World* reported.

The sport had never seen anything like the thrashing the Yankees administered to the rest of the American League in 1927. With a 110-44 record, they set a standard against which all great teams would be measured, capturing the pennant with an offensive display that boggled the mind. They batted over .300 as a team. Combs led the league with 231 hits. Meusel and Lazzeri each drove in more than 100 runs. And Ruth and Gehrig competed to make history. Ruth owned the record for home runs in a season, having clouted 59 in 1921. Now he and Gehrig raced for what the *New York Times* called "the hitherto unattainable height" of 60.

After Ruth hit two home runs on June 22 to give him 24 for the season, Gehrig hit three the next day to raise his total to 21. Soon Gehrig passed Ruth. Back and forth they went, lashing the ball, surpassing 40 in August and captivating fans across the country. "The most astonishing thing that has ever happened in organized baseball is the home run race between George Herman Ruth and Henry Louis Gehrig," syndicated columnist Paul Gallico wrote.

At Fenway Park on September 5, a sellout crowd stood and cheered Ruth, who had played for the Red Sox, after he smacked a ball into the right-field seats, giving him 44 for the season. Gehrig had the same total, but a day later Ruth hit three in a doubleheader to start a binge that was prodigious even by his standards. Ruth would hit 16 home runs in the Yankees' final 28 games. Gehrig could not match that pace. After keeping up all season, he hit under .300 in the final weeks. Those close to him knew his beloved mother was ill with a goiter, distracting him from his routine. (She eventually had surgery and recovered.)

With three games left in the season, Ruth had 57 homers and seemed destined to fall short of his record. But on September 29, he hit two out against Washington, tying his own record before 7,500 fans at Yankee Stadium. The next day, in the Yankees' next-to-last game of the season, he walked twice and singled before coming up in the eighth. The score was tied, 2–2, with a tough lefty, Tom Zachary, on the mound for Washington. Zachary threw a fastball for a strike. Another fastball sailed high. The third pitch was low and inside, and Ruth stepped away and swung mightily, connecting with what the *New York Times* called "a crash heard audibly in every part of the stands."

The ball started out on a low line toward the right-field foul pole before curving well into fair territory and landing halfway up the bleachers. Zachary slammed his glove on the ground in disgust as Ruth slowly circled the bases, extracting every ounce of drama from the moment. Fans tossed their hats and shredded newspapers in the air. "The spirit of celebration permeated the place," the *Times* reported.

Gehrig greeted him at the plate with a broad smile and warm handshake before stepping in to hit. He did not mind seeing his famous teammate take a bow. When Ruth trotted back out to right field for the top of the ninth, fans in the bleachers waved their handkerchiefs, and Ruth "entered into the carnival spirit and punctuated his kingly strides with a succession of snappy military salutes," the *Times* wrote.

The next day, the Yankees played their regular-season finale on Saturday afternoon against the Senators. Ruth was known to take such games off, especially with the Yankees set to start the World Series against the Pittsburgh Pirates in a few days. Gehrig could also have taken the day off; maybe the rest would have helped him shake his late-season slump. But both players told Huggins they wanted to play. Ruth was having fun, and Gehrig simply was accustomed to playing every day, having done so for more than two full seasons.

Ruth walked once in four at-bats before being lifted late in the game, which the Yankees won, 6–3. Gehrig played the whole game and hit a three-run homer, giving him 47, more than any player other than Ruth had ever hit in a season. He finished with a .373 average, higher than Ruth's .356, and 175 runs batted in, 11 more than Ruth. He easily won the balloting for the League Award, the forerunner of the Most Valuable Player award.

As Gehrig emerged, Ruth saw an opportunity. After the Yankees completed their dominant 1927 season with a four-game sweep of the Pirates in the World Series, the two players headlined a barnstorming tour arranged by Ruth's agent. Ruth and Gehrig drew crowds throughout the Midwest and California, captaining teams of local amateurs at each stop. Always, it was the "Bustin' Babes" against the "Larrupin' Lous." The tour closed in Los Angeles before 25,000 fans at Wrigley Field, the local Pacific Coast League ballpark. According to Jonathan Eig, author of *Luckiest Man*, a Gehrig biography, Ruth earned $30,000 on the tour and Gehrig made $10,000, more than his Yankees salary.

Grateful for Ruth's generosity, Gehrig readily accepted that his larger-than-life teammate would always generate more headlines, make more money, and probably hit more home runs; Gehrig would always be the sidekick. Yet inevitably, Gehrig also wanted to set himself apart from Ruth, to establish qualities for which he alone was known. Statistically, he made it a goal to drive in more runs than Ruth. "That's MY thing," he told reporters. Gehrig also sought to be dependable, ready at all times to play his best, unlike the erratic Ruth. His strength, conditioning, and lifestyle made it possible for him to play every day, as did his earnest philosophy. "I belong on the ball field," Gehrig said.

"I like to think Lou just fell into having a streak," Cal Ripken Jr. said. "That's what happened to me. I had the physicality and resiliency to play every day, so I did, and suddenly one day I had played in a thousand games in a row and it was, 'What are we going to do with this thing?' I never started out to do it, and I'm sure Lou didn't either. He had the strength to play every day, so he did."

By 1928, Gehrig's daily presence in Huggins's lineup was a certainty. That season, he and Ruth combined to hit 84 home runs and drive in 284 runs as the Yankees battled Philadelphia for the pennant. The Yankees built a large lead, lost it, and prevailed in the end. Along the way, Gehrig was ejected from two games for arguing with the umpire, and he came out of two other games early because of a sore foot. But his consecutive-game streak continued. Ruth also played in every game.

In the seventh inning of the Yankees' regular-season finale against Detroit, a ground ball took a bad hop and struck Gehrig in the face, knocking him to the ground. "He frightened everyone when he lay quite still," the *New York Times* reported, but he soon stood and was helped off the field. Fully recovered by the start of the World Series, Gehrig led the Yankees to a sweep of the Cardinals, bashing four home runs.

When the 1929 season began, the Yankees were entrenched as baseball's glamour team. They had won the past two World Series and played in three in a row. Fans flocked to their games both at home and on the road, hopeful of seeing Ruth hit one out — and if not Ruth, Gehrig.

But Connie Mack had put together a powerful Philadelphia Athletics squad featuring sluggers Al Simmons and Jimmy Foxx and pitchers Lefty Grove and George Earnshaw — the foundation of a dynasty set to emerge. The Athletics also were hungry after losing the 1928 pennant by a slim margin. When Ruth sat out games early in the season because of a hamstring injury, attributable to his being in poor shape, the Athletics roared out to a commanding lead. By mid-August, the Yankees were 15 games behind, and it was clear they would not play in their fourth straight Series.

A dip in Gehrig's performance, the first of his career, contributed to the Yankees' failure to contend. Although he drove in 125 runs, a healthy total, by the end of the season his batting average had dropped 74 points from the year before. Even when diminished, though, Gehrig's bat was preferable to any alternative on Huggins's bench. Gehrig played in every game for the fourth straight year.

As the season slipped away, Huggins was losing weight and developed a boil over his right eye. He said he was just upset about the team's failings, but he started complaining about headaches and fatigue, missed three games, and finally agreed to check into the hospital. His doctors said he had a form of blood poisoning, which turned into sepsis. His condition spiraled in the wrong direction, and shockingly, Huggins died on September 25. He was just 51 years old.

Word of his death reached the Yankees during a game in Boston. The center-field flag at Fenway Park was immediately lowered to half-staff, and a moment of silence was observed. Players wept in the Yankees' clubhouse as they spoke to reporters after the game. Gehrig was nearly inconsolable; Huggins had guided his career, helped him develop. The American League canceled all games the next day.

Ruth, ever the opportunist, campaigned to become the new manager. Other star players such as Ty Cobb and Tris Speaker had become managers later in their careers, and since Ruth had done so much for the Yankees, he figured they owed him. But Ruppert thought Ruth was immature, reportedly telling the slugger, "You can't even manage yourself, much less a team." The job went to Bob Shawkey, an easygoing former Yankees pitcher who had coached under Huggins.

If Ruth had gotten the job, Gehrig's consecutive-game streak might have ended. Ruth did not think such streaks were important enough to guarantee a player a spot in the lineup every day. What was the point? But Shawkey, a Huggins disciple, kept playing Gehrig. Why rest him? Gehrig had his finest all-around season in 1930, finishing with a .379 batting average, 41 home runs, and 179 runs batted in.

The Yankees kept pace with the Athletics early in the season, but a losing streak in July dropped them back. Shawkey was unable to discipline his former teammates, especially Ruth, who ignored most rules and any attempt at punishment. By September, the Yankees were headed for their worst record in six years. Shawkey indulged Ruth one last time, letting him pitch against the Red Sox in the season finale in Boston. Ruth threw a complete game and won.

Late in the season, Gehrig dealt with the first significant injuries of his career. His left elbow had started to hurt in July, and by late August he could barely make routine throws. The Yankees' trainer suspected a chipped elbow bone. Then, in early September, Gehrig broke the little finger on his right hand. Instead of telling Shawkey, he wrapped the finger with tape before coming to the ballpark and continued to play as if nothing were wrong.

His hitting did not suffer—his average in September was higher than in April and May—so no one could accuse him of hurting the team by playing when he was less than 100 percent. Throughout his career, he often played well when injured. But as soon as the season ended, he checked into St. Vincent's Hospital in New York. The Yankees' surgeon expected only to repair the chipped elbow bone, but X-rays revealed the broken finger Gehrig had hidden. That injury also required surgery.

As Gehrig convalesced, Ruppert shopped for a new manager; clearly, Shawkey was not right for the job. Bypassing Ruth again, the owner hired Joe McCarthy, a former Cubs manager who had instilled discipline in Chicago with a dress code and off-season exercise plan. The new skipper was under orders to "shake things up," Ruppert said, and John Kieran, the *New York Times* columnist, offered a suggestion. "It might pay Joe to yank Lou Gehrig out of the lineup for a day," Kieran wrote. "Lou hasn't missed a game in the past five seasons. McCarthy should snap this string before it becomes a worry to Lou."

10

Ripken

A SOUR YEAR

Cal Ripken Jr. was living a charmed baseball life. In his first two full seasons with the Orioles, he had won the Rookie of the Year and Most Valuable Player awards and played on a World Series winner, catching the last out of the clincher. Any of those achievements would constitute a career highlight for most players, but Ripken experienced them all by age 23. As the 1988 season began, he was, at 27, a five-time All-Star who had never missed a game due to injury. Even with the Orioles coming off back-to-back losing seasons, his father was his manager, his brother was his double-play partner, and his best friend batted behind him every night.

In 1988, though, his charmed life soured. The Orioles' decline reached such a nadir they became fodder for talk-show comedians. Ripken was a subject of trade talks. His offensive production, which had tailed off in 1987, continued to settle at a more modest level. And worst of all, his father's long-sought major league managerial opportunity ended abruptly.

After watching the team lose 95 games in 1987, the Orioles' owner, Edward Bennett Williams, had fired Hank Peters, the general manager, and also canned the minor league director and several influential scouts. Senior was retained as manager and gamely expressed optimism during spring training, but his hold on the job was tenuous given the team's weak pitching staff and Williams's obvious dissatisfaction with the status quo.

Sure enough, after just six games, all defeats, Senior was fired. The Orioles had lost twice at home to the Milwaukee Brewers to start the season, including a 12–0 embarrassment on Opening Day, and then dropped four to the Indians in Cleveland by a combined 28–6 score. Even though the season was just a week old, Williams and his new general manager, Roland Hemond, had seen enough. Hours before the Orioles played the Kansas City Royals at Memorial Stadium on April 12, Senior was called into a meeting and told to clear out his office.

It was the quickest in-season firing in major league history, and it staggered both of Senior's sons. Bill heard the news on the radio as he drove to the ballpark for the game. "I was on Cold Spring Lane, about a mile away," he said, vividly recalling the moment more than two decades later. Twenty-three years old and still relatively new to the majors, Bill was mostly confused. The Orioles' trainer, Ralph Salvon, pulled him into an office when he reached the clubhouse. "Senior had told Ralph to tell me he was a big boy and could handle himself. I should just worry about taking care of myself," Bill said.

When Junior arrived shortly thereafter, the brothers exchanged a wordless look. "It was a blank stare, like, 'What just happened?'" Bill said. "I think it is probably fair to say Junior was more pissed. He had a deeper understanding than I did at that point. He knew it wasn't fair, that we were 0-6 for a reason, that Senior wasn't given the horses to do anything with, which quickly became more evident."

Not surprisingly, while playing for the team that had just fired his father, Junior went into a funk. "He was still a young man. What happened with his dad bitterly disappointed him," his agent, Ron Shapiro, said. Having already started the season slowly, he did not get a hit for a week after the firing, dropping his average to .047. For the season, he had two hits in 43 at-bats.

Meanwhile, the Orioles continued to flounder under Senior's replacement, Frank Robinson, a Hall of Fame outfielder from the team's glory years in the 1960s. By late April, Baltimore had played 21 games and lost them all, an unimaginable situation for a team that had won the World Series just five years earlier. On the cover of *Sports Illustrated,* under the headline THE AGONY OF THE ORIOLES, Bill was pictured sitting in a dugout with his eyes closed, resting a bat against his forehead — a portrait of despair.

Years later, Junior would recall the first months of the 1988 season as "a very difficult time." He found refuge in the sport's daily rituals, the rhythmic grind of pregame infield and batting practice followed by a game.

Senior's tutelage had produced a player as meticulous about his craft as an accountant poring over financial ledgers. In Junior's opinion, you could not play a game without thoroughly preparing for it, and that preparation included honing his swing in batting practice and fielding dozens of ground balls.

Many other players regarded the pregame work as drudgery and occasionally concocted reasons to skip it, but Ripken embraced it. "I think he even spurred Dad into making us do more of it when Dad was managing," Bill recalled. While fans gawked at his growing consecutive-game and consecutive-inning streaks, teammates and opponents gawked at his devotion to batting and infield practice.

"The most amazing thing was watching how hard he worked every day on preparing to play, just quietly going about his business," said Mickey Tettleton, a catcher who joined the Orioles early in the 1988 season after being released by the Oakland Athletics. "It was a rough season for us, but you would never know from watching him. He was out there taking ground balls in the afternoon, never skirted that. And he never shut it down in a game, like if we were losing. He stayed focused and intense, never gave up even a single at-bat."

To Tettleton, who played 14 years in the major leagues, the root of Ripken's commitment was easy to discern. "He just loved the game so much, everything about it, playing, competing every night, even in a bad year," Tettleton said. "It was infectious. Even though we were losing, guys enjoyed being around one another. We would hang out in the clubhouse after games, talk baseball. He made it easy. He very well could have been one of those bigger-than-life figures, but he was just one of the guys."

After his slow start, Ripken heated up, his average soaring to .316 by May, but then he slumped again and was back under .240 by early June. The highs and lows were dizzying, but Robinson continued to play him every day. The last-place Orioles had little else going for them. "A real pleasure I had was coming to the ballpark every day and knowing I could write his name in the lineup without checking with him or the trainer," Robinson recalled.

One night, Ripken crashed into the Orioles' third baseman, Rick Schu, while chasing a pop foul down the left-field line. "Both guys went for it. The collision was pretty violent. They went down hard and stayed down," recalled Roland Hemond, who would hold the Orioles' general manager job from 1988 through 1995. "My first thought was, 'Well, this might be it for Cal and the streak.' Rick told me later he didn't care whether he was injured, just whether Cal got up. And Cal eventually did, like always."

On June 25, 1988, Ripken became the sixth major leaguer to play in a thousand straight games. When the first to do it, Everett Scott, reached that threshold in 1923, he received a hero's treatment in Washington even though he played for the visiting Yankees. The U.S. secretary of the navy gave a speech. A marine band played. Scott received a commemorative gold medallion from the American League. But when Ripken reached a thousand in a row, also as a visiting player, his achievement received no mention during the game at Boston's Fenway Park, and even his teammates did not congratulate him. "I don't remember it. We didn't throw a party. I don't even think we talked about it," Bill Ripken said.

Unlike Scott, Ripken was not the consecutive-game record holder. In fact, he needed to play in every game for another seven seasons to reach Gehrig's record. He was not even halfway there, and Hemond, a veteran executive, did not believe he would make it. It was just too likely he would get injured at some point in the next seven years, Hemond thought. Players pulled muscles, shattered bones, and suffered other debilitating injuries. Every pitch brought the chance that it was your turn. Ripken was determined and strong, but surely the odds would catch up with him.

"It was admirable, what Cal had done to get that far, a thousand in a row," Hemond said years later. "But to envision him going on and breaking the record, it was difficult to comprehend that was even humanly possible."

After 21 straight losses, the Orioles finally recorded their first win of 1988 on April 29, defeating the White Sox in Chicago, 9–0. Four days later, at their first home game since they snapped the losing streak, a sellout crowd packed Memorial Stadium for a "Fantastic Fans Night" promotion, billed as a chance for Baltimore to show support for its beleaguered club, now the city's only major league sports team, with football's Colts gone.

With more than 50,000 fans on hand, it felt like a World Series game. Taking a microphone before the huge crowd, Maryland's governor, William Donald Schaefer, announced the state had just signed a deal to build a new ballpark for the Orioles in downtown Baltimore. Initially stunned, the fans loosed a roar. Schaefer's news quashed long-simmering rumors about the team possibly moving to Washington, where Edward Bennett Williams resided.

The Orioles won the game, sending the fans home delighted. But once the euphoria of that exciting night wore off, it was clear Baltimore was in for a long, grim summer. By late May, the Orioles had played 47 games and won nine. "We weren't having any fun at all on the field," Ripken recalled. His baseball life had gone from charming to depressing, from sweet to stressful, and increasingly uncertain. Although the Orioles' future in Baltimore was now set, Ripken's was not. Shapiro had negotiated a multiyear contract for him before the season, but he turned it down, instead signing a one-year deal that enabled him to become a free agent after the 1988 season. It appeared he was willing to move on. Senior's firing only increased the perception in the industry that he was unhappy in Baltimore.

During spring training before the 1988 season, the Toronto Blue Jays had offered to trade slugger George Bell to the Orioles in exchange for Ripken. Bell, the American League's reigning Most Valuable Player, was unhappy about being moved from the outfield to the designated hitter role. Toronto's general manager was Pat Gillick, the former Orioles minor leaguer who had played with Senior in the early 1960s. Now an aggressive, forward-thinking roster architect, Gillick envisioned Ripken as a third baseman.

Hemond was unwilling to make the deal, but his phone continued to ring during the season. The Boston Red Sox, Pittsburgh Pirates, and Houston Astros all called with offers for Ripken that the media reported. Ripken was distracted and conflicted. Though upset about Senior, he had been in the Orioles organization for a decade. Rumors about his departure made him nervous. "It's very unsettling," he said later. "I was disturbed that I might be traded."

As stress built inside him, he idly picked up a wad of tape and squeezed it one day while Richie Bancells taped his ankles before a game at the Metrodome in Minneapolis. An idea came to him. When he and his siblings had spent their summers around Senior's minor league teams years earlier, they had played baseball for hours inside clubhouses and under concession stands, using balls made of tape. Why not re-create that now? A game of "tape ball" might make for a lighthearted break from the Orioles' grim season.

Ripken approached the gangly teenagers who worked in the visitors' clubhouse in Minnesota. "I suggested that we could go down to the field later that night, after the game, and play tape ball," Ripken recalled. "Needless to say, they were pretty excited."

That night, long after the last pitch of the game between the Orioles and Minnesota Twins, Junior, Bill, a few teammates, and the clubhouse boys made their way to the field. The empty Metrodome was dimly lit. "It was 2 a.m., maybe 3 a.m.," Ripken recalled. "We picked sides and played. Home plate was out in the infield, near second. We ran around, styled when we hit home runs. It was so healing to go back and be in touch with how you started to love this game."

Tape ball games became routine when the Orioles played in Minnesota. "We'd be running, diving, sliding. There were big collisions at first base. The clubhouse kids had all these burns. There were potential injury risks all over the place. But boy, we had fun," Ripken recalled.

His Orioles teammates smiled and shook their heads when they heard about it. They were not surprised. Junior was reserved in public, but they knew a side of him the media and fans never glimpsed. "He's the biggest kid ever, basically," Bill said. Ripken was mischievous, constantly inventing games and dares to help break up the monotony of the long season.

"People would never know that about him because he's so diplomatic in public. But there was always something going on," recalled Brady Anderson, an outfielder who joined the Orioles in 1988. "Looking back, it was a coping mechanism. Somehow, play was his way of releasing stress. It was nonstop with him . . . not resting, annoying someone in the training room, joking around, competing at something stupid."

Ripken enlivened batting practice with games of "500," in which players accrued points while shagging flies. At the Metrodome, he and teammates competed to see who could use the fewest steps to traverse a steep concrete stairway connecting the clubhouse and dugout. "Wearing metal cleats, probably not the smartest idea," Ripken said. During a rain delay in Baltimore one night, while their teammates dozed or watched television,

Ripken and Anderson competed to see who could jump the highest from a standstill. "We did that for over an hour," Anderson said.

When pitcher Ben McDonald, a Louisiana Cajun with a fun-loving spirit, joined the Orioles several years later, he was surprised to discover their well-mannered shortstop was so like-minded. "Junior and I had a lot of wrestling matches," McDonald recalled, chuckling at the memory.

One of the group's favorite contests centered on, of all things, pain tolerance. Players would form coalitions and plot sneak attacks on an unsuspecting teammate, hoping to inflict enough pain that he would relent and cry uncle. Ripken was a frequent attacker, but when others ganged up on him and drove their knuckles into his chest, he stubbornly refused to submit.

"We went at it all the time," McDonald said. "Cal was a big, strong guy. People didn't realize that. One time he grabbed [pitcher] Rick Sutcliffe, another big guy, and we couldn't pry Sut loose from him. I'm a big guy myself. It got pretty intense."

The school-yard behavior theoretically jeopardized Ripken's consecutive-game streak, but he did not care.

"I never saw an ounce of caution in him," McDonald said. "I mean, I wasn't going to be the stupid guy who broke his finger wrestling in the clubhouse and ended the streak. But oh, man, we did so much stuff. We were like little kids let loose. With the streak going on, we'd go to water parks on the road and come flying down these crazy rides. We played tape ball in the Metrodome in the middle of the night. If we had said we were going to go parasailing or jump out of an airplane, I'm talking right in the middle of the streak, Junior would have been the first one out of the plane."

Several years later, when he was in sight of Gehrig's record, Ripken smiled when reporters speculated that he exercised caution to avoid an injury that might end his streak. "It blew me away that people thought I had to live a careful life," Ripken said. "Shoot, I played basketball through the off-season, got stitches, a broken nose, blew out my ankle. But reporters would ask [my wife] Kelly, 'Do you cut up his food so he doesn't have to use a knife?' She was funny, she'd say, 'Yeah, I do all that stuff. We have soap on a rope in the shower. We don't want him slipping on a bar of soap, so he wears it around his neck.' She was joking."

· · ·

Instead of trading Ripken in 1988, the Orioles traded Mike Boddicker to the Red Sox for Anderson, then a 24-year-old on the cusp of a major league career. A breezy, chatty Southern Californian, Anderson struck up a friendship with Ripken as the Orioles wobbled to the end of a miserable season.

One day in batting practice, Ripken took his cuts before a game and then went to the outfield and shagged flies alone. "He clearly needed to be by himself," Anderson recalled. "I didn't know any better, so I went up to talk to him."

Ripken shook his head. "Not now," he said.

Anderson asked what was wrong, straining to imagine what could possibly be bothering his highly decorated teammate. "He already had a World Series ring, an MVP award. I was just getting to the majors," Anderson recalled. "But now he's standing there in the outfield and starts talking about it, his consecutive-game streak. It was on his mind."

Ripken asked Anderson whether he thought it was important, and if so, why? Anderson had an opinion; he had studied baseball history and knew about Gehrig's streak. "I had a sense for it," Anderson recalled. "Mostly, I talked and he just kind of listened. I said it's an amazing record that reflects so many great qualities. Even then, I thought, 'You know, he's probably going to make a run at it.' I talked that day like it was a foregone conclusion. We talked about his potential legacy."

After that first outfield conversation, Anderson and Ripken did not discuss the subject again for years. "It wasn't like he was sitting around thinking about it," Anderson said. "Maybe he didn't even know why he brought it up that day. He was still seven years away. But it was out there."

Indeed, Gehrig's record was not a forgotten milestone stashed in baseball's attic. Though more than a half century old, it was part of the modern conversation. Just a few years earlier, Steve Garvey, a first baseman for the Los Angeles Dodgers, had established the National League consecutive-game record by playing in 1,207 games in a row. Until a broken finger ended his run, Garvey had spoken unabashedly about wanting to keep going until he passed Gehrig. Ripken said that was never his motivation, but by 1988 it was evident he was, if anything, a viable candidate to catch Gehrig because he possessed some important qualities.

Physical Strength

"Cal was probably the strongest guy I ever played with, from a physical standpoint. I think that got lost a little bit as his streak grew," Ken Singleton said. "I played basketball with him in the off-season, and if you found yourself alongside him underneath the basket and tried to move him out, you couldn't budge him. I mean, I couldn't, and I'm not small myself. Cal was just a tough dude. He played a dangerous position and was in a lot of collisions, but in the years I played with him, most of the guys who collided with Cal came out second best."

Mickey Tettleton vouched for that. The catcher eventually departed Baltimore in a trade and played seven more years for other teams. What was it like sliding into Ripken at second base?

"Like sliding into a tree," Tettleton said. "You couldn't budge him."

Smart Positioning

"Shortstop can be dangerous with all the collisions at second base, but Cal handled himself so well around the bag, was always positioned well, with his legs under him, on plays at second as well as on backhand plays in the hole," Richie Bancells said. "You get hurt when your body is vulnerable, and he minimized that. And it didn't hurt that he was six-foot-four and 220 pounds, which was unheard-of, that size at that position."

General Good Health

"The illness factor, never getting one that knocked him out, that's probably more impressive than the injury factor," Bancells said. "You can get into a whole lot of science. Some people just have good immune systems. There were days when Junior came to the park with a fever, but where it would knock other people down, he would go, 'I can get through it; I'll be all right. Let's get through the game and we'll deal with it afterward.' When the bell rang, so to speak, it was time to play. And the ironic thing was, he was never a guy to take a pill. He never came looking for an Advil."

Toughness

"Certain injuries and illnesses, you're just not going to play through them, and he didn't have any of those," Anderson said. "But he had some that would have kept other guys out a few weeks, especially injuries — a knee, an ankle, a wrist — and he just grinded through them. He was a little bit superhuman in his ability to recuperate, recover, and get out there and play."

Off-Season Conditioning

Ripken was ahead of a trend that developed as free agency pushed salaries higher. When his career began, many players worked jobs in the off-season and used spring training to get in shape for playing 162 games. Ripken worked out in the off-season.

"The season itself was such a grind. Once it started, you just tried to hold on to what you had physically, as opposed to building yourself up," he said. "The off-season, I thought, was for building yourself up to get ready for that. When I came to spring training, I was in the best shape I'd be in all year."

He drew up a regimen every off-season, relying on Bancells's expertise. "He would ask questions: 'Would this be beneficial? Would that be beneficial? Why does something function this way? How can I improve this?'" Bancells said. "It's funny. A lot of guys play this game, but they don't see the efficiency of their body as a tool that makes them money. Cal was ahead of his time. He thoroughly understood that for him to be on the field for all those games during the season, his body had to be in great shape when he came to camp."

The basketball games he orchestrated attained urban-legend status around Baltimore. Ripken invited teammates, other pro athletes, and former college basketball players to join him for full-court games that became intensely competitive. Playing near the basket because of his size,

Ripken battled for rebounds, drove hard to the basket, and exchanged elbows.

"I loved how 'basketball legs' made you feel in baseball. It was great training. And it was fun," Ripken recalled. "You could keep your weight down if you did it regularly. I always believed it was a necessary part of building your strength up during the off-season."

Bancells said, "His thought was, 'If you're going to stay in shape in the off-season, let's make it fun.' He understood from asking about his body that basketball could help make him quicker, help him move laterally, help hand eye coordination. It was also a big cardiovascular workout and an anaerobic workout."

Though Bancells had not played basketball since high school, he was a regular at Ripken's games, which were played in a high school gym until Ripken built a suburban home with an indoor basketball court. "They were intense, physical, competitive games," Bancells said. "The next day, you knew you had played."

Mindset

Junior was always quick to credit Senior and Eddie Murray with helping him understand the importance of being available every day, but Ron Shapiro and Bill Ripken believe Junior deserved the credit.

Shapiro, who also represented Murray, said, "Eddie may have refined Cal's approach, but he didn't impact it, because Eddie's approach embodied Senior's. Eddie was a great reinforcement but not an originator of the Cal Ripken approach to baseball and hard work."

As for Senior's influence, Bill Ripken said, "Sure, Dad was the way he was, and Junior got whatever he got from that. But Junior took what Dad was all about and magnified it tenfold. I don't think Dad possibly could have imagined what Junior was able to pull off because of what was instilled in him. Junior took it and ran with it to a vastly higher level."

Around the All-Star break in 1988, Ripken made a decision, authorizing Shapiro to negotiate a long-term contract for him with the Orioles. "I don't believe his father was going to let him get upset enough that he left," Shapiro recalled. On July 28, he signed a three-year contract worth more than $6 million. "Cal is the rock on which we're rebuilding our club," said Larry Lucchino, the team's president.

That rebuilding effort was going to be a major construction job. The Orioles ended 1988 with 107 defeats, the most for them in any season since they began playing in Baltimore in 1954. Ripken was on the field for just about all of it, starting every game and finishing all but two. Although his .262 average, 23 home runs, and 81 runs batted in did not match his output from earlier in his career, his determination to be available every day had been tested like never before. When Robinson pulled him after the third inning of the season finale on October 2, letting him watch the rest of the game from the visitors' dugout in Toronto, it was almost an act of mercy. The Blue Jays already had a seven-run lead. Ripken had experienced enough dismal baseball for one year, the manager thought. Maybe he did not want a break, but he had earned one.

11

Gehrig

A FRIEND'S INFLUENCE

As a young player, Lou Gehrig witnessed the last months of Everett Scott's consecutive-game streak, planting in his head the idea that such an accomplishment existed. Then, in the early 1930s, Gehrig came in contact with another consecutive-game stalwart — Joe Sewell, a diminutive infielder who was the only major leaguer other than Scott to have played in a thousand straight games.

A vestige of baseball's dead-ball past, Sewell was a 32-year-old contact hitter, renowned for not striking out, when he joined the Yankees in 1931 after a decade with the Cleveland Indians. With him batting in front of Ruth and Gehrig and a new manager, Joe McCarthy, running the club, the Yankees hoped to finally overcome the Philadelphia Athletics, who had captured the American League pennant in 1929 and 1930.

The son of a horse-and-buggy country doctor, Sewell had grown up on the family farm in Titus, Alabama, in the early 1900s, spending countless hours tossing up rocks and hitting them with a broomstick. It was just his way to kill time, but the idle practice sharpened his batting eye and shaped his career, Sewell said later.

When he enrolled at the University of Alabama, expecting to become a doctor himself, he took premed classes, joined a fraternity, and was elected class president, never entertaining the idea of a pro baseball career. Though he stood only five feet six, he excelled as a middle infielder for the Crimson Tide varsity, setting records on Southeastern Conference championship teams. A pro scout spotted him playing shortstop in a semipro summer circuit, the Tennessee Coal and Iron League, after his graduation in 1920. Impressed with Sewell's quick hands and knack for making contact, the scout convinced Sewell to sign a contract with the New Orleans Pelicans of the Southern Association. Within months, he received a surprising call-up to the major leagues when the Indians purchased his contract. Locked in a pennant race with the Yankees and White Sox, they suddenly needed a shortstop. A chain of events set off by a horrific tragedy had left them shorthanded.

On August 16, 1920, Carl Mays, a pitcher for the Yankees, threw a fastball at the Polo Grounds that sailed up and in on Ray Chapman, the Indians' star shortstop. Chapman did not duck; he probably never saw the scuffed-up ball. It hit his skull with a thwack so loud that Mays thought it had hit his bat. The ball caromed into play, right to Mays, who picked it up and threw to first to record the out, while Chapman dropped to the dirt, blood oozing from his left ear. Instinctively, he tried to stand and run, but he lost consciousness and collapsed as players from both teams raced to the plate, alarmed. Chapman was carried from the field, his skull severely fractured. He died the next morning.

The sport mourned the shocking death of a player who was popular with teammates and opponents alike. In an unprecedented gesture, other teams offered to loan the Indians a shortstop. Cleveland politely declined and gave the job to Harry Lunte, a light-hitting reserve, but then quickly determined he was not a suitable replacement. When Lunte pulled a thigh muscle in early September, the Indians turned to Sewell.

It should have been an exciting day, but Sewell was heartsick. "Ray Chapman was my hero," he recalled later. "I felt the Indians' pennant hopes died with his passing. I made up my mind as I traveled north on the train that I would forget I was Joe Sewell and imagine I was Chapman fighting to bring honor and glory to Cleveland."

He arrived in Cleveland with little more than a new suit of clothes, bought during a stopover in Cincinnati. Tris Speaker, the Indians' star center fielder, was in his first season as a player-manager. A 32-year-old Texan who had worked on a ranch before playing pro baseball, Speaker felt an affinity for Sewell and let him watch several games from the bench before putting him in the lineup. "Are you sure?" Sewell asked, feeling unprepared. But he was ready. Borrowing a 40-ounce black bat from a teammate, he knocked a triple in his first at-bat. "When I got to third, I thought, 'Shucks, this ain't so tough,'" he said years later.

He collected 23 hits in the Indians' final 22 games, and they won the pennant, but since he had been added to the roster so late, he was not eligible to play in the World Series. The Indians asked for an exemption because of Chapman's death, and the National League champions, the Brooklyn Robins, agreed to waive the roster rule. Sewell struggled in the Series, but the Indians won.

The next year, he became the team's everyday shortstop and hit .318 while striking out just 17 times in almost 700 plate appearances. All those hours spent hitting rocks with a broomstick had paid off. The job was his. By late in the 1922 season, Sewell had played in more than 300 straight games.

Speaker, however, was not a proponent of playing streaks. A major league star since 1909, he had played a full season of games only once. He believed in players taking at least one short respite every season, and he gave Sewell one in early September 1922, sitting the young shortstop for a weekend of games in Chicago even though Sewell was hitting .304.

After that, however, Sewell never rested, not even while committing a startling 59 errors in 1923. Ordinarily, a shortstop that mistake-prone would sit on the bench now and then, but Speaker needed Sewell's bat. He hit .353 and drove in 109 runs while committing all those errors. The next year, he led the American League with 45 doubles. In 1925, he hit .336 and, amazingly, struck out just four times in almost 700 plate appearances. In 1926, he batted .324 and struck out just six times.

After the 1926 season, Speaker faced game-fixing allegations and re-signed. His replacement, Jack McAllister, continued to play Sewell every day. With Everett Scott's streak having ended in 1925, Sewell now owned the longest active consecutive-game streak in the majors — 784 straight games by the end of the 1927 season.

The Indians had become also-rans, lagging behind the powerful Yankees. In 1928, they hired a new manager, Roger Peckinpaugh, a former shortstop for the Yankees and Red Sox who valued defense. Sewell's run as the everyday shortstop ended. He played third base part-time that season and shifted permanently the next year.

On June 16, 1929, he became the second major leaguer, after Scott, to play in a thousand straight games. His streak was up to 1,091 by the end of the season, and Sewell said he planned to keep going until he passed Scott and became the all-time "iron man." It was a goal that seemed attainable, he said. Other than that weekend in 1922 when Speaker rested him, he had never missed a game since becoming a major leaguer.

Early in the 1930 season, though, he ran a high fever while on a road trip. To keep his streak alive in St. Louis on April 29, he batted in the top of the first and left the game after grounding out. The Associated Press sent out a story stating that his pursuit of Everett Scott's consecutive-game record was "in jeopardy."

He still had a high fever the next day, but Peckinpaugh let him play, and he socked a line drive into right field in the top of the first. The ball landed in the grass and rolled to the wall as Sewell raced around the bases, mustering his flagging strength. As soon as he stopped at third, he bent at the waist and signaled that he needed to come out. A pinch runner replaced him.

The next day, the Indians took a train to Boston, and Sewell's condition did not improve. When he woke with the same high fever on May 2, hours before the opener of a series with the Red Sox, he decided enough was enough—he was too sick to keep going. His streak ended at 1,103 games, 204 shy of Scott's record.

The Associated Press erroneously reported that Sewell's streak had "started in 1920 and until yesterday he participated in every ball game played by the Indians during this ten-year period." In fact, he had missed that weekend in Chicago in 1922. If Speaker had played him then, he would have owned the record now, not Scott.

Sewell missed eight games due to his illness, and when he returned, Peckinpaugh reduced his role, making him a part-time player. His average dropped to .289, and at the end of the 1930 season, he asked the Indians for his release, thinking he could still hit as an everyday player for some team. The Indians obliged his request. Sewell went home to Tuscaloosa, Alabama, and fielded offers. Connie Mack mailed a contract from Philadelphia and telegraphed, "Don't sign with anyone else until you get it." The Yankees sent a scout to Sewell's home to emphasize how much they wanted him.

The Yankees won out, and in his first year with baseball's big-name club, he played third base and batted second. Joe McCarthy did not play him in every game, but he only missed about one per week while proving that, indeed, he could still perform at a high level, hitting .302 and scoring 102 runs, his career high.

In an era when teams asked players to share hotel rooms on road trips, Sewell and Gehrig became roommates. Sewell was four years older, and he was married and from the South, unlike Gehrig, a single New Yorker, but they had a lot in common. Both had gone to college. Both were "straight arrows." They spent evenings talking baseball in the hotel lobby or their room while their teammates hit the bars. "Joe is the rural type, in bed by 10 and up at six," one sportswriter reported. Gehrig kept the same hours.

They were opposites in size and as hitters — Gehrig a broad-shouldered slugger, Sewell a slender contact specialist — but they were alike in their desire to play every day. When Sewell's consecutive-game streak ended in 1929, Gehrig's became the longest active streak in the majors at more than 700 games.

Gehrig respected his new teammate and heeded Sewell's advice about the importance of making contact at the plate. Up to that point in his career, Gehrig, like Ruth and other power hitters, had piled up strikeouts, averaging more than 73 per season as he "swung for the fences." But he struck out just 56 times in 1931, Sewell's first season in New York, and lowered that to 38 in 1932. Never again, in fact, would Gehrig strike out as often as he did early in his career, and though he never credited Sewell, his roommate's influence seems obvious.

No record exists of their discussing consecutive-game streaks, but considering how much time they spent together, it is likely the subject came up. By the time the Yankees released Sewell after the 1933 season, Gehrig had played through a back ailment and broken bones and had set a record for consecutive playing.

Sewell was 34 when the Yankees dropped him. This time, there was no rush to Tuscaloosa to sign him. His bat was declining. His speed was diminished. It was not unusual for a major leaguer to keep playing beyond age 34 — Ruth was still going at 38 — but Sewell never played again. Insiders wondered if he had worn himself out by taking so few breaks during his career.

Stationed across the infield from him for three years in the early 1930s, Gehrig had an intimate view of Sewell's decline. But Gehrig obviously did not buy the theory that Sewell's consecutive-game streak had hastened his demise. Ignoring the whispers, Gehrig kept playing every day.

· · ·

On May 9, 1932, the Yankees had a home game scheduled against the St. Louis Browns, with the first pitch at 3:30 p.m. Gehrig usually arrived at Yankee Stadium several hours early, in time to change into his uniform and take part in pregame drills, but on this Monday, he never went to the ballpark. He went to court instead.

His mother, Christina, had been in a car accident, and a passenger riding with her had filed a lawsuit seeking $40,000 in damages. The case was due to be heard that afternoon. Gehrig had played in 1,060 straight games, but his court date was more important. Christina had to testify, and Gehrig was not about to let his mother experience that alone. He also might have to testify, as he had been in the car when the accident occurred.

Around noon, the Yankees announced they were postponing the game and rescheduling it as part of a doubleheader on July 10. Their rationale was "threatening weather conditions," the *New York Times* reported. But while it was a cool, cloudy day in New York, with the forecast calling for rain, no drops ever fell. The Yankees and Browns could have played.

Conspiracy theorists have long speculated that the Yankees' owner, Jacob Ruppert, called off the game to protect Gehrig's streak, knowing the first baseman had a court date and might not be available. Ruppert certainly liked the streak and thought it was important. Asked why he kept it up, Gehrig told *New York World-Telegram* sportswriter Dan Daniel, "I am interested in it, the fans seem to be, and Ruppert mentions it often enough for me to believe I ought to go as far as I can with it." Ruppert wanted the Yankees in the headlines. He had traded for Ruth, turned the team into a winner, and built Yankee Stadium. Gehrig's impressive streak seemed to be part of that narrative.

But it is doubtful Ruppert postponed the May 9 game just to preserve Gehrig's streak. Given the gloomy weather forecast and the fact that the Browns were baseball's worst team, the game would have drawn a paltry crowd; when the teams played the next day at Yankee Stadium, they drew so few fans that no attendance was listed. Played in warmer weather, as part of a July doubleheader, the game would attract a much larger crowd and bring in more cash.

In the years before television revenue reconfigured baseball economics, teams depended heavily on ticket sales. It is interesting to speculate about Gehrig's streak possibly having received a dubious stay of execution, but Ruppert often postponed early-season games and rescheduled them for summertime dates when more fans would attend. In 1932, 7 of the Yankees' first 25 games were pushed back. When the May 9 game was made up on July 10, the Yankees sold 31,000 tickets. From a financial standpoint, Ruppert's decision was a no-brainer.

And even if the game had gone on as scheduled on May 9, Gehrig probably would have made it to the ballpark in time to keep his streak going. He was never called to testify.

As Dan Daniel recounted the story later, Gehrig did not know he was nearing Everett Scott's consecutive-game record. Daniel is the one who told him.

According to Daniel, the two ate breakfast together at the Yankees' hotel in Washington on July 4, 1933, and then chatted in the lobby afterward.

"Do you have any idea how many games in a row you've played?" Daniel asked.

"No, I don't," Gehrig replied. "I do know that I started in 1925 and this is 1933, so I guess it's somewhere in the hundreds."

Daniel's eyebrows went up. "No, it's more than that," he said. He promised to identify the number and let Gehrig know.

It took a precise eye to determine exactly where the Iron Horse's streak stood. Many sportswriters did not recall that he had pinch-hit the day before he became a regular in the Yankees lineup in 1925. More recently, during the 1932 season, a game between the Yankees and Tigers had to be replayed after the Yankees batted out of order and the Tigers successfully protested, and Will Harridge, president of the American League, ruled that *both* the invalidated game and the replayed game would count toward Gehrig's streak.

The day after Daniel brought it up in Washington, he told the first baseman the streak had stood at 1,197 straight games when the 1933 season began, so Gehrig was now within 25 games or so of Scott's all-time record of 1,307.

It is unknown whether Gehrig actually kept count before that conversation, but he did afterward. Several weeks later, he corrected the Yankees press corps when it reported he had played in 1,293 straight games. "The published dope on my consecutive-game record is incorrect," he told reporters, standing by his locker before a game. "I have played in 1,294 straight games since June 1, 1925. The generally accepted total is short by one. The writers have overlooked that I was a pinch hitter the day before I broke in as a regular on the Yankees. Walter Johnson was pitching and we were getting our fifth straight defeat. I'm sorry to say I flied out to Goose Goslin."

He reached into his wallet and pulled out a frayed newspaper clipping containing a box score from June 2, 1925, his first game as a regular and the second game of his streak. The writers printed corrections. Gehrig continued playing.

The reporters' focus on his individual achievement did not come at a good time. The Yankees and Senators had battled all season for first place in the American League, but now the pitching-rich Senators had pulled ahead. The Yankees trailed by 5½ games when they traveled to St. Louis to play the lowly Browns.

On Wednesday, August 16, Gehrig tied Scott's record before a meager crowd at Sportsman's Park. There was no mention of his achievement at the park. In fact, the home team celebrated "Rogers Hornsby Day," in honor of the longtime major league infielder, whom the Browns had just hired as player-manager. The Yankees lost badly, 13–3, to fall 6½ games out.

"Though individual distinction came to Gehrig, gloom was the lot of the McCarthymen," the *New York Times*' James P. Dawson wrote.

The next day, Gehrig received much more attention as he became baseball's all-time Ironman, running his streak to 1,308 games before another small crowd at Sportsman's Park.

After the first inning, both teams gathered around home plate for a ceremony. Will Harridge spoke first and gave "eloquent testimonial to a ball player who has established a remarkable record," St. Louis sportswriter Sid Keener reported. E. G. Brands, editor of the *Sporting News*, then stepped to the microphone, congratulated Gehrig, and presented him with a silver statuette commemorating the achievement. Gehrig smiled and posed for pictures with Joe Sewell. Harridge had invited Everett Scott, who now ran a bowling alley in Fort Wayne, Indiana, but Scott had sent a telegram saying it was "impossible" for him to attend.

After the brief ceremony, the game resumed. Ruth hit a home run and Gehrig added a triple. The Yankees took a lead into the bottom of the ninth, but Hornsby smacked a home run to force extra innings, and the

Browns won in the 10th. The Yankees were now 7½ games out, their pennant prospects fading fast.

When reporters asked the 37-year-old Hornsby about Gehrig after the game, he crinkled his ruddy face. Known as "the Rajah," Hornsby was a down-home Texan who sprinkled his conversations with plainspoken country colloquialisms. "All I know about the guy," he growled, "is he didn't get that record sitting on the bench!"

Sid Keener translated Hornsby's comment in a column the next day: "He was speaking his own language and no doubt hoping his expression would hit home with his own players. It is known that there are many athletes in the business who are always eager to take a vacation. They have scratched an ankle, twisted a wrist slightly, fallen into a brief batting slump, and things are generally in bad shape with them. They want a 'time out.' Ball players of that type will never get along with Hornsby."

In a *New York Times* column, John Kieran, who had covered both Scott and Gehrig, made it clear that he was more impressed with the Iron Horse's endurance record. Scott, Kieran wrote, was "a careful chap" who wore padded shoes and "never slammed into a wall in pursuit of foul flies." Deacon "would play shortstop and let it go at that." By contrast, Kieran wrote, Gehrig "doesn't wear special shoes" and "in his endeavor to win a ball game" will "run into walls, fall into boxes and plunge down dugout steps in pursuit of foul flies." Collisions "with players or furniture mean nothing to him," Kieran wrote, adding that the first baseman "seemed to be made of steel and concrete."

Hours after Gehrig broke the record, he received a telegram from Ruppert. It read: "Accept my heartiest congratulations upon the splendid record of continuous service which you have just completed. My best wishes are with you for many additional years of success."

Though now one of baseball's biggest stars, Gehrig had changed little since he joined the Yankees as a naïve youngster in the 1920s. Still unmarried, he spent many nights with his parents at the home he had bought for them in New Rochelle, a New York suburb. He dated little. His mother's opinions still influenced his tastes and behaviors.

In 1932, though, he began dating Eleanor Twitchell, an attractive, spirited brunette from Chicago. They had met before but became reacquainted at a party in Chicago during the 1932 World Series. By the middle of the 1933 season, their relationship was serious enough that they discussed getting married.

It was a delicate situation. Gehrig's mother resented having to share his affections after controlling them for so long. But Gehrig was giddily happy. When the Yankees played at Comiskey Park in June 1933, a Chicago paper reported that Twitchell sat in a box by the Yankees' dugout and "posed for a few thousand photographs while Lou smiled by her side" before the game. A rumor that "Lou and his adored one" had "secretly taken their vows" was "emphatically denied," but Gehrig confirmed their intention to marry after the season.

A few months later, Eleanor moved to New York. She and Gehrig found an apartment in New Rochelle, near where Gehrig's parents lived. As contractors renovated it for the couple, the Yankees were wrapping up a disappointing season; they would finish well behind the Senators.

On September 28, Gehrig ran his streak to 1,348 straight games with a brief appearance against the Senators at Yankee Stadium. He walked in the first and singled in the third, then came out of the game and watched the rest of the Yankees' 11–9 win from the dugout. Ruth replaced him at first base because of a "hankering to clown" at a different position, one newspaper reported.

The next day, hours before the Yankees played the Senators again, Gehrig and Eleanor abruptly decided to get married—immediately. The mayor of New Rochelle was called in to officiate. Some reports said the ceremony took place at City Hall, while others placed it at the couple's apartment. Either way, it came together so quickly that Gehrig's mother did not attend, a clear indication of which woman in his life now held more sway.

After the noontime ceremony, Gehrig and Eleanor hustled to Yankee Stadium for the game. Even on his wedding day, Gehrig wanted to play. He told his teammates and the press his news. McCarthy congratulated him and put him in the lineup. He went hitless in four at-bats but drove in two runs on sacrifice flies. That night, he took Eleanor out to dinner. Then he played another game the next afternoon.

12

Ironmen

THE BLESSING OF GOOD FORTUNE

Hours after he became baseball's all-time consecutive-game leader in St. Louis in 1933, Gehrig sat at the desk in his hotel room and wrote a thank-you note to the *Sporting News*, which had given him a silver statuette that afternoon.

"Permit me to express my sincere thanks and appreciation for the beautiful trophy which you so kindly presented to me at the game at Sportsman's Park," he wrote. "I'll treasure it as long as I live, along with such honors that baseball has been good enough to give me. However, the continuous game record I have broken required good luck and plenty of breaks more than any outstanding quality of the player. There are so many things likely to keep a player out of a game, twisted ankles, sprains, charley horses, illnesses, etc., that my record proves, more than anything else, that I have been particularly gifted by good fortune."

The *Sporting News* published his note, and many fans surely smiled when they read it. It was classic Gehrig, so humble and gentlemanly. Babe Ruth would never have admitted he was more lucky than good! But Gehrig meant it. The accepted narrative about his streak was that it was a product of his being tough, determined, and resilient, all of which was true. But the gift of "good fortune" also played a role, and Gehrig knew it. His humility was not falsely ginned up for public consumption.

A couple of years earlier, he had accompanied other major leaguers, including Lefty Grove and Mickey Cochrane, on a goodwill tour of Japan after the 1931 season. Their powerful squad swept all 17 games it played against Japanese college teams and commercial clubs, often winning by more than 10 runs as fans filled ballparks in hopes of seeing Gehrig or another American clout a home run, a feat seldom seen in Japan.

Midway through the tour, the Americans faced a crafty pitcher from Keio University whose tosses dove, spun, and darted around the plate. Misreading a curveball's break, Gehrig leaned in too far, and the ball hit his right hand where it gripped the bat. He stepped away, shaking his hand in pain, and immediately left the game. X-rays revealed two broken bones. Unable to play, Gehrig watched the rest of the tour from the dugout with his hand bandaged.

At the time, he had played in 1,042 straight regular-season games, 19 World Series games, and dozens of exhibitions, all without sitting one out. Missing a game was a new experience, and he did not like it, having wanted to put on a show in Japan. But the injury illustrated his good fortune. When a pitch hit you in the wrong place, it did not matter how strong you were or whether you were determined to play every day. You had no choice but to sit and watch.

Physically, baseball was not nearly as dangerous as football, which Gehrig played in high school and college. Still, players were hit by pitches and spiked on the bases all the time. Pulled muscles and broken bones were commonplace. Gehrig had experienced his share of injuries, but none that forced him to miss a game. When one finally did, he was playing an exhibition game in November more than 6,000 miles from home, not taking on an American League opponent in a regular-season game. His consecutive-game streak was not impacted.

Yes, he was lucky.

"You need luck to play in a lot of games in a row, no doubt about it," said Billy Williams, a Hall of Fame outfielder for the Chicago Cubs, in an interview for this book. "So many things can happen. You slide hard going into second and get hurt. You run into the fence chasing a line drive and get hurt. You get beaned in the head at the plate. You can get knocked out of the lineup almost anytime, in almost any way. The odds are it will catch up with you at some point unless you have some luck."

Williams, a career .290 hitter who set the National League consecutive-game record in 1969 and held it for 14 years, said a streak is similarly under constant threat away from the ballpark. "Just regular life, stuff happens. You sleep funny and wake up with a stiff neck, so you can't swing the bat. I had to deal with that. Or you catch the flu, and there goes your streak. You can play through a lot of things, but not everything," Williams said.

The presence of luck, both good and bad, in almost infinite iterations, is evident in every streak. Steve Brodie stayed healthy for long enough to almost pass George Pinkney and set a record in 1897 (not that he knew it), but a sore arm ended his streak. Fred Luderus established a threshold for Everett Scott to pass in 1919, but only because Al Munro Elias talked Luderus's manager into keeping his streak going. Scott admitted that "a good percentage of luck" helped him play in 1,307 straight games. There was the time he played after being knocked out cold during batting practice. There was the time he was told not to play when a nasty boil arose on his head, seemingly ending his streak until a storm washed out that day's game and his boil burst, enabling him to play the next day — and, as it turned out, every day for another four years.

Richie Ashburn, a fleet outfielder for the Philadelphia Phillies destined for the Hall of Fame, thought luck was on his side as he ran up a playing streak of 730 straight games in the early 1950s. But then he collided with a teammate while chasing a line drive in an exhibition game and suffered a leg injury that ended his streak. Steve Garvey also thought luck was on his side until he emerged from a play at the plate with a broken finger in 1983, abruptly ending the fourth-longest streak in history.

"A freak play in so many ways," Garvey recalled in an interview. "The pitcher throws a wild pitch past the catcher. I'm on third base and start for the plate. I would have made it easily except the ball caroms off the part of the façade behind home that is exposed concrete, not padded. So it bounces right back to the catcher, who throws it to the pitcher covering home in plenty of time. I'm dead. The pitcher straddles the plate, which they teach you not to do, and I tried to slide around him instead of into him and possibly injure him. My thumb gets caught and . . . that's it."

His wistfulness still evident more than three decades later, Garvey cited the ways in which the play was unfortunate for him. "If the ball doesn't carom off the brick; if the pitcher doesn't straddle the plate; if the pitcher doesn't throw a wild pitch in the first place, then I keep playing," he said.

Garvey assessed the calculus of a streak as "75 percent philosophy, determination, and will, 20 percent divinity, and 5 percent luck." And as Billy Williams noted, some of that luck and divinity is needed off the field. Gus Suhr, a first baseman for the Pittsburgh Pirates in the 1930s, experienced enough good fortune on the field to set a National League consecutive-game record that would stand for more than two decades. But it might have stood for longer if not for a telegram he received in 1936.

A product of the same San Francisco sandlots that produced Joe DiMaggio and Tony Lazzeri, Suhr was a lanky ballplayer with movie-star looks — a square jaw, dark hair, and dimples that creased his cheeks. Nimble in the field and consistent at the plate, he was a steadying force on unpredictable Pittsburgh teams. His streak began on September 11, 1931, and Pie Traynor, the Pirates' venerable player-manager, quickly learned to rely on him. Suhr banged out 10 home runs, 11 triples, and 31 doubles in 1933. The next year, he drove in 103 runs.

Gehrig's streak had become newsworthy at the time, increasing the attention paid to feats of endurance, and in 1935 sportswriters noticed Suhr was approaching the National League consecutive-game record, held by Eddie Brown, an outfielder who had played in 618 straight games for the Brooklyn Robins and Boston Braves in the 1920s. Although that streak paled next to Gehrig's, it was a league record, and Suhr was unabashed about wanting to break it. Traynor helped him do it.

After a torn thumbnail forced him to sit out the first eight innings of a game against the Giants on May 20, 1935, Suhr asked Traynor if he could play the top of the ninth in right field, just enough to constitute an official appearance and keep his streak going. On September 15 and September 16 of that season, he tied and broke Brown's record, again by playing just a half inning of defense each time.

Overall, Suhr did not start 9 of the Pirates' last 14 games in 1935, but his brief appearances, either as a defensive replacement or pinch hitter, kept his streak going. After driving in 118 runs and making the National League All-Star team in 1936, he passed 800 games in a row early in the 1937 season, having set a goal of becoming the first National League player to surpass a thousand games in a row. Then, in early June, while in Boston to play the Braves, he received a telegram bearing the news that his mother had died in California.

Suhr could not make it to the West Coast in time for the funeral, but he felt uncomfortable playing while his mother was being laid to rest. He decided to honor her by sitting out a three-game series against the Giants at the Polo Grounds. On June 5, 1937, Suhr missed a game for the first time in six years, ending his streak at 822 games. He spent the day with relatives in Brooklyn.

After missing those three games, Suhr played in every game for the rest of the 1937 season, ending with a .278 average and 97 runs batted in. Then he played in every game in 1938 until late in the season. If not for his mother's death, he would have joined Gehrig, Scott, and Sewell as the only major leaguers between 1876 and 1969 to play in more than a thousand games in a row.

In an interview for this book, Ripken described his Orioles teammate Eddie Murray as an "Ironman without the status of being an Ironman," meaning he was available as often as Ripken and similarly in the lineup day after day, month after month, and year after year, yet he sat out just enough games to keep him from becoming known for his endurance. "It's really no different. Eddie played in almost every game, almost every year," Ripken said.

Indeed, while with the Orioles in his prime, from 1977 through 1988, Murray appeared in 96.6 percent of the team's games. He missed fewer than five games in seven seasons, including 1984, when, like Ripken, he achieved perfect attendance. After playing in a Baltimore win over Cleveland on April 17, 1985, he had streaks of 171 straight games and 1,539 straight innings. But that night he learned his sister had died and left the club to be with his family for the funeral in California.

When he returned after missing five games, he started a new streak, playing in every game for the rest of the 1985 season and every game in 1986 until early July, when a hamstring pull ended his run at 230 straight games. He had played with the injury for a week, serving as the designated hitter in three games and pinch-hitting twice, until it became clear he really needed to take time off and let his hamstring heal. When he went on the disabled list — for the first time in his career — he had missed just one of the Orioles' previous 400 games. Yet his younger teammate was the budding Ironman.

Over the years, numerous major leaguers have, like Murray, shared the attitude Ripken and Gehrig possessed about playing every day, but experienced bad luck in some form — an illness, an injury, a family event, a managerial decision — that limited their consecutive-game achievement. Del Pratt, an infielder for the Browns, Yankees, Red Sox, and Tigers between 1912 and 1924, played six full seasons of games, but never more than 363 in a row. The Chicago Cubs' Ernie Banks played as many full seasons (six) as his teammate Billy Williams, but only Williams is remembered as an Ironman.

Lou Brock, an outfielder for the Cubs and Cardinals who is among the most prolific base stealers in history, never completed a full season of games, but he missed few — usually when the manager demanded that he sit out a contest that he could have played. "You never saw Lou in the trainer's room, and I mean that, never," said Tim McCarver, a catcher for the Cardinals in the 1960s, who played 21 years in the major leagues and later became a prominent television broadcaster. "You couldn't hurt Lou. That's a tremendous compliment to have that said about him, that you couldn't hurt him, which meant he was always available."

McCarver stated that players such as Brock and Murray were just as durable as Gehrig and Ripken even though they never set records. "If a guy plays 155 games a year, it's the equivalent of playing 162," McCarver said. "That's not to diminish what Gehrig and Ripken did, which was more than admirable. But what was really important was they were available for all those games. The same was and is true for many other players who only missed a few games. The only difference is their managers or front offices made the choice not to play them."

Of the many developments that can end a streak, a managerial decision can most frustrate a player. His manager rests him, thinking he needs a break because he is tired, slumping, or has a poor record against the opposing team's starting pitcher; any one of a number of rationales can be cited. Regardless, the player has no control over the decision. The manager makes it, ostensibly for the good of the team.

On August 6, 1955, Chicago's feisty All-Star second baseman, Nellie Fox, sat out a game against the Orioles in Baltimore, but not by choice. He had played in 274 straight games at the time and was hitting .305 on a team jockeying with the Yankees and Indians for first place in the American League. He did not want to miss the game; in fact, he was furious about it. But his manager, Marty Marion, was adamant. "Guys need rest. They're dragging," Marion told reporters. The White Sox were on a 19-game road trip.

With Fox out of the lineup, the Sox quickly fell six runs behind. Fox paced back and forth in the dugout, muttering and swearing. He later called it "the most miserable day I ever spent in baseball," to which Marion responded, "It was the most miserable day of my life, too, having to listen to him gripe from the bench."

When Fox returned to Marion's lineup the next day, a *Chicago Tribune* headline blared SOX RESTORE LITTLE NELL TO 2D. Neither Marion nor his successor, Al Lopez, who took over in 1957, dared rest Fox again. He was an indispensable leadoff man, the heart of the club. When the White Sox won the American League pennant in 1959, Fox hit .306 and was voted the league's MVP.

His playing streak reached 600 games in a row during the pennant-winning 1959 season, and it stood at 798 on September 4, 1960, when Fox checked into the hospital with a high fever, ending what would have been the longest consecutive-game streak since Gehrig's — 1,098 games — if Marion had not forced him to sit out that game in Baltimore.

Without question, Pete Rose is the ultimate "Ironman without the status of being an Ironman." The all-time major league hits leader is not often referenced with Ripken and Gehrig only because of what an Ironman is perceived to be — that is, someone who plays in hundreds or thousands of games consecutively. But using other metrics, Rose compares favorably with Ripken and Gehrig as an exemplar of extreme endurance — more favorably than do Scott, Garvey, Williams, and others renowned as Ironmen.

Games Played in a Career

Rose holds the major league record, having participated in 3,562 games over 24 seasons. He played in 561 more games than Ripken, who is No. 8 on the all-time list, and almost 1,400 more games than Gehrig, who is tied for No. 159.

Full Seasons of Games

Ripken holds the record, having achieved perfect attendance in 15 seasons. Gehrig did it 13 times. Then comes Rose with 10, which is more than Garvey, Scott, or Joe Sewell, each of whom did it 8 times.

Best Decade

Ripken and Gehrig are the only major leaguers to play an entire decade without taking a day off. But Rose almost did it between 1973 and 1982, sitting out just 4 games. Billy Williams missed 10 games in his best decade. Nellie Fox missed 15.

In the accepted Ironman metric, though, Rose lags behind the others. His longest playing streak was 745 games. It is the 12th-longest streak in history, hardly a triviality, and Rose also had a run of 678 games, making him the only player with two of the 20 longest streaks. Still, his best is well short of the thresholds set by Ripken and Gehrig.

As one of the sport's most decorated players, Rose surely had other matters on his mind besides playing streaks. Yet he made it clear that he did care about them, indicating that he valued what they represented and regretted the injuries and managerial decisions that denied him a record-setting streak.

He eventually left the sport in disgrace, banished for gambling, denied a place in the Hall of Fame. If not the most polarizing player in history, he is close. But long after Rose's career ended, many of those he played with and against still respected the determination and tenacity he consistently exhibited, even if he irritated them at times. And Rose, like many from their generation, could hardly bear to watch current players *not* try to play every day, citing various aches and pains as a reason to sit out.

"Pete had an interesting idea: players should be paid on a day-to-day basis, getting their money every day if they said they were available to play. That would change things, wouldn't it?" Tim McCarver said. "It's an extreme idea, and obviously it's never going to happen, but that's Pete. He was a guy who was always ready to go."

A Cincinnati native, Rose was the son of a bank teller who had been a standout athlete, best known as a barrel-chested, rugged halfback on a semipro football team. When Rose first broke into the majors, playing for his hometown Reds in the early 1960s, he exhibited a style that borrowed liberally from his father's sport, playing with such rugged abandon that the Reds' veterans initially thought he was kidding. Who was this young guy sprinting all-out to first after drawing a walk? A bubble-gum-chomping infielder with a crew cut and dark eyes that blazed with intensity, he dove wildly for balls, slid headfirst on steals, and sprinted to and from the dugout between innings. Whitey Ford, the New York Yankees' ace pitcher, mockingly called him "Charlie Hustle" after observing him dashing around the field during a spring training game.

But rather than take offense at the nickname, Rose adopted it, believing it aptly described his game. He always hustled, and he always played. In his debut season with the Reds in 1963, he batted .273, missed just five games, and was voted the National League Rookie of the Year. Two years later, he batted .312, made the All-Star team for the first time, and played in every game of a season for the first time.

With the same thick chest and sturdy legs that were a boon to his father on the football field, Rose was built to handle the rigors of a long season without taking breaks. From 1963 through 1971, he sat out just three games per season on average while becoming one of baseball's signature players, a two-time batting champion who routinely surpassed 200 hits in a season. "Charlie Hustle" was a perennial All-Star on Cincinnati teams that won three division titles and two National League pennants. In 1973, he batted .338 and was voted the league's Most Valuable Player.

His all-out style kept him from building a lengthy playing streak, however. In 1968, after becoming an outfielder, he tore up his hand trying to make a leaping grab at the wall and missed some games. In 1970, he ran over catcher Ray Fosse while scoring the winning run in the All-Star Game, fracturing Fosse's shoulder and knocking himself out with a bruised knee.

Somewhat counterintuitively, Rose did not routinely begin playing full seasons of games until he was in his 30s. He started in 1974, with the Reds on the cusp of greatness as the "Big Red Machine." The next year, he hit .317 and again played in every game as the Reds won a division title and the National League pennant and defeated the Boston Red Sox in the World Series. In 1976, as the Reds repeated as World Series champs, Rose played a full season for the third straight year, hitting .323.

By the start of the 1978 season, he was closing in on 700 straight games. It was the longest consecutive-game streak in Reds history, and Rose was proud of it. "I've always thought the two things that mark a good athlete are consistency and durability, and that's why I like to play every day," he would say later.

But on May 7, 1978, two days after collecting his 3,000th career hit, he came down with a virus and was out of manager Sparky Anderson's lineup for the second game of a doubleheader against Montreal. The Reds fell behind early, then rallied to take a 4–2 lead. Anderson told Rose to get ready to bat for the pitcher in the bottom of the seventh, a maneuver that would extend his streak. But when the pitcher, Doug Bair, retired the Expos in order in the top of the seventh, Anderson let Bair bat and kept Rose on the bench. The fans booed and chanted, "We want Pete!" They knew his streak was on the line. But Anderson prioritized keeping a hot pitcher on the mound and winning the game over Rose's streak, which ended that night at 678 straight games.

"It's nice to have a streak like that, but it doesn't mean that much," Rose told reporters after the game. "Sparky told me, 'I'm glad these streaks of yours are coming to an end or you're going to get me lynched.'"

Rose was back in the lineup the next day, and a month later he singled twice in a win over the Cubs on June 14, beginning what would become another of his signature achievements: a 44-game hitting streak, the game's longest since Joe DiMaggio's in 1941. Though Rose fell short of DiMaggio's mark of 56, his streak equaled Wee Willie Keeler's National League record, set in 1897.

Rose never denied that he wanted to set individual records. When reporters interviewed him, he always knew his statistics, how he ranked among the league leaders, and where he stood on various all-time lists. He had accomplished a lot. In 1978, shortly after his famous hitting streak, he became a free agent and signed a four-year deal with the Philadelphia Phillies worth $3.2 million, making him the highest-paid athlete in team sports, quite a feat for a 37-year-old.

Having never won a World Series, the Phillies signed Rose hoping he could put them over the top. They had a nucleus of veteran talent that had recently earned several division titles but had always fallen short in the postseason. In his first year, Rose hit .331 and played in every game, but the Phillies finished fourth in the National League East, a major disappointment. The next year, Rose again played in every game, and though his .282 average was his lowest since his rookie year, the Phillies finally realized their dream, winning the World Series.

In 1981, Rose led the National League in hits in a season shortened by a labor dispute. He turned 40 that year, though, and his talents began to ebb. His average dropped to .271 in 1982 and sank even lower early in 1983. Paul Owens, the Phillies' manager, still played him every day, but it took a handful of pinch-hitting appearances and late-game defensive stints to keep his consecutive-game streak going.

As usual, Rose knew his numbers. "If it wasn't for me missing a game with the flu in 1978 when I was with the Reds, I'd be close to 1,400 straight games," he told reporters. "I had 678 straight that time. I've only missed nine games since the 1970 All-Star Game, only three because of injury."

On August 24, 1983, Rose sat out the early innings of a game against the Giants in San Francisco. With the score tied in the bottom of the ninth, Owens told him to get ready to hit in the top of the 10th. But the Phillies' ace pitcher, Steve Carlton, gave up a home run that ended the game, also ending Rose's streak at 745 straight games.

Asked by reporters if he was disappointed to see his streak end, Rose nodded. "Sure, it meant something to me," he said. "I've always come to the ballpark ready to play, for 21 years."

But he was not upset with Owens. "They just didn't need me today," he said with a trace of melancholy.

His bad luck.

13

Ripken

A GUIDING PHILOSOPHY

In the bottom of the sixth inning of the Orioles' first game in 1989, Cal Ripken stepped to the plate to face Roger Clemens, Boston's ace right-hander. The Orioles trailed, 3–1, and a comeback against Clemens seemed unlikely, but the packed house at Memorial Stadium still stood and encouraged Ripken with a roar. There was one out in the inning, with runners on second and third. It was exactly the kind of situation Eddie Murray had thrived in for a decade as Baltimore's cleanup hitter, but Murray was gone now, having been traded to the Los Angeles Dodgers during the off-season. Ripken batted cleanup for the Orioles.

Murray's departure was not a shock. His relationship with the organization had deteriorated after Edward Bennett Williams publicly criticized his work ethic shortly after his mother and sister died suddenly in 1986. Murray demanded and received an apology from the outspoken lawyer, but the marriage between the Orioles and one of their finest players was crumbling. To enhance their rebuilding effort, they traded him for two relief pitchers and a hot shortstop prospect.

Now, just six innings into the season, Ripken needed to deliver as the team's new cleanup hitter. He took Clemens's first pitch for a strike, worked the count to two balls and two strikes, and dug in. Clemens fired a fastball, hoping to send Ripken back to the dugout. Ripken put his thick torso in motion, swung hard, and hit the ball squarely. It flew off his bat in a high arc toward left field. When it cleared the outfield fence, the fans loosed a shattering roar. With one swing, Ripken had put the Orioles ahead.

As Ripken circled the bases, it was difficult for him not to take stock of his circumstances. After slogging through turbulence on and off the field in 1988, he was in a better place now. He had married his longtime girlfriend during the off-season. His new contract tied him to the Orioles for the next three years. And in a surprise that delighted him, the Orioles had rehired his father as the third-base coach under manager Frank Robinson. With great joy, Ripken gave Senior's hand a firm slap as he rounded third on his way around the bases following his home run off Clemens.

Little was expected of the Orioles in 1989. They were coming off a disastrous season, and their best hitter now played for the Dodgers. But a crop of young players and a can-do vibe infiltrated their clubhouse. Mickey Tettleton emerged as a productive slugger, helping ease the effects of Murray's departure. A pair of young outfielders, Brady Anderson and Mike Devereaux, chased down line drives headed for the gaps. A left-handed starter, Jeff Ballard, deftly mixed speeds and won 18 games. Gregg Olson, a young closer, embarrassed hitters with a nasty curveball.

Improbably, after losing 107 games the year before, the Orioles shot to the top of the American League East early in the season and maintained the lead through much of the summer. Ripken's role in the resurgence did not unfold exactly as expected. After hitting a home run in the first game, he hit only two more in all of April and May. He still drove in his share of runs, but Tettleton replaced him as the cleanup hitter, and his average slipped as the season wore on. His defense emerged as the standout aspect of his game.

Though he lacked the quickness of most shortstops, he had sure hands, a strong arm, and, most important, an analytical approach that turned defense into a science. Before every pitch, he took into account the batter, the pitcher, the count, and the pitch call, and positioned himself where he thought the ball was most likely to travel if hit. Sometimes he even factored in the weather, such as whether the wind was carrying balls.

He never wrote down his thoughts or findings, just reacted instinctively inning after inning and game after game. Few shortstops were in the right position more consistently. He committed just 8 errors in 1989, down from 21 the year before. The only reason he did not win a Gold Glove, given to the best defensive player in the league at each position, was that Toronto's brilliant shortstop, Tony Fernandez, committed just 6 errors.

Putting his knowledge and instincts to use with the manager's blessing,

Ripken also quarterbacked the infield and sometimes even positioned the Orioles' young outfielders before a pitch. "There was never a doubt that I wanted him on the field at all times," Frank Robinson said, "and believe me, so did our pitchers and everyone else on the team."

But while his defense was superb, his offensive production waned as the Toronto Blue Jays rallied and challenged the Orioles for the division title. In September, when his team needed him most, Ripken hit .198. Toronto overtook the Orioles and held on to win the division.

Ripken ended the season with 21 home runs and 93 runs batted in, solid production, but his final average of .257 reflected his ongoing struggle with consistency. In his first three years with the Orioles, he had hit .297 and averaged 27 home runs and 99 runs batted in. But his average was down 40 points and his production totals were lower in his three most recent seasons. He was not yet 30, still in his prime, but his years as an offensive force were becoming a distant memory.

Nonetheless, Robinson, like Weaver, Altobelli, and Senior, always found a rationale for playing Ripken every day, regardless of how the shortstop hit. By the end of the 1989 season, Ripken had played in 1,250 straight games.

"It's true he wasn't hitting well for quite a period of time, but what I liked about Cal was he could help us in other ways, especially with his defense," Frank Robinson recalled. "He made his teammates around him better, especially in the infield. He was into the game. He kept everyone on their toes, told them how to play certain hitters. He helped us win games in ways other than just offense. I never considered resting him."

On August 7, 1989, a sweltering Monday night, 36,000 fans came to Memorial Stadium for the Orioles' game against Minnesota. Baltimore was still leading the American League East at the time, and enthusiasm was running high.

After the Twins scored a run in the top of the first, their starting pitcher, Roy Smith, opened the bottom of the first by striking out Mike Devereaux and Phil Bradley, the Orioles' first two batters. In each case, the third strike was called, raising doubts in the Baltimore dugout about the accuracy of home-plate umpire Drew Coble's strike zone.

Ripken stepped into the batter's box. Smith threw a fastball away, aiming for the outside corner. Coble's hand went up, signaling a strike. Ripken muttered his disagreement loudly enough for Coble to hear. When Smith hit the same spot with his next pitch, another fastball, Coble's hand went up again, strike two. Ripken continued to mutter. Coble told him to pipe down.

That infuriated Ripken, who turned and unleashed a stream of obscenities. Coble quickly raised his right thumb, ejecting the shortstop from the game.

"He can argue balls and strikes, but what he can't do is call me what he called me," Coble told reporters later.

Another American League umpire, Tim Welke, had ejected Ripken on September 25, 1987, also for arguing balls and strikes in the bottom of the first. In 1996, Al Clark would become the third umpire to eject Ripken during his consecutive-game streak.

"In our opinion, Cal wasn't the greatest guy for umpires," Clark said. "He always thought he was right, could be pretty arrogant about it. If we called something against him, let's just say he didn't have the respect for umpires that other players had. I think he got it from his father, who really didn't like umpires at all. But that doesn't diminish the respect we had for Cal and how he played the game."

When Coble ejected him after calling two strikes on him on that hot night in 1989, Frank Robinson had to summon a pinch hitter to finish his at-bat. Rene Gonzales, the first Oriole to hit for Ripken in more than seven years, struck out.

Though he had barely played, Ripken still received credit for appearing in the game, extending his streak to 1,198 straight games. The streak would not have ended even if he had failed to fulfill the requirements for an appearance. According to the major league rule that sets the parameters for appearances, "the streak shall be extended" if a player on a consecutive-game run is "ejected from a game by an umpire before he can comply with the requirements of this rule."

While Ripken left the clubhouse through a dugout exit to avoid talking to reporters after the Orioles lost to Minnesota, Coble gave his side of the story. The contested pitches were strikes, he said, "dead on the outside corner." But Orioles fans in the front rows abused him all night after he tossed Ripken. "I was called every name in the book," Coble said. "That's the most miserable two and a half hours of my life. That's like throwing God out of Sunday school."

Coble's reference to God indicated the respect Ripken now commanded throughout baseball, at least partly because he had played in so many games in a row. That did not mean he received a deity's treatment at home, though. "The way I remember it, thirteen hundred through eighteen hundred was all negative," Ripken said, referring to the time that encompassed those consecutive games in his streak.

The starting date for that period was June 3, 1990, when he reached 1,300 games in a row. One week later, on a warm, cloudy Sunday afternoon at Memorial Stadium, the Orioles played the Yankees. It should have been a celebratory occasion. By reaching 1,307 straight games, Ripken had equaled Everett Scott's consecutive-game threshold, set 65 years earlier. Now only Gehrig's streak was longer. Yet Ripken received a lukewarm reaction from his hometown fans. After he struck out in the bottom of the fifth, he heard boos as he returned to the dugout. When the inning ended and it was noted on the scoreboard that the game was official and Ripken had tied Scott, only polite applause sounded.

Why the modest reaction? Ripken was slumping miserably, his average for the season down to .217. He had gone through rough times before, but this was the worst. Some fans believed he needed to take a day off to collect himself, and they were lighting up radio talk-show boards with their opinions. Ripken's streak was getting in the way, they said, and he should sit for the sake of the team.

"The streak was being examined not for what it was, but for all these other things," Ripken recalled. "People were looking at your intentions, calling you selfish. Meanwhile, the Orioles were going through a rebuilding process, making it easy to blame anyone for anything. For a lot of people, the answer was, 'He's playing too much; he needs to come out; he's obsessed with the streak.'"

It did not help that the Orioles as a whole also were floundering. After a slow start dropped them six games out, they briefly rallied, then collapsed before the All-Star break, prompting speculation that their surprising 1989 performance had been a fluke. Ripken continued to excel on defense; he would commit just three errors all season. But his bat was so tepid that Frank Robinson dropped him to sixth in the order.

Were his years of playing every day really taking a toll? Ripken did not believe it. He did not feel tired. His play in the field was superb. He tinkered with his batting stance, changing where he put his hands and

Brooklyn third baseman George Pinkney, "tender and high-bred" according to one sportswriter, was the greatest Ironman of the nineteenth century.

National Baseball Hall of Fame Library; Cooperstown, New York

A sore arm in 1897 ended Steve Brodie's consecutive-game streak just shy of the all-time record. He probably did not even know he was close.

National Baseball Hall of Fame Library; Cooperstown, New York

Joe "Ironman" McGinnity earned his nickname for pitching both ends of doubleheaders, not for building a consecutive-game streak.

George Eastman House / Getty Images

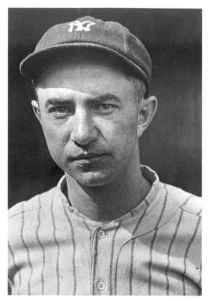

Everett "Deacon" Scott brought the idea of baseball endurance into the limelight. Lou Gehrig broke his record in 1933.

National Baseball Hall of Fame Library; Cooperstown, New York

Early in his Yankees career, Lou Gehrig admired his larger-than-life teammate, Babe Ruth. But that changed.

MPI / Getty Images

Gehrig conveyed the classic image of strength in the years before weight training and performance-enhancing drugs sculpted inhuman physiques.

National Baseball Hall of Fame Library; Cooperstown, New York

Gehrig is helped off the field after getting knocked out by a fastball to the forehead during a 1934 exhibition game in Norfolk, Virginia.

Bettmann / Getty Images

Gehrig receives a trophy in a mid-game ceremony after breaking Everett Scott's consecutive-game record in St. Louis in 1933.

Bettmann / Getty Images

Gehrig peers out from the dugout at Briggs Stadium in Detroit on May 2, 1939, the day he took himself out of the lineup, ending his Ironman streak at 2,130 games.

Bettmann / Getty Images

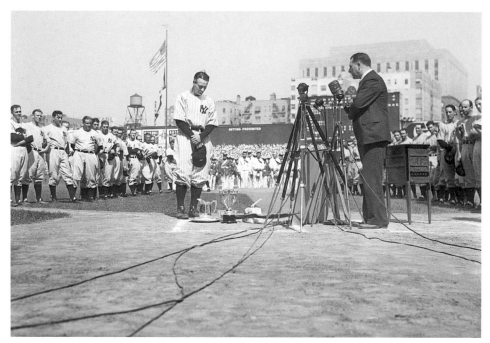

Gehrig, head bowed and belt cinched tight around his gaunt waist, listens to a speech on July 4, 1939, after which he stated that he was "the luckiest man on the face of the earth."

Bettmann / Getty Images

Gus Suhr, a first baseman for the Pittsburgh Pirates, held the National League consecutive-game record for 22 years.

National Baseball Hall of Fame Library; Cooperstown, New York

The Washington Senators' Eddie Yost played in 829 straight games, taking a few shortcuts along the way.

National Baseball Hall of Fame Library; Cooperstown, New York

Stan Musial set the National League consecutive-game record in 1957 despite having
not played in a game in Pittsburgh two years
earlier.

National Baseball Hall of Fame Library,
Cooperstown, New York

Even while setting the National League consecutive-game record, Billy Williams wondered
aloud why he was doing it.

National Baseball Hall of Fame Library;
Cooperstown, New York

Pete Rose compares with Ripken and Gehrig
as an Ironman in several statistical categories,
but was not known for his endurance.

National Baseball Hall of Fame Library;
Cooperstown, New York

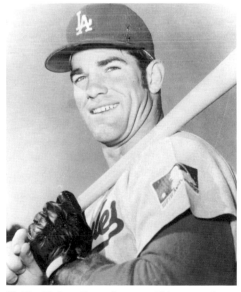

Unlike Ripken, Steve Garvey said he wanted to
break Gehrig's Ironman mark. He fell short, but
has held the National League record since 1983.

National Baseball Hall of Fame Library;
Cooperstown, New York

When Cal Ripken Sr. (center) managed Cal Ripken Jr. (left) and Bill Ripken (right) in Baltimore in 1987, he became the first major league skipper to manage two of his sons.

Bettmann / Getty Images

Sliding into Ripken at second base was "like sliding into a tree," one player said. His size and strength made him a candidate to play every day.

The Sporting News / Getty Images

Eddie Murray (center) exchanges a celebratory hand-slap with Ripken. He convinced his younger teammate that it was important to play every day.

Bettmann / Getty Images

Cal Ripken Jr. exchanges greetings with fans on his "victory lap" around Camden Yards on the night he broke Gehrig's record.

Brian Bahr / AFP / Getty Images

The day after Ripken broke
Gehrig's record, he paraded
through the streets of Baltimore
on a float.

The Sporting News / Getty Images

Consecutive-game streaks have
all but disappeared, but several
players in the new century,
such as Miguel Tejada, have
possessed the urge to play
every day.

*National Baseball Hall of Fame Library;
Cooperstown, New York*

how he aligned his feet. He had never gone to anyone other than Senior for batting advice; maybe it was time to try an entirely new approach. He certainly was seeing fewer juicy pitches now that he no longer batted in front of Murray.

The truth was Ripken never wanted to sit out even one trip to home plate, much less an entire game. He always found value in an at-bat, even near the end of a lopsided win or loss.

"If you were swinging well, you didn't want to stop; you wanted to get in that last at-bat so you felt good going into the next game," he recalled. "By the same token, if you were going bad, it was an opportunity to try something, 'Let me get a little closer to the plate; let me spread out a little bit; let me open up; look for this, look for that.' Maybe you found something you could use the next day, and you went into that game with hope as opposed to thinking, 'I'm stinking.' I firmly believed there was huge value in both of those. I never thought you could solve your problems by not playing."

Frank Robinson agreed that the streak was not the problem. One of the greatest hitters ever, Robinson believed Ripken was lunging at pitches, a sign of frustration.

Nonetheless, Ripken said years later that Robinson considered ending the streak in 1990. "He told me later that he would leave the house thinking, 'This is it, the day I'm going to stop it,'" Ripken said for this book. "He probably believed I was struggling and maybe he could put someone in there and get a couple of hits out of them, but ultimately it was to fix me. Because there is a theory that if you take a couple of days off, you clear your head.

"But at the moment of truth, when Frank was at the park and sat down to make out the lineup for that day's game, he told me, 'I thought about all the things you did in the course of the game, not just hitting and fielding, all the things you did of value, and I didn't want to replace you.' That was probably the highest compliment you could get. Even when I wasn't hitting and you think [sitting] might benefit me in the big picture, at the moment of truth, sitting in his office, he didn't want to do it."

In an interview for this book, Frank Robinson denied the streak was in jeopardy that year. "I never thought about giving him a day off," Robinson said. "The first thing I did every day was write in his name, then fill in around him."

The manager was not a proponent of giving a slumping player a break. "I don't think one day off makes any difference. I really don't," Robinson said. "We all have that thought, 'Give the guy a day off, let him relax.' But how can he relax when he's at the ballpark watching a game, watching his teammates, and he's not out there? I don't really think there's a lot to be gained."

Ripken played on, and he heated up as the Orioles surged after the All-Star break, climbing to within four games of first place. But neither he nor the team stayed hot. By late August, the Orioles were 10 games out and fading fast, and Ripken was in another slump. He ended up hitting .250 for the season, his career low.

After the 1990 season, his streak stood at 1,411 straight games. It infuriated him to be accused of putting his interests ahead of the team's, maintaining the streak because he wanted to pass Gehrig, regardless if the Orioles suffered. Ripken vehemently denied that charge. A truly selfish player, Ripken believed, ducked tough pitchers to protect his average, citing a headache, a sore hamstring, or the need for a day off. Ripken never used that dubious tactic.

Also, he thought, he had never resorted to artifice to keep his streak going. Unlike many of his consecutive-game predecessors, including Gehrig, he never used a pinch-hitting appearance or brief defensive stint to extend his streak. He also never agreed to serve as the Orioles' designated hitter on days when he did not feel his best.

"I never once played for the sake of extending the streak, and the best evidence of that is I started every game in the field," he recalled. "There were times when you had to challenge yourself injury-wise and ask if you should play, if you deserved to play, but I was always able to go."

There certainly were times when his brother Bill came to the ballpark wondering whether Junior would play, only to realize he always played. "He hit so many balls off his shins and ankles," Bill recalled. "You'd look at him after the game, and he'd have his foot in an ice bucket with a big, nasty, bright purple bruise. You'd see him limp out of there. But when he came back the next day, the limp was almost gone. There were times during the off-season when he sprained his ankle playing basketball and there was no way he could have played the next day. But during the season, he always found a way to play, actually found a way fairly easily not just to play, but to play and be productive."

Ripken said, "My guiding philosophy was that playing every day for your team was the most honorable thing you could do. They were counting on you. You had a challenge that day, and you came to the ballpark to meet that challenge. You played. That was the highest level you could achieve. I had the physicality and resiliency to do it, and the streak evolved out of that. You're just playing, using your approach, what you think is right, and all of a sudden, you were at a thousand games and now there was this thing. People think my goal in life was to build the streak and break Gehrig's record, but the opposite was true. I would rather have had more hits, more home runs. The streak just happened."

Doubts about his intentions never ebbed. Brooks Robinson, a friend and admirer of Ripken's, said in a 1999 interview, "There probably were times when he should have sat out for a game or two." But Robinson also said he understood Ripken's desire to play every day: "It's a wonderful trait, it really is, because with all the money and multiyear contracts in the game, I've seen plenty of guys say, 'Well, I'm not feeling too good today. I won't play.' It happens all the time. But Cal still went out there. He didn't set out to break the record, no question about that. It was just the way it happened."

Disappointed with his 1990 season, Ripken played more basketball in the off-season, lifted more weights, took hours of extra batting practice, and asked Frank Robinson for hitting advice. Robinson said he left his body in poor position to drive the ball when he lunged at pitches. Robinson also told him to focus on hitting to all fields and stop trying to carry the offense.

Like a researcher in a science lab, Ripken tinkered with different stances for hours in the batting cage. When the 1991 season began, he debuted a crouching stance. The new mechanics and new approach reenergized his bat. He hit .338 in April. On Memorial Day, he ranked among the league leaders in home runs and runs batted in. "He's fundamentally sound and relaxed," Robinson said. Ripken conceded he had been "stubborn" and should have changed his approach sooner. "The problem has been me," he said.

In July, he put on a show at the All-Star Game in Toronto. In the Home Run Derby on Monday, he took 22 swings and hit 12 balls into the seats, including three in a row at one point. He hit another home run in the

All-Star Game the next night. Continuing to bash the ball the rest of the season, he finished with a .323 average, 34 home runs, and 114 runs batted in, a performance that earned him the American League MVP award for a second time. He also finally won the Gold Glove at shortstop, his first.

His soaring performance eliminated any doubts about whether he belonged in the sport's elite class of stars. Those doubts had arisen as his hitting sagged after his breathtaking early years, but now he was a two-time MVP and nine-time All-Star with a Gold Glove and 259 career home runs — an impressive record.

Meanwhile, the 1991 season unfolded with few, if any, calls for Ripken to end his streak for the good of the team, which he quietly found amusing. The task of playing a full season was the same as in the years when he hit .250. The wear on his body was identical, as was the challenge of maintaining his focus.

Ripken believed his stellar season validated his belief that his consecutive-game streak had no bearing on how he played. As he saw it, other factors impacted his hitting, for better or worse, and his defense never suffered. There was no reason for him to stop.

Ripken's second MVP season came in a down year for the Orioles, who started slowly and wound up with 95 losses. Frank Robinson paid for the dismal performance. Fired as manager on May 23, he soon accepted a job as the team's assistant general manager.

The new manager, Johnny Oates, had played for Senior in the Orioles' minor league system in the 1960s and 1970s and gone on to play for five teams in 11 years as a catcher in the major leagues. A pleasant, deeply spiritual southerner from Richmond, Virginia, Oates had turned to coaching and managing after his playing career ended and had risen through the ranks, exhibiting energy and thoroughness. The Orioles hoped those qualities would help their record.

When Oates played Ripken at shortstop on May 24, 1991, his first day as manager, Ripken's playing streak inched forward to 1,449 straight games — long enough that no manager would dare stop it now without Ripken's consent. But Oates was especially supportive of his shortstop's desire to play every day. Oates viewed Senior as a mentor and role model; Senior's relentlessness and attention to detail as a minor league manager had influenced Oates years earlier. Now that he was getting his first shot as a major league manager, Oates thought it was wonderfully fitting that Senior was his third-base coach and Senior's son was his shortstop. The streak was safe as long as Oates managed the Orioles.

Oates had first met Junior as an exuberant youngster running around minor league clubhouses two decades earlier, and in some ways, Oates felt, Junior was no different now. He never even took a day off from infield or batting practice, much less a game.

A month into Oates's tenure, Ripken went four days without a hit and asked Oates if he could take extra batting practice before a game in Kansas City. Oates suggested he take the day off from infield practice instead; maybe that would help him feel fresher for the game. "He hasn't missed infield or batting practice in ten years," Oates said later. But Ripken did not want to change the pregame routine he had followed for so long. He not only took batting practice and infield practice, but he also went to the outfield afterward to shag flies as others hit.

As batting practice rolled on, the Orioles' Sam Horn stepped into the cage. Known for bashing prodigious home runs — more before games than during them — Horn knocked a succession of balls toward the fence. Turning to see where they landed, Oates squinted in disbelief. Ripken and the Orioles' second baseman, Tim Hulett, were standing by the fence, taking turns attempting to make leaping catches of Horn's blasts before they cleared the fence.

The Orioles moved into their new ballpark in downtown Baltimore in 1992. Architectural critics hailed its groundbreaking blend of old and new influences; its brick façade and wrought-iron railings conjuring up turn-of-the-century baseball; its luxury boxes and giant video scoreboard representing the latest in modern amenities. Oriole Park at Camden Yards would influence an entire generation of ballparks as other cities attempted to replicate Baltimore's jewel.

The new home seemed to energize the Orioles. A laughingstock when they began the season with 21 straight losses just four years earlier, they now played in front of packed houses every night and, with Oates in command, won enough to warrant the support.

Early in the season, they traveled to Toronto for a series against the Blue Jays. It was the scene of Ripken's All-Star triumph the year before, and fans applauded as he stepped to the plate in the top of the first. Toronto's starter, Jack Morris, promptly hit him with a pitch. The ball struck Ripken's "funny bone," the nerve in the back of his elbow. His throwing hand went numb.

A few innings later, the Blue Jays' Dave Winfield slashed a ground ball up the middle with two out and two runners on base. Ripken glided to his left, scooped up the ball, and threw toward first. "With no feeling in my hand, I had no clue where it would go," he recalled. The throw was on target and beat Winfield to the bag for an out that appeared routine. But Ripken was shaken.

"I've often wondered what would have happened if I hadn't made that particular throw," he recalled. "If I had thrown the ball away and two runs scored, and that continued; at some point, you would have to say, 'I'm hurting the team because I can't make the plays.' As it was, getting hit did affect my throwing all season. I had to figure out how to adjust my aim, because the ball wasn't traveling the same way."

It was the start of a rough season for him. After establishing career highs at the plate in 1991, Ripken regressed in 1992. His elbow hurt. His crouching stance stopped working. His confidence wavered. His average plummeted. After getting hit with a fastball in July, he did not hit a home run for 73 games, a staggering falloff for a player who had dominated the Home Run Derby at the All-Star Game the year before.

He also was distracted. His contract was due to expire after the season, and Ron Shapiro was trying to negotiate a long-term deal with the Orioles. Unhappy with what he felt was a low offer, Shapiro told the media Ripken might become a free agent and sign with the Yankees. Baltimore fans were agitated by the prospect of their native son wearing pinstripes when he broke Gehrig's record. Shapiro also said Ripken and his wife would not mind a change of scenery because they lacked privacy off the field.

In the end, he decided to stay, signing a five-year, $30.5 million contract with the Orioles in late August. The deal made him the game's highest-paid player. "In my heart, I always wanted to be an Oriole, and I can say this now, I never wanted to be anything else," Ripken said at the time.

Hours after the deal was announced before a game at Camden Yards, he hit into a double play and was booed on his 32nd birthday.

14

Gehrig

PLAYING HURT

At the outset of the 1934 season, Gehrig picked right up where he had left off in 1933 and battered American League pitching, driving in 18 runs in the Yankees' first 17 games. But Ruth could no longer come close to matching his younger teammate. Now 39, Ruth still hit an occasional home run, but his average dropped, and he trudged around the outfield covering far less ground, his gut bulging over his uniform belt. It was almost embarrassing.

Finally, Gehrig had become the Yankees hitter opponents most feared. A cartoon in the *New York Daily News* depicted him emerging from Ruth's shadow, a sentiment Gehrig appreciated. But he also could not help wondering if he would always be measured in relation to Ruth. Could he ever separate himself?

His consecutive-game streak certainly was one way. It was a unique achievement. Gehrig owned the all-time record. And even though he believed it was partly attributable to "good fortune," as he had written in his note to the *Sporting News,* he also believed it reflected admirable qualities. You had to be committed, determined, and tough. Gehrig had played with broken bones and back pain. As he watched Ruth's years of overindulgence exact a toll, he was proud that he stayed in shape and was always available to play, and he liked that an appreciation for his approach was growing.

"Lou lives by copy-book maxims. He has all the sturdy virtues. He doesn't drink. He goes to bed early and gets up early. He is straightforward and upstanding. He has worked hard and he has prospered. He has been a great ball player on a great club. He is clearly entitled to all the honors they may bestow upon him," John Kieran wrote in the *New York Times.*

Without announcing his intention, Gehrig resolved to continue playing every day for as long as he could. He was just 30, healthy and bullishly strong. He could keep going for years, he believed. If the acclaim he already received was any indication, the streak could help him forge a legacy apart from Ruth.

As if to prove he could play through any issue, he came to Yankee Stadium on May 10, 1934, with a miserable cold. But instead of asking off, as many players would have, he slammed two home runs and a pair of doubles in the first five innings against the White Sox, driving in seven runs before McCarthy finally took him out. "Fans wondered what he would have done at bat if he had been in perfect health," the *New York Times* wrote, adding that Gehrig surely would keep playing every day, "cold or no cold."

A little over a month later, 55,000 fans came to Yankee Stadium for a doubleheader against Detroit. The teams were one game apart at the top of the American League standings. The Yankees won the first game as Gehrig knocked in a run and Ruth struck out twice. But in the fourth inning of the second game, Gehrig fouled a pitch off his right big toe. He played the rest of the game with a noticeable limp, and X-rays taken that night revealed a chipped bone. "Lou was urged to take a few days off," one newspaper reported. But he decided to keep playing after the Yankees' orthopedic surgeon explained that he could not make the injury worse.

"If it was my left foot, it would be different," he told reporters. "I get most of my drive off my left foot, and it's my left foot that I use in touching the bag when fielding around first base. Of course, it hurts when I run, but that's all right. At this particular point, I think it is best I stay in the lineup. If I thought I was hurting the team any, I wouldn't care about that consecutive-game mark. I'd get out."

He limped through a loss to the Tigers on June 18, but no one dared suggest that he was "hurting the team any." He hit a long home run to right field, scored twice, and handled 13 fielding chances without an error. After the game, one newspaper reported that "a good deal of pain was attached to Lou's Iron Man stunt" and "despite his eagerness to play, the injury may yet force him to the sidelines."

It did not. After a well-timed off day for the Yankees, Gehrig played both games of a doubleheader against Cleveland on June 20. Although he still limped, he hit a home run in the first game and reached base four times in the second as the Yankees won twice. Afterward, he smiled as he told reporters it would take more than a broken toe to end his streak, which now stood at 1,406 straight games.

In late June 1934, the Yankees traveled to Washington for a series against the Senators that included three games over four days. On the off day, they traveled to Norfolk, Virginia, to play an exhibition against one of the franchise's minor league affiliates. It was the last thing the players wanted to do; they had played games for nine straight days. Gehrig's broken toe was not healed, but management wanted him to play in Norfolk, where the Yankees' visit was the big event of the summer.

A sellout crowd filled Norfolk's ballpark. The home team's starting pitcher, Ray White, was a hard-throwing right-hander who, like Gehrig, had attended Columbia University and played on the baseball team. But White was not a fan of Gehrig's. The two had been introduced several years earlier, and when they saw each other later, Gehrig acted as if he did not know White. Gehrig probably was not shunning the youngster — he could be awkward socially — but White took it personally. After yielding a home run to Gehrig in spring training in 1934, White hit him with a pitch in Gehrig's next at-bat. Now, months later, White was determined to get the best of Gehrig.

He probably was too excited. The Yankees' leadoff batter, Myril Hoag, hit White's first pitch for a home run. Then Ruth singled, bringing Gehrig to the plate. White fired his best pitch, a searing fastball. Gehrig swung his thick torso, made contact, and watched the ball soar out of the park. As Gehrig circled the bases, White watched him disgustedly, hands on hips.

The Norfolk club staged its own rally in the bottom of the inning, scoring four runs, but White was still fuming when Gehrig batted again in the top of the second. The pitcher hurled another fastball, this time up and in, intending to send a message. Gehrig waited too late to react, and the ball hit him squarely in the face, just above his right eye. He collapsed next to home plate.

Doc Painter, the Yankees' trainer, raced from the dugout to attend to Gehrig. "Lying still as death itself," according to the *New York Post*, Gehrig did not stir while Painter dabbed him with a wet towel for several minutes. Finally, he sat up. Bill Dickey, the Yankees' catcher, provided a shoulder to lean on as he staggered off the field. Norfolk's team doctor examined him in the clubhouse and said he had "a moderate concussion." Gehrig returned to the Monticello Hotel, where the Yankees had spent the night. He showered, dressed, and drank a beer at the bar, joking with a reporter that it would take more than a blow to the head to stop him.

That evening, the Yankees took a boat back to Washington. The next morning, Gehrig woke with a headache and a purple bruise on his forehead. But X-rays revealed no fractures, and Gehrig told McCarthy he wanted to play against the Senators that afternoon.

Shortly before the players left for the ballpark, a reporter came across Ruth in the lobby of the team hotel.

"How's Gehrig?" the reporter asked.

Ruth waved a hand dismissively. "You can't hurt that guy unless you go to work on him with an axe," Ruth said.

The date was June 30, 1934, a Saturday. The Yankees were in first place. Gehrig had played in 1,414 straight games. When he came to bat in the top of the first, he drove a fastball into the gap between left field and center. The ball dropped to the ground and rolled to the wall. Gehrig sprinted around first and second and reached third standing up.

When he batted again in the third inning, he knocked another triple, this time to deep center field. In the top of the fifth, he slugged his third triple in as many at-bats. Fans at Griffith Stadium could only shake their heads at Gehrig's show, unaware that he had a bruise on his forehead and probably never should have set foot on the diamond. Gehrig's teammates also shook their heads, marveling at his ability to not just play but also excel with an injury.

When heavy rains washed the teams from the field before the end of the fifth, the game was called off before it became official, wiping its statistics from the record books. Gehrig's three-triple performance vanished from the books, but those who saw it knew, as Gehrig had joked the day before, that it was going to take more than a fastball to the head to stop him.

In mid-July, the Yankees traveled to Detroit for a crucial four-game series. They were in first place, a half game ahead of the Tigers. The four games would draw close to 90,000 fans to Navin Field, the Tigers' intimate park near downtown.

Gehrig drove in his 90th run of the season in the series opener, which the Tigers won, then complained after the game that his back was sore and needed treatment. The Yankees were not alarmed. They believed Gehrig had chronic lumbago, a lower-back ailment that was a form of rheumatism. He experienced intermittent pain in his back and legs and always played through it.

The next night, though, he suffered a setback. Facing Tommy Bridges, a Detroit pitcher whose arsenal included a renowned curveball, Gehrig swung awkwardly at a breaking pitch on the outside corner. He made contact, but as the ball sailed away, "the rest of my back went with it," Gehrig said later.

The ball landed in shallow center field for a single as Gehrig stumbled, almost falling, while running to first. He could barely stand but stayed in the game, taking second when the next batter singled. Dickey followed with a line drive that Detroit's second baseman, Charlie Gehringer, grabbed. Gehringer stepped on the bag to double off Gehrig, who could not move nearly fast enough to get back to the bag.

Returning to the dugout after that play, Gehrig told McCarthy he needed to come out of the game. His departure produced a sizable shuffle. McCarthy moved third baseman Jack Saltzgaver to first, moved shortstop Frank Crosetti to third, and brought Red Rolfe off the bench to play shortstop — a hint of the finagling McCarthy hardly ever faced because Gehrig played every day.

That evening, Doc Painter worked on Gehrig's back in his hotel room, applying a heat treatment and massage. But his back felt no better the next morning. "I had to fall out of bed to get up. Doc had to dress me," Gehrig said in a 1939 interview. The date was July 14, 1934. Gehrig had played in 1,426 straight games. He later admitted he "wanted to remain in bed" and not play because of the searing back pain, but "club officials urged me not to break the [streak]." In a 1936 interview with St. Louis sportswriter Sid Keener, Gehrig recalled: "I had sent word to McCarthy that I was down for good this time. He came running up to my hotel room. He wouldn't let me end the record. He helped dress me and had me carried out to the park where my teammates aided me in putting on my uniform."

Warming up, he experienced pain so intense it "made breathing difficult and swinging a bat torture," the *New York Times* reported. Soaked in sweat, Gehrig reportedly told McCarthy he "could not go nine" innings. But McCarthy "insisted" on Gehrig making at least one plate appearance to extend the streak, Gehrig told Keener.

McCarthy's lineup had Gehrig batting first and playing shortstop, a position he had never manned. When the game began, he hobbled to the plate, bent at the waist, and lunged at the first pitch. The ball popped lightly off his bat and landed in short right field for a single. Gehrig trudged to first and stopped on the bag. McCarthy sent Rolfe in to run for him. Gehrig limped to the dugout, his day over.

The box score for the game, which Detroit won, 12–11, listed Gehrig as the Yankees' starting shortstop. But he never played there. Rolfe played all nine innings at shortstop, while Saltzgaver manned first. But Gehrig's lone at-bat meant he had played. His consecutive-game streak continued.

The *New York Times* reported the curious scene without rendering a judgment. Some sportswriters lauded Gehrig, suggesting the stunt illustrated his toughness. But Bud Shaver, an editor and columnist for the *Detroit Times*, was appalled.

"Instead of enhancing his reputation for durability, Gehrig sullied it," Shaver wrote. "He also impugned his reputation for sensibility. If a man is too ill to play, the sensible thing to do is refrain from playing. His physical handicaps are apt to be disastrous for his teammates. Records preserved in the manner in which Gehrig preserved his at Navin Field prove nothing except the absurdity of most records."

If anything, the maneuver forever quashed the myth that Gehrig did not care about his streak. Although he insisted it was the team's idea for him to play, he went along with a stunt derived strictly to get him through a tough day with his streak intact.

The next day, his back still hurt, but when Doc Painter wrapped a tight swath of adhesive tape around his torso, he found he could move relatively freely without collapsing. McCarthy put him at his usual spots, batting third and playing first base. Facing Schoolboy Rowe, a tough right-handed pitcher in the middle of a personal 16-game winning streak, Gehrig could not take full swings, but he could push his bat at the ball. In an 8–3 defeat for the Yankees, Gehrig singled in each of his four trips to the plate.

The Tigers eventually pulled away in the standings, winning 14 games in a row at one point to lock up the pennant. Gehrig did his best to keep the Yankees in contention. Despite a concussion, fractured toe, and lumbago, he led the American League in batting average (.363), home runs (49), and runs batted in (165), capturing the Triple Crown for the only time in his career. It was a feat Ruth never achieved.

On the next-to-last day of the season, Gehrig and McCarthy again executed a dubious maneuver to extend his playing streak. In the second game of a doubleheader in Washington on September 29, Gehrig batted in the top of the first, drew a walk, and left for a pinch runner. Though listed as the starting first baseman in the box score, he never took the field.

Three years later, Gehrig reiterated in an interview that it was McCarthy and the Yankees who wanted him to extend his streak with such stunts. The manager practically begged him that day in Detroit, Gehrig said, identifying that occasion as "the closest I ever came" to ending his streak. "And it's as close as I want to come," he said. "I'll take those broken fingers and busted toes, but no more sore backs for me."

On the last day of the 1934 season, Ruth played what many believed was his final major league game, going hitless against the Senators in Washington. A band from St. Mary's Industrial School for Boys in nearby Baltimore serenaded its famous alum. The Senators presented him with a scroll signed by President Franklin Roosevelt, cabinet members, and fans. After Washington's 5–3 win, Ruth gave a short speech and told reporters he would continue in baseball "as long as I can do anybody any good."

He wanted to manage. He had played on while his talents ebbed, enduring the indignity of Ruppert's cutting his salary, because he thought Ruppert might fire McCarthy, opening the door for him to take over. Ruth thought he deserved the chance as a reward for his contributions to the franchise. He had made the Yankees into the colossus they now were, he believed.

But Ruth had misread the situation. After dealing with Ruth's indiscretions and outright rebelliousness for years, Ruppert was not about to put him in charge. Before the 1934 season, Ruppert had offered to let him manage the franchise's minor league affiliate in Newark, New Jersey, privately believing Ruth would dislike the job and give up on his dream of managing the Yankees. But Ruth turned down the Newark job, opting to continue playing for the Yankees. "I'm a big leaguer," he groused.

What Ruppert really wanted was a graceful parting with his larger-than-life star. It finally happened, not so gracefully, after the 1934 season, in which Ruth hit 22 home runs, less than half of Gehrig's total, while dealing with multiple injuries and ailments. Even Ruth could see that his time in New York was up. "I'm through with the Yankees unless I can manage them," he conceded, and Ruppert was not about to let that happen.

Gehrig was glad to see him go. When Gehrig first broke in with the Yankees, he had admired Ruth's talent and celebrity. It was exciting for him when they became friends. After Ruth hit 60 home runs in 1927, he was asked if he could do it again. "I don't know, but if I don't, I know who will: that bozo over there," he said, pointing to Gehrig. The compliment, delivered as only Ruth could, meant the world to Gehrig at the time. But as he matured, Gehrig was increasingly annoyed by Ruth. Gehrig would never chase women, drink all night before playing, or take the field with a hangover. His disdain was evident to any observer paying close attention. Whenever Ruth scored a run, Gehrig turned his back rather than congratulate his teammate at home plate.

Their relationship disintegrated into outright hostility after the 1934 season. Both players were on an All-Star team that toured Japan. On the boat ride over, it was rumored that Ruth flirted with Eleanor Gehrig one day in his cabin. Later that winter, a visit by Ruth's wife to Gehrig's mother in New Rochelle led to more trouble.

Ruth had always enjoyed "Mom Gehrig," as everyone called her, and she, in turn, had enjoyed Ruth's lighthearted banter. She also had liked Ruth's first wife, Helen, and their daughter, Dorothy. In the years when Ruth and Gehrig got along well, Ruth occasionally tagged along when Gehrig visited his parents, often bringing Dorothy. Ruth even surprised Mom Gehrig with a puppy once.

But Ruth visited little after his marriage to Helen fell apart, mostly due to his infidelities, and Mom Gehrig did not like his second wife, Claire, a former showgirl. Undeterred, Claire visited Mom Gehrig one day after the 1934 season. She brought Julia, her 17-year-old daughter from a previous marriage, as well as Dorothy, now a 12-year-old tomboy. Julia dressed more stylishly than Dorothy, and Mom Gehrig noted the difference and later made a comment about it being a shame. The comment got back to

Ruth, who told Gehrig his mother should mind her own business. Gehrig was furious. No one criticized his mother.

Although Gehrig's wife found it silly that the two could not get along, Gehrig was adamant about distancing himself from Ruth. Equally angry, Ruth forbade anyone in his family to speak to anyone in Gehrig's family.

Finished as teammates, Ruth and Gehrig were also finished as friends.

It was a testy time for Ruth. He had no job in baseball now that the Yankees were done with him. The Senators considered hiring him as their manager, but his high salary demand scuttled the idea. Connie Mack also considered hiring him to manage in Philadelphia, hoping his presence would sell tickets, but Mack eventually decided against it. Ruth finally found a home when the National League's miserable Boston Braves signed him. Barely able to pay their ballpark rent, the Braves would do anything to sell a few tickets. Ruth's contract made him a player-coach and executive vice president, and he expected he would eventually get to manage.

But his return to Boston did not go well. Horribly out of shape, he slumped early in the season. His outfield play was abominable. The Braves were in a shambles. Ruth soon wanted no part of any of it. Within days of his last great performance, a three-homer game in Pittsburgh in late May, he retired.

The Yankees did not miss him. McCarthy named Gehrig the team's captain in 1935. A splendid rookie outfielder, Joe DiMaggio, joined the club in 1936. Although the Yankees finished second in 1935, they reclaimed the top spot in the American League in 1936 and defeated the Giants in the World Series. An era of unparalleled success lay just ahead.

In the summer of 1935, Grantland Rice cornered Gehrig for an interview before a game at Yankee Stadium. "How much longer is this thing going to go on?" Rice asked, referring to Gehrig's endurance streak, which had surpassed 1,500 games earlier that season.

"I haven't thought much about it. It's become a habit and you get used to a habit. I've been lucky," Gehrig told Rice.

His streak had survived several challenges, and another soon arose. On June 8, the Yankees were at Fenway Park for a doubleheader. In the bottom of the first inning of the opener, Carl Reynolds, a Boston outfielder, reached first base on a walk and took a large lead. After a pitch to the next batter, Bill Dickey, the Yankees' catcher, snapped a throw to first, trying to catch Reynolds. The throw sailed inside the baseline, and as Gehrig reached for it, Reynolds crashed into him while retreating to the bag. Gehrig was briefly knocked unconscious, and when he came to his senses, he reported feeling intense pain in his right shoulder. "I thought for sure it had been fractured," he said later.

He talked McCarthy into letting him stay in the game and initially seemed fine. In the top of the second, he walked, stole second, and scored on a hit. But his shoulder throbbed, and he finally left the game after six innings. In the second game, he played all nine innings, reached base three times in four plate appearances, and drove in a run, but his right arm "hung almost limp at his side," the *New York Sun* reported.

His shoulder still ached when he arrived at Fenway Park the next day for a game against the Red Sox. "I would not have been able to play," he said later. Fortunately, the game was postponed by rain. The Yankees also had the next day off as they traveled by train to St. Louis for a series with the Browns.

In the first game in St. Louis, Gehrig cracked a double, scored twice, and handled a dozen chances in the field without an error. Three days had passed since the collision that knocked him out and injured his shoulder, but he was fine now. "The extra day off gave me time to mend and keep my record going," he explained.

Gehrig churned on. On August 8, 1935, he hit a home run while running his streak to 1,600 games. On June 5, 1936, he reached 1,700 straight, again hitting a home run to commemorate the occasion.

By now, he was accustomed to playing in pain. During a 1936 interview with Sid Keener, he held up his gnarled right hand. The pinky resembled "a piece of granger twist tobacco," Keener wrote, with "heavy knots" on the knuckles and a "badly bent" tip.

"This finger has been fractured four times," Gehrig told Keener. "But what's a broken finger when you're with a ball club fighting for a pennant?"

According to the *Brooklyn Daily Eagle*, Gehrig had suffered "more than enough injuries that would have stopped the ordinary ballplayer who welcomes a respite from his work. Gehrig has been hit in the head three times; broken almost all of his fingers; the toe on his right foot has been fractured; he tore a muscle in his right leg; and a few years ago his shoulder was thrown out of kilter in a collision. But nothing has been able to stop him."

In 1936, Gehrig came out of one game when the Yankees were 23 runs ahead, and also took off several at-bats after the Yankees clinched the pennant in September. Otherwise, he always played. He was 33 years old, and by the end of the season, his streak stood at 1,808 straight games. He had surpassed the record of his predecessor, Everett Scott, by more than 500 games.

But as impressive as it was, his feat had detractors, including, of all people, Everett Scott, Gehrig's former teammate, whose record Gehrig had broken. "Gehrig can probably stay in there for a good many more games, barring injury, if he cares to," Scott told the *Fort Wayne Journal Gazette*, "but I believe he would be wise to take a rest when he feels that he needs it. It's the old legs that begin to feel the strain, sooner or later."

Before the 1936 season, Ruth offered sportswriter Bill Corum a similar opinion, stating that Gehrig should end the streak and focus on his hitting rather than playing every day. In January 1937, Ruth fired an even harsher shot. "I think Lou's making one of the worst mistakes a ballplayer can make by trying to keep up that 'Iron Man' stuff," Ruth said. "He's already cut three years off his baseball life with it."

Gehrig "ought to learn how to sit on the bench and rest," Ruth continued, because the Yankees "aren't going to pay off on how many games in a row he's played. The next two years will tell his fate. When his legs go, they'll go in a hurry. The average fan doesn't realize the effect a single charley horse can have on your legs. If Lou stays out there every day and never rests his legs, one bad charley horse might start him downhill."

The comments angered Gehrig. He felt he knew what his body could tolerate — a lot more than Ruth's body, which had broken down at least partly because Ruth did not take care of himself. Gehrig stayed in much better shape.

Ruth's sour grapes convinced Gehrig to keep his streak going. When he summoned the press to what was billed as a "tea party" at the Commodore Hotel in New York in January 1937, reporters expected him to state his case for making the $40,000 salary he wanted from the Yankees that season. But once he had the press around him, Gehrig used the platform to reflect on his streak, his career goals, and his legacy. It was evident he was miffed about Ruth's comments.

"I have played in 1,808 straight games and plan to stretch that string to 2,500," he declared. "That's my five-year plan. Some people think I'm crazy to play day in and day out. But I know myself better than other people know me. I get enough off days during the season to prevent my going stale. I am only 33 and I don't have to begin worrying about my legs — not just yet. I'm not going to endanger my health or the success of our ball club by sticking in the lineup when I am not fit. But just so long as I am fit, I will hang on grimly to my determination to play in 2,500 straight games."

His overall goal, he said, was to play long enough to break "about a dozen records which lie within my grasp," including the major league career marks for runs scored and runs batted in. The home run record, held by Ruth, was insurmountable, he acknowledged, but "I plan to join the 3,000-hit club."

In a one-on-one interview after the event, sportswriter Dan Daniel asked Gehrig to name the greatest player he had seen. It was a trick question. The obvious answer was Ruth. But Gehrig named Honus Wagner, the Pittsburgh Pirates' shortstop, calling him "a marvelous player who went along doing a grand job without any thought of himself. He was a team man all of the time."

Not once did Gehrig mention Ruth's name — neither in his "tea party" remarks nor in his interview with Daniel. His distaste was evident. The comment about Wagner's having no "thought of himself" was an obvious slap at Ruth.

Until now, Gehrig's motivation for playing every day had been to help his team. But now it was personal.

15

Ironmen

SHENANIGANS

By the 1950s, consecutive-game streaks had become the oddball in the family of baseball feats — not a black sheep so much as a crazy, complicated cousin, beloved by some, irksome to others.

On one hand, the public and many players viewed them as a worthwhile achievement. Five of the 15 longest streaks in history began or ended in the 1950s, and fans faithfully responded with swells of applause, appreciating the toughness and dedication required. Gehrig's "Iron Man stunt" was still a vivid memory, having ended not that long ago. In deference to Gehrig, streaks were treated with respect.

But they also had accumulated a set of detractors, skeptics who believed it was a silly, pointless goal, and certainly an odd thing to become known for. Youngsters playing imaginary games in their backyards dreamed of hitting home runs and winning the World Series, right? They did not envision themselves simply playing in hundreds of games in a row.

Babe Ruth had chided Gehrig for caring about the streak. A columnist in Detroit had eviscerated Gehrig after watching him stumble to the plate, bat leadoff, and leave a game in 1934, all for the sake of extending his streak. "Records preserved in the manner in which Gehrig preserved his at Navin Field prove nothing except the absurdity of most records," the columnist wrote. Gus Suhr had extended his league-record streak with even more "token" appearances that raised questions about his feat's legitimacy. Everett Scott later wondered aloud why he had bothered to play in so many games in a row.

Obviously, it was a challenge for a player to stay healthy enough and productive enough that his manager kept him in the lineup for years. But did his resolve to take zero days off really make his team better? The correlation was not always clear. Miller Huggins wanted to end Scott's streak several years before he did. Suhr admitted in hindsight that he should have rested more for the sake of the team.

Anyone skeptical of the legitimacy and importance of consecutive-game streaks was handed plenty of ammunition in the 1950s. The contrivances reached a new threshold of dubiousness. Eddie Yost, the Washington Senators' third baseman, somehow kept a long streak going for nine days without stepping into the batter's box. Stan Musial, the St. Louis Cardinals' magnificent right fielder, quietly engineered what sounded like an act of sporting chicanery, extending his career-longest streak one night without setting foot on the diamond.

Yost had played in more than 800 games in a row when he began resorting to manipulations to keep his streak intact late in the 1954 season. Twenty-seven years old at the time, he was, like Gehrig, a German American from New York, born in Brooklyn, raised in Queens. Having grown up cheering for the Yankees, and Gehrig in particular, he enjoyed that he was now being compared to his hero as an exemplar of endurance.

Yost had made his major league debut as a 17-year-old in 1944 when the Senators, their roster ravaged by the war effort, signed him and brought him straight to Washington. After spending the next two years in the navy, he resumed his baseball career, expecting to hone his skills in the minors. But the GI Bill contained a provision that guaranteed returning servicemen the jobs they had left behind, so he stayed in the majors. Within a year, he was the Senators' regular third baseman.

Although he did not hit for a high average, the five-foot-ten, thick-chested Yost possessed a keen eye at the plate. He had "a precise sense of the strike zone," the *New York Times* wrote, and could foul off strikes for hours, it seemed. Fans began calling him "the Walking Man," and not because he resembled Auguste Rodin's headless bronze sculpture of the same name. No one in the major leagues, not even Ted Williams, drew more bases on balls.

His consecutive-game streak began on July 8, 1949, when he returned from an ankle sprain so severe he had walked on crutches for weeks. The Senators' trainer wrapped his ankle with tape before every game, and he was able to play the rest of that season without taking a break. The next year, he played a full schedule for the first time, starting each of the Senators' 155 games on a still-tender ankle bulging with tape. He collected 169 hits and 141 walks, finishing with a .440 on-base percentage. The OBP (as on-base percentage would become known) statistic received no attention at the time, but Yost's season ranked with the best performances of Ruth, Gehrig, and Williams.

After playing another full season in 1951, Yost continued to bat lead-off for the Senators in 1952 even when a slump dropped his average below .200. He would lead the American League in walks that year. "Every time I look up, that feller is on base," said Casey Stengel, the Yankees' manager, who put Yost on the American League All-Star team even though he was hitting only .196 at the time.

Paul Richards, manager of the Chicago White Sox, grew so frustrated watching his pitchers walk Yost that he started fining them $25 per walk. (They rang up almost $600 in fines.) Yost also irritated the Yankees, who tried to trade for him after the 1952 season.

"All I hear from other clubs when they talk trade is Yost, Yost, Yost," Washington's owner, Clark Griffith, said. "They look at his batting average and think they can make a deal for him. But I wouldn't swap him for Mickey Mantle even up, and to prove it, I'm paying him almost twice as much as the Yankees pay Mantle."

Yost received a $21,000 salary in 1953 after pointing out to Griffith that the club did not have to pay a backup third baseman because of his consecutive-game streak. He had played in more than 800 straight games by September 17, 1954, when Russ Kemmerer, a pitcher for the Red Sox, hit him in the head with a fastball at Washington's Griffith Stadium in the bottom of the fourth inning.

After spending the night in the hospital, Yost returned to the ballpark the next day. His head still throbbed, and it certainly was not crucial that he play; the Senators were 43½ games out of first place. But Yost wanted to preserve his streak, later admitting his goal was "to get to a thousand" games in a row.

Just as Joe McCarthy helped Gehrig in the 1930s, Washington's manager, Bucky Harris, devised a plan that enabled Yost to keep his streak going. Hours after leaving the hospital, he was on Harris's lineup card and stationed at third base when the game against the Red Sox began. After two Boston players batted in the top of the first, Harris pulled him from the field. It was the briefest of workdays, but it extended Yost's streak.

Since 1912, both major leagues had accepted that "all appearances by a player in a championship game count as a game played," according to *Total Baseball,* the modern encyclopedia. The next day, Yost was on the field for just four at-bats by the Red Sox before Harris pulled him. But his streak continued.

Leaving Washington after that game, the Senators ended the 1954 season with series in New York and Boston. Yost never batted but appeared in every game. One day in New York, he was on the bench as Roy Dietzel started at third base, batted in the top of the first, and played the field in the bottom of the first. Yost then replaced Dietzel in the field in the bottom of the second for two batters before being replaced himself. One day in Boston, he was out of the lineup for the first game of a doubleheader but took the field with two out in the bottom of the first. Standing at third base with his glove on, he watched a Washington pitcher issue an intentional walk, then was taken out of the game. In the second game that day, a catcher, Bob Oldis, was the Senators' leadoff hitter and third baseman and batted in the top of the first. Yost replaced Oldis at third in the bottom of the first and again lasted two batters before being replaced himself.

By the end of the season, Yost had played in 813 straight games. If his teammates or the media thought poorly of the tactics he had used to keep his streak going, their gripes did not receive a public airing. No one suggested that his streak had become a contrivance, or that Yost had selfishly put his interests ahead of his team's. Since they last won a pennant in 1932, the Senators had become also-rans. Why not let one of their players have some fun? Nothing was at stake.

At spring training the next year, Yost was the subject of a flattering *Sporting News* profile authored by *Washington Post* sports columnist Shirley Povich and headlined YOUNG IRON MAN YOST KEEPS STROLLING. Povich noted that Yost had used "token appearances" to keep his consecutive-game streak going but did not criticize him. Gehrig had also done that, Povich wrote, and what mattered was Yost's overall durability.

But early in the 1955 season, Yost came down with tonsillitis, ran a fever, and felt too weak to play nine innings. The Senators' new manager, Charlie Dressen, helped him keep his streak going. Yost played third base for an inning on May 11, 1955, to reach 829 straight games. But he still had a fever and felt miserable the next day. Dressen asked what he wanted to do. The Senators were playing the Cleveland Indians.

"Bench me. I'm not doing the team any good with these token appearances. It's no way to keep a record going," Yost said.

He was not listed on the lineup card. The Senators scored a run in the first inning and added another in the third. The game moved along quickly. Soon it was the sixth, and many in the crowd of 9,653 were aware Yost's streak was on the line.

"We want Yost! We want Yost!" the fans chanted.

Yost sat quietly in the dugout until Dressen approached him in the eighth. "Want to play?" the manager asked.

"No, I've had it," Yost said.

When Yost's streak ended, Stan Musial's consecutive-game streak became the longest active streak in the major leagues. He had played in more than 500 games in a row for the Cardinals.

Musial, like Rose, was a classic "Ironman without the status of being an Ironman." Endurance was an underrated hallmark of his brilliant 22-year major league career. By the end of it, he would complete more full seasons without a day off (nine) than any player in history except Ripken, Gehrig, and Rose. In 1955, he was 34 years old and closing in on 13 straight seasons of hitting .300 or better, and he had missed just 14 games since breaking in with the Cardinals in 1941. Yet his absences had been timed just right (or wrong) to prevent him from building a notable playing streak.

By late in the 1955 season, though, he was within 250 games of Gus Suhr's National League consecutive-game record, by now two decades old. When sportswriters asked him about it, he shrugged. That record was small potatoes for a player who would win three Most Valuable Player awards and capture seven National League batting titles. Unlike Everett Scott, Musial was not obsessed with consecutive-game history. Now that a record was within sight, though, he cared enough to go to some lengths to keep his streak alive.

On August 29 at Ebbets Field, the Brooklyn Dodgers' ace right-hander, Johnny Podres, tried to back him off the plate with an inside fastball. The pitch sailed up and in, and when Musial raised his right arm to protect his head, the ball struck his right hand at 90 mph, raising "a painful bruise," the *Sporting News* reported, and prompting "fears" that Musial's consecutive-game streak was over. But for the Cardinals' next game, the opener of a series in Pittsburgh on August 30, their manager, Harry Walker, put

Musial in the lineup, batting fifth — two slots below his usual perch. He played right field in the bottom of the first, enough to constitute an official appearance. When he was due to bat in the top of the second, a pinch hitter replaced him. He had barely played, but his streak continued.

The next day, Musial's bruised hand was still sore. According to a *Sporting News* article authored by St. Louis sportswriter Bob Broeg two years later, Walker approached the umpires several hours before the first pitch and asked if Musial could extend his streak simply by appearing on Walker's lineup card. The umpires said yes, that would suffice. Walker returned to the visitors' clubhouse at Forbes Field and proposed the idea to Musial, who "objected mildly in the presence of this writer, insisting he felt up to giving it a try," Broeg later wrote. Undeterred by Musial's misgivings, Walker proceeded with his plan, telling reporters later he feared Musial might "aggravate the injury" if he played.

Musial was in the St. Louis lineup as the starting right fielder and No. 5 hitter. As the dismal matchup between the seventh- and eighth-place teams began before 6,379 fans, the Cardinals' Ken Boyer led off the top of the first with a single. The next two batters made outs before Rip Repulski also singled. Musial was due to bat, but Pete Whisenant hit for him and flied out to end the inning. Musial was out of the game without having played, but the National League still credited him with an appearance, extending his streak.

Walker had exploited a gray area produced by the lack of language in the major league rule book specifying what constituted an appearance. Although statisticians had used "accepted" criteria since 1907, the rule book would not contain specific language until 1973. Up to that time, league officials and umpires rendered ad hoc judgments. Musial's situation was rare, perhaps unprecedented, but when pressed, the umpires and league ruled that a place in the starting lineup did constitute an appearance.

With his hand improved, Musial played all nine innings the next night at Forbes Field, and by the end of the season, his streak stood at 618 straight games. But it was alive only because of a record-keeping loophole that Scott, Gehrig, and Suhr never exploited. Whenever they kept their streaks alive with "token" appearances, they always batted at least once or briefly played in the field. Either they did not know a "starting lineup" loophole existed or they found it unsporting.

The absence of clarity seems impossible today, when so much scrutiny is paid to every statistical development, even the smallest detail. But Musial's phantom appearance was a throwback to when inconsistencies were common in baseball. In the dead-ball era, a player with all zeros on his statistical line often was not listed in a box score and thus did not receive credit for playing in a game, even if he did. That could be why Gehrig always made sure he took an at-bat to keep his streak going.

Musial's misgivings about that night in Pittsburgh became more pronounced. As he neared Suhr's record two years later, he said he was tempted to sit out a game "to show that while I appreciate the record, it didn't mean enough for me to have tried to gain it unfairly." But he persisted. In 1956, the *Sporting News* reported that "Iron Man Musial" had an "impressive" consecutive-game streak and was intent on breaking Suhr's record. That he had used a loophole to keep it alive was not mentioned. At spring training in 1957, the Cardinals' manager, Fred Hutchinson, referred to strategies he would use "after Musial set the record" later that year, as if there were no doubt he would.

Musial's run almost ended after he wrenched his back in the first game of the 1957 season, but the injury responded to treatment and he continued to play, reaching his goal of 823 games in a row on June 12, 1957. The Cardinals played the Phillies in Philadelphia. Musial hit a single and double and scored twice. After the Cardinals' 4–0 win, his teammates presented him with a cake inscribed IRON MAN STAN 823.

The *Sporting News* reported that Musial was "deluged" with telegrams, including one from Suhr, who had held the record for 22 years. "Congratulations on breaking the National League record for consecutive games played. Rooting for you to get 3,000 base hits," wrote Suhr, now living in Millbrae, California.

Contacted by reporters, Suhr suggested Musial should start taking days off. Looking back at his career, Suhr said, he believed he would have been more effective late in seasons if he had sat out games along the way. The *Sporting News* seconded the idea in an editorial, writing that Musial "would be wise to think about" Suhr's advice. Musial agreed. Soon after he set the record, he said he would start sitting out the second games of doubleheaders. At 36, he was too old to play in absolutely every game.

On July 21, he played in the first game of a doubleheader in Pittsburgh, then sat out the second game, expecting his streak would end. The Cardinals built an 11–2 lead without him, but the game was halted by a local curfew before the top of the ninth, so it did not go into the books just yet. The final inning would be played when the Cardinals returned to Pittsburgh the next month. Until then, it was not an official game.

After his streak received that stay of execution, Musial changed his mind and wanted to keep going — not because of the record so much as the fact that the Cardinals needed him. They were in a pennant race, and Musial would end up hitting .351 for the season, earning his seventh batting title. He was so important to the club's fortunes that he could not afford to take a game off. Four times between July 28 and August 20, he played both ends of a doubleheader.

On August 22, he stepped into the batter's box in the fifth inning in Philadelphia before 22,000 fans. Jack Sanford, a rookie right-hander, was pitching for the Phillies. With no outs, a runner on first, and the Cardinals up by two runs, Sanford threw a curveball high and away. Reaching for it, Musial swung hard and missed. Pain shot through his shoulder. He completed the at-bat, tapping a soft grounder that produced a force play at second, leaving him on first. He then scored on a double. But his shoulder ached so badly that he left the game.

X-rays revealed a chipped bone. It was not an injury he could play through. His streak was over. As he watched from the dugout the next night, Joe Cunningham played first base for the Cardinals. Musial would not return to the lineup until mid-September, a major reason they failed to win the pennant.

Four days after he injured his shoulder, he made a token appearance strictly for the sake of his just-concluded streak. The date was August 26, 1957. The Cardinals were back in Pittsburgh, set to play a scheduled game as well as the final inning of the game that had been halted by the local curfew a month earlier. Once concluded, the "curfew game" would go into the books as having been played on July 22. Musial had sat it out before, but now, as it was completed more than a month later, he entered as a pinch runner, ran the bases, and played the bottom of the ninth at first base, all with a chipped shoulder bone.

By playing that inning, he added 33 games to the final accounting of his streak. If he had not taken advantage of the rare second chance to play in the curfew game, his streak would have ended at 862 games on July 22. But when he received credit for playing in that game, it meant he had played in every game until he injured his shoulder on August 22. His National League record went into the books at 895 straight games.

The shenanigans of the mid-1950s did not continue. It was almost as if Yost's gyrations and Musial's remark about "unfairly" setting the record chilled the idea of extending streaks through extreme manipulations. From then on, the players who set streak records, including Billy Williams, Steve Garvey, and Cal Ripken Jr., started the vast majority of their games (Ripken started every one), and when they did sit out, they always batted once or played a full inning of defense to keep their streak going.

It helped when an official definition of an appearance finally graced the rule book in 1973, after the American League voted in the designated hitter and there was speculation that a "designated runner" rule might also soon be approved. Feeling compelled to define an appearance in a changing landscape, baseball authored Rule 10.24, labeling it "Guidelines for Cumulative Performance Records." The new rule included this paragraph: "A consecutive game playing streak shall be extended if the player plays one half inning on defense, or if he completes a time at bat by reaching base or being put out. A pinch running appearance only shall not extend the streak. If a player is ejected from a game by an umpire before he can comply with the requirements of this rule, his streak shall continue." (The rule number was later changed to 10.23, and more recently to 9.23.)

The "starting lineup" loophole was addressed several years later with this clause in Rule 10.21: "When a player listed in the starting lineup for the visiting club is substituted for before he plays defensively, he shall not receive credit in the defensive statistics (fielding), unless he actually plays that position during a game. All such players, however, shall be credited with one game played (in 'batting' statistics) as long as they are announced into the game or listed on the official lineup card." (The rule was later changed to 10.20, and more recently to 9.20.)

The rules enacted in the 1970s made it official that a player could receive credit for an appearance just by making the starting lineup. But he could not use such an appearance to extend a consecutive-game streak. If those rules had existed in 1955, Musial's streak would have ended on the night he did not play in Pittsburgh.

16

Ripken

TOUGHING IT OUT

Hard feelings brewed early when the Orioles and Seattle Mariners met at Camden Yards on June 6, 1993. It was a sunny Sunday afternoon, the customary sellout crowd in place, the Orioles gunning for a three-game series sweep. When their first two batters, Harold Reynolds and Mark McLemore, tried to bunt in the bottom of the first, Seattle's starter, Chris Bosio, threw inside on McLemore and behind Reynolds. Talk of retaliation circulated in the Baltimore dugout.

The Orioles built a 5–1 lead behind their ace right-hander, Mike Mussina, with Seattle's only run coming on a home run by catcher Bill Haselman. When Haselman stepped into the batter's box in the top of the seventh, Mussina threw inside, trying to back him off the plate, and hit him. Haselman dropped his bat and charged the mound, ready to brawl. The Mariners and Orioles raced from their dugouts and met in the middle of the diamond, and a melee ensued.

Ripken sprinted to the mound to keep Haselman from injuring Mussina, but the Orioles' first baseman, Paul Carey, reached the mound first and grabbed Haselman, so Ripken turned to confront the Seattle players coming from their dugout. His cleats slipped as he turned, and he felt a pop in his right knee as several thousand pounds of Mariners bowled him over. He ended up on his back, on the bottom of the pile, suspecting he was injured.

When the brawl ended, he tested his knee and, adrenaline pumping, was able to continue. It did not even hurt after the game. He iced the knee and headed home, thinking he had suffered no more than a minor sprain.

But when he swung out of bed the next morning, he almost toppled over when he put his feet on the floor. His knee could not bear his weight. He had played in 1,790 straight games.

"We'll see, but I don't think I can play tonight," he told his wife, Kelly.

"Can't you pinch-hit?" she asked.

Ripken smiled and asked, "You, too?" He had always said he would never resort to artifice to extend the streak.

"I thought it was so important to you," Kelly said.

"If I can't play, I can live with that," Ripken said. "I'm not going to play just for that. If it ends because of this, I'll be at peace with myself. I can accept it."

He understood Kelly simply was suggesting a way to keep the streak going, but he was not going down that road. If the injury limited him, he would sit out.

He called Richie Bancells with the news that his knee had given out. "I knew something was up when he called that early," recalled Bancells, who told Ripken to see the team doctor that morning and then come to Camden Yards for treatment. The Orioles were playing Oakland that night.

An MRI revealed a sprained medial collateral ligament, which meant Ripken might have trouble moving from side to side. "I didn't think there was any way he could play," Bancells said. "But he came to the park, and we treated it all afternoon."

Word filtered out of the trainer's room that the streak was in jeopardy. "Cal might not make it tonight. His knee is really stiff," Johnny Oates, the manager, told Roland Hemond, the general manager, in a midafternoon phone call. Arriving for the game, players whispered to each other to keep from tipping off the media.

After several hours of treatment, Bancells led Ripken to an indoor batting cage under the stands, where Ripken took some swings and Bancells rolled balls to him, making him move from side to side. He reported that the knee hurt but it was starting to feel better. When Bancells explained that Ripken could further damage the knee if he played, Ripken just shrugged. "I think I'll play. Let's wrap it up and deal with it after the game," he said.

As Hemond watched from an office overlooking the field, Ripken emerged from the dugout several hours before the game and ran wind sprints down the right-field line. Then he took infield practice. Hemond smiled. The streak would continue.

Ripken was at shortstop when the game began, but he was worried about his knee holding up. Seldom, if ever, had he thought, "Don't hit a ball to me," but this once, he hoped to give his knee a couple of innings before it was tested. Naturally, Oakland's first batter, Lance Blankenship, hit a scorching ground ball, heavy with topspin, sending Ripken scurrying to his right. Deep in the hole when he grabbed it, he planted his right foot, putting his weight on his injured knee, and hurled the ball on a taut line across the diamond. The throw had enough zip to beat Blankenship to first.

The knee had passed its test.

It was still sore two nights later when, expecting Oakland's Bob Welch to throw a breaking ball away, Ripken leaned over the plate and was hit on the left wrist. He cursed under his breath as he jogged to first, thinking he had been hit in response to an inside fastball thrown at Oakland's catcher, Terry Steinbach, in the top of the inning. After advancing to second on a ground out, Ripken tried to score on a single, rounding third and heading for the plate. As the throw from the outfield reached Steinbach, Ripken plowed violently into him, decking him with a forearm to the jaw. Steinbach held on to the ball to record the out, but he was so dazed by the collision that he had to leave the game.

It was the kind of play that could easily produce hard feelings, but rather than hold it against Ripken, Steinbach saluted him. "A person like him, especially chasing that record, might be more reserved. Not him," Steinbach said later. "He's always very aggressive. He does what it takes to win."

If games 1,300 through 1,800 were the toughest period of the streak for Ripken, when everything was "all negative," the nadir of that difficult stretch came early in the 1993 season.

Ripken's familial support system on the field was gone, having been eradicated in the off-season when the Orioles fired his father and released his brother. Senior had been the team's third-base coach for four years, and though Oates, the manager, admired him, some in the organization believed he was still bitter about being fired as manager in 1988. He turned down the team's offer of a job in the minor league system. Bill, whose playing time had dwindled, signed with the Texas Rangers.

Now the only Ripken wearing an Orioles uniform, Junior was coming off a 1992 season in which he had batted a modest .251 and set career lows for home runs and runs batted in. Early in 1993, he experienced more struggles. Through 47 games, he was batting .199 with four home runs. The rest of the Orioles floundered along with him. Expected to contend in the American League East, they lost 10 of their first 14 games and were 10 games out of first place by Memorial Day, disappointing the sellout crowds packing Camden Yards.

Skepticism about Ripken's streak echoed in Baltimore, on radio talk shows, in newspaper columns, and in the stands. There was no doubt he would continue to play every day, but was that really best for the team? The question was being asked throughout baseball, not just locally. Bobby Bonds, a former star outfielder, now a hitting coach for the San Francisco Giants, vented to a Bay Area newspaper, calling it "idiotic" for Ripken to play through such a slump. Bonds, the father of superstar Barry Bonds, added, "He's doing it for a record, but I think he's stupid for doing it. Is he helping the team or hurting the team? He's probably hurting the team. He wants to break Gehrig's record even if it costs Baltimore the pennant. If I were his manager, he would be out of there."

But Bonds was not his manager. Johnny Oates was, and Oates, ever supportive of Ripken's Ironman status, kept playing him every day. "If the good Lord wants Cal to have a day off, He'll make it rain," Oates said. When reporters asked the manager why that made sense even with Ripken struggling, he explained that Ripken's defense was as airtight as ever, and offensively, Oates said, Ripken almost always ended the season with at least 20 home runs and 80 runs batted in, no matter how badly he struggled at times.

"I wanted him in there. I was always going to make sure Cal played. And I don't think it ever hurt us in a single game," Oates said later.

Ripken remained committed to playing every day, but he was increasingly frustrated by the attention and scrutiny. His streak had become such a huge story that everywhere he turned, it seemed, reporters wanted to talk to him and fans wanted his autograph. Ripken recoiled from the scene, taking measures to wall himself off.

In his perfect world, he could play every day without anyone making a fuss about it. Reporters would not corner him in the clubhouse and ask questions — sometimes questions he had already heard many times. Fans would not chase after him and ask for his signature when he had a game to prepare for. He did not mind obliging fans and, in fact, signed autographs until his hand hurt, but when he found it difficult to focus on what mattered most to him, preparing and playing, he became irritated.

Pete Rose had given daily press conferences both before and after games when he made his run at Joe DiMaggio's consecutive-game hitting streak in 1978. "I loved the limelight," Rose said. Two daily press conferences sounded like a nightmare to Ripken. Wanting to be left alone to do his job, he spent more and more time before and after games in the trainer's room, where reporters were not allowed. He and Richie Bancells talked about their families, movies, the headlines, gossip, anything but the streak. "We never talked about it. I taped his ankles every day and we never discussed the streak," Bancells said.

Actually, Bancells recalled, the subject came up once, when Ripken suddenly blurted, "What's the big deal? It's the manager who puts me in the lineup." After Ripken said that, Bancells recalled, "he looked at me and said, 'You come to work every day, too.' He equated playing shortstop every day with being a welder going to work every day, or being an athletic trainer coming to work every day to tape ankles. He minimized the whole thing. No one believes that, but it was true. His mindset was more of a blue-collar-type thing, a working-class-type thing, where you worked every day, which came directly from his dad."

But if Ripken really believed he was no different from a welder, he was the only person who thought that. The interest in him and his streak had grown so intense that on the road he stayed under an assumed name at the team hotel and was besieged for autographs in the lobby. Zealous fans even chased him on taxi rides to and from games, hoping to obtain his signature when he jumped out. One night when he returned to his hotel room after a game, he walked down the hall for ice, and two fans jumped out from behind the dispenser and asked for autographs.

Feeling overwhelmed, Ripken asked his teammates if they cared whether he stayed apart from them on the road, in a different hotel. They said they did not mind. Ripken then asked the front office if he could try that. The club acceded to his request, somewhat reluctantly. Ripken began staying in different hotels, still under an assumed name, and traveled to and from games in limousines with dark windows, protecting his identity.

He liked the new arrangement, finding that he had fewer distractions and could focus on playing. But the media had a field day when it uncovered his plan, suggesting it was the ultimate example of Ripken's believing he was bigger and more important than the team. When he slumped at the plate early in the 1993 season, *Washington Post* columnist Tony Kornheiser wrote of him, "What's the excuse this year, the limo was late?"

On June 28, 1993, *Sports Illustrated* published a long feature on Ripken's situation titled "Solitary Man: It's a Long, Lonely Haul to Lou Gehrig's Record for Besieged Oriole Shortstop Cal Ripken Jr." Sportswriter Tom Verducci depicted a bristling Ripken avoiding the press and taking late-night rides down dark alleys to avoid fans. "Yes, I think Cal has withdrawn," Ron Shapiro, Ripken's agent, told Verducci. "There's a tremendous burden created by the public and created within Cal."

Ripken admitted to Verducci that he was frustrated that his streak was becoming so big that it was starting to overshadow everything else he had accomplished. "That's become my identity; that's what people see when they see me," he said. He also was frustrated by the perception that he was selfish: "The worst part is you spend 11 years building a reputation as a team player, helping people out, and all of a sudden, because you stay at another hotel for other reasons, people take that away from you. Now you're selfish and putting yourself apart from the team. All you want to do is to be able to walk freely, without problems."

With characteristic bluntness, Rose boiled the situation down to its bare essence. "I think the streak is a good thing for baseball, but it's a better thing for baseball if the player is productive," he told Verducci. "If Cal Ripken plays like Cal Ripken should last year, the Orioles probably win the pennant. Unless he has a decent year, people will say he's just trying for the record. If he hits .215, is the streak a good thing? Any pressure he's getting is created by himself because of his low batting average and statistics."

But just when Ripken felt the world was closing in on him—criticism swirling, his average dipping—he perked up. Although he hated the perception that he was intentionally pursuing Gehrig, he realized he was fighting a losing battle after he injured his knee in the brawl and his wife suggested he pinch-hit to keep the streak going. If his wife, who knew him best, thought he wanted the record that badly, he could not expect Bobby Bonds or anyone else to understand his philosophy. Once he realized that, he felt liberated.

There had been speculation that he might get booed at the 1993 All-Star Game in Baltimore, his hometown fans turning on him and his .215 average. Instead, his ears rang with thunderous cheers that night. That encouraged him, as did his teammates' unyielding support.

"He was our shortstop, one of the best in history defensively and certainly one of the best offensively. Why would you want him out of the lineup?" Brady Anderson said for this book. "Who was going to replace him? That made it even more comical. It wasn't like Ozzie Smith was on the bench. Come on, the criticism of him was a joke. We never thought he should take a day off."

Ben McDonald agreed that support for Ripken never wavered inside the Orioles' clubhouse, even if it did outside. "I never heard any of the players say anything," McDonald said. "I heard the talk, we all did, when he was slumping, that the manager should think about giving him a day off. We didn't talk about it much, but when we did, Cal was funny, he'd say, 'What good would one day do?' A week, maybe, could do something, but not one day. What was the point of that? But from a player's standpoint, we had too much respect for him to question it. We knew how hard it was to go out and play every day. I never heard anyone say one word."

McDonald, as part of the Orioles' starting rotation, had a vested interest in Ripken's staying on the field. "As a pitcher, I didn't care what he hit. I wanted him behind me" in the field, McDonald said. "It was so reassuring to have him there. I don't know that he was the fastest or quickest guy to play shortstop, but he was certainly the smartest. He knew every hitter like the back of his hand, knew how to get them out, what their tendencies were. I could turn to him for advice during a game, turn to him for anything. He made so many plays. I used to say to him, 'Don't ever take a day off.' All of the pitchers felt the same way."

After hitting bottom early in the season, Ripken finished 1993 on a roll, batting 63 points higher in the second half of the season. You could almost sense him fighting the perception that he only cared about the streak. He dove headlong to catch a pop-up, injuring his shoulder. He ran over his friend and former teammate Bob Melvin in a violent home-plate collision. But he never missed an inning.

Asked by an interviewer what he thought about Ripken's pursuit of Gehrig, Jon Miller, the Orioles' radio play-by-play man, posed a question of his own: "I'm amazed at the things that get attributed to Cal because of the streak. Every time there has been a brawl or near brawl, he has been one of the first guys out there. If the streak is so important to him, what's he doing out there?"

Even as the controversy continued, the majority of people *inside* the game respected him and his dedication to playing every day. "I was in the opposing clubhouse by then, and all I heard was respect," said Mickey Tettleton, a former Orioles teammate. "Players knew how hard it was for him to do what he was doing. And they appreciated not just what he was doing, but how he was doing it. He really respected the people he played against. That was clear. He never showed anyone up, just played hard. The stuff Senior taught him. That garnered him a lot of support."

On December 31, 1993, baseball's collective bargaining agreement expired, with no new deal in sight. The owners wanted to implement a salary cap to ease what they claimed was a worsening financial situation. The players did not want the owners setting limits on their earning power. The sides continued to negotiate as the 1994 season opened, but after years of hostility and mistrust, they did not get far. In June, the owners failed to make a scheduled payment to the players' pension and benefit fund. In July, the players set August 12 as a strike date.

While it lasted, the 1994 season was an eyepopper. The San Francisco Giants' Matt Williams was challenging Roger Maris's single-season home run record. The San Diego Padres' Tony Gwynn was trying to become the first .400 hitter since Ted Williams, in 1941. The Montreal Expos, who had never played in a World Series, dominated the National League, and the Yankees, after a decade of mediocrity, were back on top, forging the American League's best record. Fans ignored the gathering labor clouds as the average attendance at a major league game soared to a record 31,600.

In Baltimore, Peter Angelos had bought the team and green-lighted the signing of expensive free agents such as first baseman Rafael Palmeiro and closer Lee Smith. They blended with the existing core, led by Mussina and McDonald, and the Orioles, playing to sold-out houses at home, won often enough to stay close to the Yankees. Ripken, now 33, was the oldest player in the lineup, but a vital piece. Batting cleanup behind Palmeiro, he saw more juicy pitches, hit .340 in April, and slugged his 300th career home run in May.

On May 14, his playing streak reached 1,930 straight games, leaving him exactly 200 shy of the record. Catching Gehrig was no longer a distant reality, too far away to reckon. Ripken was getting close. The shrill public debate quieted. As Pete Rose had suggested, there was nothing to talk about when Ripken performed well. His average soared over .300 in June and stayed there. By early August, he had more than 70 runs batted in, putting him on pace to surpass 100 for the season.

He was originally scheduled to reach 2,000 straight games on a Saturday night in late July, at home — a perfect setting for a celebration. But several weeks before that, the last two games of a series in Seattle were postponed when acoustic tiles fell from the ceiling of the Kingdome. Now Ripken would reach 2,000 on the road, in Minnesota, on August 1.

The day before, the Orioles finished a homestand with an afternoon game against Toronto in front of 47,674 fans. There was unease in the stands because the Orioles were slipping farther behind the Yankees in the standings, but as they took the field in the top of the fifth, it was noted on the scoreboard that game 1,999 of Ripken's streak was about to become official. The fans stood and cheered, sustaining the noise for so long that Ripken doffed his cap. "They really got into it," Ripken wrote later.

The Blue Jays also applauded in the visitors' dugout, but when Ripken batted in the bottom of the sixth, Toronto's pitcher threw behind him and then hit him on the butt — payback for Ben McDonald throwing behind a Toronto batter in the fourth.

The next night, in a half-empty Metrodome, Ripken became the only major league player other than Gehrig to reach 2,000 straight games. On the day Gehrig hit that threshold, his wife, Eleanor, had suggested he sit out to give his streak a memorable end. Gehrig did not like the idea and played. Ripken's wife did not offer such a suggestion, but she did fly in to commemorate the occasion. Surprising her husband, she sat behind the dugout.

As Ripken approached the plate in the top of the first, the public-address announcer noted that this was game number 2,000. The crowd stood and applauded. Ripken waved, stepped out of the batter's box, and took off his helmet to acknowledge the appreciation. The reaction from another team's fans surprised him — as did the long ovation the day before in Baltimore

"I was pleasantly surprised [by both]," he wrote later. "I never wanted whatever hoopla there was, but it was gratifying that everyone seemed to be behind me now. It's true that I was hitting .315 and driving in runs, but I like to think that people finally understood what the streak was all about. For quite a few years I'd been thinking of it as a negative, mainly; I'd had to defend playing every day. Now it seemed like the streak had turned into a positive thing for me and for baseball."

Ten days later, after the games of August 11, the players went on strike, halting the season. Negotiations continued without success. On September 14, Bud Selig, the sport's commissioner, canceled the rest of the season and the postseason. There would be no World Series in 1994. It was one of baseball's saddest days.

The dispute continued through the off-season, jeopardizing the start of the 1995 season. Ripken's streak was swept into the issue. The owners devised a plan to use non-union "replacement" players. Though the product would be inferior, pro football's owners had used the ploy in 1987 when their season was halted by a work stoppage, and it had caused cracks in the union. Now, if the Orioles fielded a replacement squad and played officially sanctioned games without Ripken, his streak would end at 2,009 straight games.

The owners knew fans would be furious if Ripken fell short for that reason. They hoped the union would be more likely to settle as a result. It was a situation without precedent. Several prominent players said they would support Ripken by crossing the picket line and playing just to keep his streak going; it was that important.

But Ripken, a long-standing union member, traveled to New York, met with the union's leadership, and explained that he would not cross any picket line. "If they use replacement players, it's not major league baseball and I won't be playing," he told reporters.

That meant Gene Budig, the president of the American League, would decide the fate of Ripken's streak if replacement-player baseball became a reality. Would those games actually count? Budig gauged the feelings of several prominent figures in the game and discovered that Ripken had a lot of support. "I wouldn't do anything to jeopardize that streak," Oakland manager Tony La Russa said. "I'd rather not play [replacement] games and wait for the thing to get settled."

In a further complication, Peter Angelos would not cooperate with the replacement-player scheme. The Orioles' owner had made his fortune defending union members in class-action lawsuits against corporations, so unlike most of his fellow owners, he was pro-union. He would not field a team of replacement players, he said, and if other teams did, the Orioles would forfeit their games. So would a forfeit end Ripken's streak?

On March 31, 1995, hours before Budig had to rule, a federal judge, Sonia Sotomayor, destined for the U.S. Supreme Court, effectively ended the dispute by granting an injunction sought by the National Labor Relations Board against the owners on a charge of unfair labor practices. The players voted to end the strike, and the owners reluctantly let them come back to work under the terms of the old collective bargaining agreement. Replacement-player baseball would not happen.

The American League announced a regular-season schedule beginning in late April, with each team playing 144 games. If Ripken did not sit any out, he would tie Gehrig's record on September 5 and break it on September 6 when the Orioles played the California Angels at Camden Yards.

Suddenly, the prospect of his making history was real. The countdown began.

17

Gehrig

A TRAGIC TURN

After negotiating a $39,000 salary with the Yankees in 1938, Gehrig experienced a miserable spring training. He could not drive the ball. Hits eluded him. One day, he swung so hard at strike three that he spun around and fell, drawing laughter. The Yankees were alarmed, and so was Gehrig. At one point, he sat out three straight games.

Once the season started, he fared little better. After a month, he was hitting under .200 with just two home runs. Manager Joe McCarthy dropped him to fifth in the batting order, then sixth. Some sportswriters suggested he had reached the inevitable point where his skills declined, perhaps exacerbated by his years of playing every day. No one imagined he was experiencing the stirrings of a fatal disease.

McCarthy never considered resting him. Gehrig was his captain. With DiMaggio replacing Ruth and Gehrig setting the tone, the Yankees had adopted a professional, businesslike approach. DiMaggio gracefully roamed the outfield and smacked home runs, but Gehrig was the heart of the squad. Even if he finally was showing his age, his struggles would not last for long, McCarthy figured. The manager recalled Gehrig slumping horribly early in 1937 and ending up with his usual terrific statistics.

Sure enough, Gehrig snapped out of his funk. When he drove in a run with a long double in Cleveland on May 22, he brought his average to .270. But his back tightened up as he legged out the hit. A trainer massaged his back on the field, enabling him to stay in the game and score on a subsequent hit, but he came out after that. The Yankees said it was just another flare-up of his lumbago. Gehrig disagreed, saying a cold had "settled" in his back.

The next day's game was rained out, likely sparing him from extending his streak with another brief, early appearance. His back ached. But after the extra rest, he played all nine innings and hit a double in a loss to the Indians on May 24.

By playing both ends of a doubleheader at Yankee Stadium on May 30, he ran his streak to 1,999 games. The next morning, according to Jonathan Eig's Gehrig biography, LUCKIEST MAN, Eleanor made a bold suggestion as the couple ate breakfast.

"Don't go to the stadium today. Tell them anything you want, but skip it," she said.

She stated her case. Gehrig had already proved that no player in history could match his endurance, she said. Stopping the streak now, just shy of 2,000, would be memorable. Why wait for it to end on a more depressing note, because of injury or age?

Gehrig, according to Eig's book, replied that it was an interesting idea, but "you know I can't just skip it." After playing through so many injuries and illnesses, he was not going to end the streak on a day when he felt great. He still believed he could reach 2,500 games in a row. Although he had started slowly that season, he was heating up. He kissed Eleanor good-bye and headed to the ballpark in the Bronx.

On a sunny afternoon, just 6,000 fans came to see Gehrig reach the biggest of round numbers — 2,000 games in a row. The Yankees did not hold a ceremony either before the game or when the game became official. No actors or politicians gave speeches or presented Gehrig with a trophy or commemorative coin. Gehrig collected one hit, a single, in four at-bats and drove in a run as the Yankees pounded the Red Sox, 12–5. Gehrig posed for a few pictures, but that was all that marked the day as different.

When reporters surrounded him after the game, the conversation turned, as usual, to why he kept going. Perhaps because he now knew even his wife thought it might be time to stop, Gehrig reacted coolly. "I don't see why anyone should attack my record. I have never belittled anyone else's," he said. "I intend to play every day and shall continue to give my best to my employers and the fans."

The Yankees soon found the form that had produced back-to-back World Series triumphs. With a run of 20 wins in 24 games, they took first place in early July and quickly grew a lead. Their third straight pennant was assured. But Gehrig played an increasingly minor role and dealt with more injuries. Another lumbago attack forced him out of one game. On July 17, he reached for a low throw from pitcher Spud Chandler, and the ball glanced off his left thumb. The team doctor wanted him to get an X-ray, but he refused, saying, "I'll shake it off. That's what I've always done." When he finally relented, the X-ray revealed a fractured bone in the thumb as well as "several old fractures Gehrig knew nothing about," one newspaper reported.

After an off day, Gehrig wore a splint on his thumb during batting practice before the Yankees played Cleveland on July 19. He removed the splint for the game and played all nine innings, going hitless in four at bats. Asked if the injury might end his streak, Gehrig replied, "I would play in this series if I had no thumb at all." He went on: "Oh, it hurts, but I can grip a bat and handle a ball all right, and there's no reason why I shouldn't play."

He eventually heated up, collecting four hits in one game and pushing his average near .300 by late July. But though he had almost 100 runs batted in, he was troubled by his inability to drive the ball. Most of his hits were singles now rather than doubles or home runs. Trying to reignite his power, he heeded McCarthy's suggestion to use a lighter bat — 33 ounces instead of 38 — but that did not help. Nor did adopting a new approach in which he relied on his hands and arms rather than his legs. He hit just three home runs in the Yankees' last 30 games.

Near the end of the season, the Yankees played a batch of doubleheaders. Gehrig obviously was tired. At his "tea party" at the Commodore Hotel the year before, he had said he would no longer resort to stunts like the one he pulled in Detroit to keep his streak alive. "I don't believe in making a practice of that sort of thing. I don't want to cheapen the record. If I can't play through [a game], we will let it lapse," he had said. But when the time came, late in the 1938 season, he could not bring himself to do it.

On September 19, he did not feel like playing against the Browns in St. Louis. The Yankees had clinched the pennant the day before and celebrated into the night. Now fewer than a thousand fans were on hand for a Monday afternoon game at Sportsman's Park. Gehrig did not come up to bat in the top of the first, then played first base in the bottom of the inning. When it was his turn to bat in the top of the second, his backup, Babe Dahlgren, pinch-hit for him. He was done for the day without a plate appearance.

After the game, which the Yankees lost, 13–0, there was no mention of Gehrig's being injured or ill. The team did not explain why he had left the game early. Ten days later, Gehrig made another token appearance in the second game of a doubleheader against the Athletics in Philadelphia. After he had played the whole first game, collecting a hit and scoring a run, McCarthy put him at his usual spot in the lineup for the second game. Gehrig watched the Yankees go down in order in the top of the first, then played the field in the bottom of the inning. But when it was his turn to bat in the top of the second, Dahlgren hit for him. For the second time, he was out of a game without having batted.

The Yankees easily swept the Chicago Cubs in the World Series, winning four games by a combined score of 22–9. Gehrig played every inning, extending his World Series consecutive-game streak to 34. After losing in his inaugural appearance in the Fall Classic in 1926, he and the Yankees had triumphed in 1927, 1928, 1932, 1936, 1937, and, now, 1938.

A lifetime .361 hitter in the Series, Gehrig usually led the Yankees in October. But he was quiet this time, collecting just four singles against the Cubs. Of the Yankees' big hitters, he was the only one who failed to knock a home run. Of course, with DiMaggio and Dickey sandwiching him in the order, the club no longer depended heavily on him.

In the top of the fourth inning of the first game, a scene unfolded that, in McCarthy's opinion, made it clear that Gehrig's playing days were just about over. Gehrig bashed a hit to deep right field, seemingly an easy double. But the Cubs' right fielder scooped up the ball and hurled it to the second baseman, who passed it on to the shortstop covering second. Gehrig was out by three feet. He could no longer leg out a double.

In the final game, played at Yankee Stadium on October 9, 1938, Gehrig batted fifth and played first. With the Yankees leading, 4–3, in the bottom of the eighth, Gehrig batted with one out and DiMaggio on first. Vance Page, a tall right-hander for the Cubs, threw a high fastball. Gehrig swung and connected. The ball headed for right field on a line and sank to the grass for a single. DiMaggio reached third on the play, and both he and Gehrig scored during a four-run rally.

In the top of the ninth, Red Ruffing, the Yankees' pitcher, allowed a leadoff single, then recorded two outs. With the Cubs down to their last out, their second baseman, Billy Herman, swung awkwardly and tapped the ball to Ruffing. The pitcher scooped it up and tossed it to Gehrig, who squeezed the final out in his mitt and raced to the mound to congratulate the pitcher and shake hands with his teammates. It was his last moment of glory on a diamond.

The winter after the 1938 season was an uneasy time for Eleanor Gehrig. She was increasingly concerned about her husband, who fell several times while ice-skating and complained enough about persistent stomach distress that she made him see a doctor, who diagnosed gallbladder trouble and put him on a bland diet.

Gehrig simply was not himself. "I thought he might have a brain tumor," she admitted later. "We were both worried but never said anything for fear of scaring the other."

When Gehrig struggled again in spring training before the 1939 season, he said it was because he had been lazy over the winter and was out of shape. He had experienced spring slumps before, but this one was the worst. He collected just three singles in his first 35 exhibition at-bats. Trying to find a rhythm, he spent extra time in the batting cage, but one day DiMaggio watched him swing and miss at 19 straight pitches, a startling scene. When he did reach base in games, he was so heavy-legged it seemed he wore ankle weights. In the field, two easy ground balls scooted through his legs. One day, he flubbed a grounder and was picked off first.

After graciously ignoring his struggles for a few weeks, the press began to acknowledge them. The *New York Herald Tribune* reported "concern" among the Yankees over whether Gehrig was his usual self. Even when he hit two home runs in a game near the end of spring training, he convinced few observers that he was now fine. Reporters openly speculated about the possible end of his playing streak, which stood at 2,122 games.

McCarthy was not going to bench him. In the manager's opinion, Gehrig deserved to decide when the streak ended, and Gehrig wanted to keep going.

On Opening Day, he went hitless in four at-bats, grounded into two double plays, and committed an error, dropping a throw as he tried to tag a runner — a play he usually made. A day later, he botched a routine ground ball, and although the official scorer did not charge him with an error, it was a mistake. There were two more mistakes the next day, a line drive that went off his glove and another that almost bowled him over.

After five games, he had one hit, a single. But then he singled twice and collected his first run batted in of the season in a win over the Athletics on April 25. "I am getting looser every day," Gehrig told sportswriter Dan Daniel. "I owe my current troubles to my own mistakes. At my age, an athlete cannot laze around all winter and hope to develop playing form in six or seven weeks of spring training. I should've jogged all through the off-season and come [to spring training] as well prepared as I am right now. That will be corrected next winter. Don't worry. I will be around then, and in 1940 as well. I am a determined man."

To those suggesting he should rest because he was struggling, he said, "Once and for all, let me make it plain that snapping my streak would only do me harm. Unbroken, that string is a tremendous incentive. I'm not tired. Taking a day off would be silly."

Privately, he was greatly concerned. He knew his body. Something was wrong. This was not just a slump. Maybe the problem would correct itself, but he was losing faith in his ability. He knew his teammates had doubts, too.

After his two-hit game against the Athletics, he went 1-for-3 with a walk against the Senators on April 29. The next day, a Sunday, the Yankees played Washington again before 23,712 fans at Yankee Stadium. It was their last home game before a two-week road trip, and it zipped along, scoreless, until the Yankees scored a run in the bottom of the seventh. After the Senators came back with three runs in the top of the eighth, the Yankees tried to rally. Gehrig came up with two men on and two out, with a chance to put his team ahead and maybe win the game — a situation in which he had long thrived. He was 0-for-3, but now he drove the ball on a line into center field. The fans rose in anticipation, thinking he had come through, but the Senators' George Case tracked the ball down and grabbed it for the third out.

Gehrig was disconsolate after the game. He was hitting .143 and had stranded runners in several at-bats in the one-run defeat. He blamed himself for the loss. In addition, in the top of the ninth, he had needed help to record a routine out: the Yankees pitcher had to race from the mound to cover first because Gehrig was so slow getting to the bag after fielding a ground ball. His streak now stood at 2,130, but he felt he had become a liability.

After an off day and an overnight train ride, the Yankees arrived in Detroit on Tuesday morning, May 2, and checked into the Book-Cadillac Hotel. Gehrig ate breakfast with Dickey and sat in the lobby next to a sportswriter, Charlie Segar, until McCarthy arrived. The manager had spent the off day with his family in Buffalo and flown in that morning. Gehrig stood up, approached McCarthy, and said, "Joe, I want to talk to you about an important matter." They went upstairs to McCarthy's room.

"Joe, I always said I would quit when I felt I was no longer any help to this team. I don't think I'm any help. When do you want me to quit?" Gehrig said.

"Today," McCarthy replied. ("I was afraid he'd get hurt. His reflexes were gone. He couldn't get out of the way of the ball," McCarthy said later.)

Gehrig hoped he would only have to miss a few games before reclaiming his spot in the lineup; maybe the rest would prove beneficial, he thought. Regardless, he wanted to end the streak. McCarthy returned to the lobby, summoned the beat writers, and delivered the stunning news: Gehrig would miss that afternoon's game at Briggs Stadium.

"Lou just told me he felt it would be best for the club if he took himself out," McCarthy said. "I asked if he really felt that way. He told me he is serious. He feels blue. He is dejected. I told him it would be as he wished. Like everybody else, I'm sorry to see it happen. I told him not to worry. Maybe the warm weather will bring him around. We'll miss him. You can't escape that fact. But I think he's doing the right thing."

Gehrig stopped in the lobby on his way to the park and spoke to the writers. Some reported he was near tears.

"I decided last Sunday night on this move," he said. "I haven't been a bit of good to the team since the season started. It's tough to see your mates on base, have a chance to win a ballgame, and not be able to do anything about it. Joe has been swell about it. He'd let me go until the cows come home. He is that considerate of my feelings, but I knew in Sunday's game that I should get out of there. I went up there four times with men on base and didn't knock any home. Maybe a rest will do me good. Maybe it won't. Who knows? Who can tell? I'm just hoping."

Gehrig took a cab to the park and dressed as if he would play. McCarthy gave his spot in the lineup to Dahlgren, a lanky 26-year-old in his first full season with the Yankees. According to a 1956 *Sports Illustrated* essay by Dahlgren, Art Fletcher, a Yankees coach, broke the news to him in the dugout during warm-ups.

"Babe, you're playing first today," Fletcher said.

"Are you kidding?" Dahlgren asked.

"Good luck, Babe," Fletcher replied.

Gehrig took the lineup card to the plate before the game, a chore that often fell to him as the team captain. As the brief meeting with the umpires broke up and Gehrig returned to the dugout, the stadium announcer, Ty Tyson, said, "How about a hand for Lou Gehrig, who played in 2,130 games in a row before he benched himself today!"

The 11,000 fans briefly sat in silence, stunned, before erupting in applause, aware they were witnessing history. Gehrig tipped his cap, ducked into the dugout, and took a long drink from a water fountain, hovering over the spigot so his teammates could not see his tears. As the fans continued to applaud, some of those teammates wept, too.

When the game began, the Yankees scored six runs in the top of the first, as if they wanted the Tigers to pay for Gehrig's disappointment. Dahlgren showed no sign of nervousness. He hit a home run in the third inning and later added a double. In the seventh, with the Yankees well ahead, Dahlgren approached Gehrig in the dugout and asked, "How about playing an inning or two to keep the streak alive?"

Gehrig replied, "They don't need me out there. You're doing fine."

When the last out of the Yankees' 22–2 win was recorded, it was official: for the first time in almost 14 years, the Yankees had played a game without Gehrig.

His consecutive-game streak had begun at the height of the Roaring Twenties and rolled through a stock market crash, the worst of the Great Depression, the end of Prohibition, and parts of three U.S. presidencies, and now was ending on the verge of a second world war. Baseball on the radio had just become popular when it started. Now games were starting to crop up on a thing called television.

In newspapers across the country, the end of Gehrig's streak vied for front-page space with the day's other news: the world's fair opening in New York, President Franklin Roosevelt's New Deal facing criticism in Washington, and German chancellor Adolf Hitler's threat to claim more

of Europe. Gehrig topped them all with his melancholy baseball tale —
surprising, bittersweet, and soon to become even sadder.

By coincidence, Wally Pipp was at Briggs Stadium to see Gehrig's streak
end. The man Gehrig replaced at first base for the Yankees in 1925 now
lived in Grand Rapids, Michigan, and had business in Detroit that day. He
was at the Book-Cadillac Hotel, visiting his former team, as the Gehrig
drama unfolded that morning.

Pipp thought Gehrig looked ill. It was not just Gehrig's failure to hit
or make routine defensive plays. He had lost weight. His thick, muscular
frame used to fill his uniform, but now his jersey hung loosely.

"The breakdown of Lou reminds me of the total breakdown of Everett
Scott in 1925, which emphasizes a fact, which Lou has denied, that playing
day after day for the record is bunk. It takes too much out of a man," Pipp
told Dan Daniel.

Gehrig remained with the club for another month, taking batting practice and sitting on the bench during games, but his only on-field appearance came in an exhibition game against the Yankees' Kansas City farm
club on June 12, 1939.

When he saw Kansas City's Ruppert Stadium filled with more than
23,000 fans that day, he felt compelled to try to play. "The crowd roared,"
the *Kansas City Times* reported, when it was announced he would start at
first base for the Yankees. But he lasted just three innings. He fell down
making one play and let another easy ground ball roll past him for a hit.
In the top of the third, he trudged to the plate, swung weakly at a fastball,
and grounded to second. McCarthy pulled him. He never played again.

The next day, the Yankees took a train to New York, and Gehrig traveled to the Mayo Clinic in Rochester, Minnesota, hoping to discover what
was wrong with him. "I can't help believe there's something," he told reporters. "It's not conceivable that I could go to pieces so suddenly. I feel
fine, feel strong, and have the urge to play, but without warning this year
I've apparently collapsed. I'd like to play some more, and I want somebody to tell me what's wrong."

A week of tests produced a stunning diagnosis. Gehrig had amyotrophic lateral sclerosis, a debilitating neurological disease marked by
rapidly developing weakness and muscle atrophy. Suddenly, his decline
made sense.

So little was known about ALS that Everett Scott mistakenly told a reporter Gehrig probably would not have become ill if only he had sat out a few more games, "Lou should have gone 100 games past me, sat one out, and then played about 125 a year. Maybe he wouldn't be in this situation," Scott said.

Trying to sound optimistic, Gehrig told his teammates that he had faith in his doctors and could beat the disease. The truth was far more sobering. ALS is a grave illness. Gehrig's life expectancy was now shorter, and there was no doubt his playing days were over.

The Yankees originally did not intend to commemorate the end of his glorious career. His teammates bought him a fishing rod, and that was it. But when the public clamored for the chance to show its support, the club scheduled "Lou Gehrig Appreciation Day" for July 4, 1939, and invited the 1927 team and other former players.

More than 61,000 fans filled Yankee Stadium that day. A doubleheader against Washington was scheduled. Colorful bunting hung from the stadium façade, as if it were a World Series game. More than a dozen former Yankees were on hand, including Tony Lazzeri, Bob Meusel, Waite Hoyt, and Everett Scott. They crammed into the home clubhouse before the first game and joked with the current players, creating a raucous scene. Gehrig almost fainted from the heat and swirl of noise. He retreated to McCarthy's office for half an hour, caught his breath, and came out gamely apologizing for not bringing a keg of beer.

During the first game, Gehrig sat quietly on the bench. The former players received applause as they found their seats behind home plate. Ruth made a grand entrance in the fourth inning, resplendent in a double-breasted cream-colored suit and white shirt with no tie.

After the game, the former players, minus Gehrig, gathered on the field and walked to the foot of a flagpole beyond the outfield fence. An army band played as a 1927 world championship pennant went up the flagpole. The fans cheered, and the players returned to home plate, where a microphone stand had been erected.

Gehrig was in the clubhouse. It was a sweltering, sunny day. He could not take the heat. Someone went to the clubhouse and told him to come to the field. When he appeared, his uniform belt cinched tight around his gaunt waist, the fans loosed a shattering roar. "Never in his 14 years had Lou ever heard such applause," one newspaper reported.

A ceremony began with remarks from the emcee, sportswriter Sid Mercer. New York's mayor, Fiorello La Guardia, praised Gehrig in a speech, as did the U.S. postmaster general, James Farley. McCarthy cried when he recounted the day Gehrig's streak ended. Ed Barrow, the Yankees' general manager, made his first appearance on the stadium field after running the team for two decades and announced that Gehrig's uniform number, 4, would be retired. No Yankee had ever received such an honor.

Gehrig stood in front of the speakers with his head bowed. He appeared to weep softly at times and dabbed his eyes with a handkerchief as he listened to the testimonials and received such gifts as a watch, ring, silver cup, silver serving set, and, most memorably, a trophy from his teammates with a poetic inscription written by *New York Times* columnist John Kieran:

> *We've been to the wars together;*
> *We took our foes as they came;*
> *And always you were the leader,*
> *And ever you played the game.*
>
> *Idol of cheering millions,*
> *Records are yours by sheaves;*
> *Iron of frame they hailed you;*
> *Decked you with laurel leaves.*
>
> *But higher than that we hold you,*
> *We who have known you best;*
> *Knowing the way you came through*
> *Every human test.*
>
> *Let this be a silent token*
> *Of lasting Friendship's gleam,*
> *And all that we've left unspoken;*
> *Your Pals of the Yankee Team.*

Ruth stepped to the microphone. He and Gehrig had stopped speaking, but the bad blood between them was forgotten now. Ruth had told an interviewer he felt awful about Gehrig's situation. In a brief speech, Ruth praised the 1927 team as "the best the Yankees ever had" and told Gehrig to relax and go catch some fish.

When Ruth gave up the microphone, no one was left to speak. But the fans wanted to hear Gehrig. "We want Lou! We want Lou!" they chanted. Gehrig had hoped to get away without speaking, but there was no chance of that happening. He stepped to the microphone. The stadium fell silent as he gathered his thoughts with his head bowed. When he spoke, his voice was thick with emotion.

"For the past two weeks, you've been reading about a bad break. Today, I consider myself the luckiest man on the face of the earth."

The crowd roared. Gehrig waited for the noise to subside and continued.

"I have been in ballparks for 17 years and have never received anything but kindness and encouragement from you fans. When you look around, wouldn't you consider it a privilege to associate yourself with such fine-looking men as are standing in uniform in the ballpark today? Sure I'm lucky. Who wouldn't consider it an honor to have known Jacob Ruppert? Also, the builder of baseball's greatest empire, Ed Barrow? To have spent six years with such a grand little fellow as Miller Huggins? To have spent the next nine years with that smart student of psychology, the best manager in baseball today, Joe McCarthy? Sure I'm lucky.

"Who wouldn't feel honored to room with such a grand guy as Bill Dickey? When the New York Giants, a team you would give your right arm to beat, and vice versa, sends you a gift — that's something. When the groundskeepers and office staff and writers and old timers and players and concessionaires all remember you with trophies — that's something. When you have a wonderful mother-in-law who takes sides with you in squabbles against her own daughter — that's something. When you have a father and mother who work all their lives so you can have an education and build your body — it's a blessing. When you have a wife who has been a tower of strength and shown more courage than you dreamed existed — that's the finest I know.

"So I close in saying that I might have had a bad break, but I have an awful lot to live for."

The crowd roared. He was done. Ruth stepped forward and wrapped an arm around him. Both men smiled as photographers snapped pictures, Ruth looking robust and positively kingly next to Gehrig's thin, pale frame.

The press box was crammed with sportswriters from around the country. The *Washington Post*'s Shirley Povich wrote that he "saw strong men weep" as Gehrig spoke. Charlie Segar, writing in the *New York Daily Mirror*, called it "the most touching scene ever enacted on a diamond." The *New York World-Telegram*'s Dan Daniel, who had covered Gehrig's entire career, said it was "a stirring testimonial which, in its manifestations of loyalty and appreciation and its emotional aspects, never before had been approached in the major leagues."

The *New York Herald Tribune*'s Richard Vidmer wrote that the scene honored "a truly great sportsman who could take his triumphs with sincere modesty and could face tragedy with a smile." Vidmer continued: "Gehrig was one of the greatest baseball players who ever lived but . . . stood for something finer . . . everything that makes sports important on the American scene."

Within two years, baseball's Ironman was dead.

18

Ironmen

IS IT REALLY A GOOD IDEA?

By playing for the Chicago Cubs against the Philadelphia Phillies on May 21, 1968, at Wrigley Field, outfielder Billy Williams ran his consecutive-game streak to 731 games. No major league outfielder had ever played in so many games in a row. Infielders such as Lou Gehrig, Everett Scott, Joe Sewell, and George Pinkney had dominated baseball's endurance tale until now.

The Phillies' Richie Ashburn had established a benchmark for outfielders with a run of 730 straight games in the 1950s, and in a coincidence, Ashburn was at Wrigley Field to see Williams pass him. Long retired from playing, he now worked as a Phillies broadcaster. "I didn't even know I had a record until I read a squib in the paper a few days ago," Ashburn said. "They didn't break endurance marks down by position when I played."

The game was halted when Williams came to bat in the bottom of the first. An announcement about his setting a record was made, and the meager matinee crowd of 4,442 fans applauded. Williams doffed his cap, stepped into the box, and tapped a weak ground ball to the pitcher.

After the game, Williams, a four-time All-Star at age 29, admitted having doubts about his habit of playing entire seasons without rest. "There's no doubt I'd get tired toward the end of a season. Then my hitting definitely would fall off," he said, referring to his experiences since 1963, when his streak began.

Actually, in 1965 and 1967, he hit higher in August and September than he did earlier in the season. He did fall off late in the season in 1966, hitting .221 in August and .250 in September, at the end of a campaign in which he hit .276 overall.

But regardless of what his statistics indicated, Williams clearly wondered whether he should play every day, mostly because his goal potentially conflicted with the team's goal. "Records like this, you don't get paid for them," Williams said. "You're paid for how you perform. And by trying to keep up the record, I not only could hurt myself, but also the ballclub. I think we have a real shot at the pennant this year, and I want to be strong in that September stretch when they need me."

Williams's comments raised fundamental questions about consecutive-game streaks. Was it really best for a player not to sit out at least a game or two every year? Would he perform better if he occasionally rested to recharge his batteries? Was he being selfish in seeking this odd form of individual glory? What was the point?

Seriously, what was the point?

Doubts about consecutive-game streaks had existed since they were deemed relevant and became recognized in the 1920s. Miller Huggins wanted to try other shortstops for several years before he ended Everett Scott's streak in 1925. Scott himself later wondered aloud why he cared about playing in so many games in a row. Babe Ruth mocked Gehrig for doing it. A Detroit columnist lambasted Gehrig for contriving to keep his streak going in 1934.

The underlying assumptions of the criticisms were (a) an Ironman streak was not important to a team's fortunes, and (b) the player probably would benefit from taking a day off.

The charge of irrelevance was difficult to refute. If you make headlines for hitting home runs, winning games on the mound, or achieving excellence in any of the game's many endeavors, you have improved your team's chances of winning. But the correlation between playing every day and winning is not obvious. You could go hitless for weeks while advancing a playing streak. Did your team benefit?

In Gehrig's case, given his offensive prowess, it was easily argued that the Yankees benefited from his playing every day for more than 14 years. Certainly, no player with similar power-hitting potential was going to come off the Yankees' bench and replace him.

Ripken faced searing criticism for continuing to play through prolonged batting slumps that, his critics believed, might have ended had he taken some days off. There is statistical evidence supporting the contention. Over his career, he hit .294 in June, .286 in July, .275 in August, and .262 in September and October, so his average dropped during the year. From that, one could conclude that he did tire and was not always at his best in the season's final weeks.

But Ripken staunchly believed the Orioles benefited from his presence every day, regardless of how he performed at the plate, and his managers and most of his teammates supported him. The case can be made that his Ironman streak was to the team's advantage.

Would occasional rest have made Ripken or Gehrig more productive? Who knows? The benefit of a day off is one of baseball's enduring mysteries. Many believe it helps. Players "definitely need an occasional break from the mental stress presented by the game," Tim McCarver said. But Ripken disagrees. "I never thought you could solve your problems by not playing," he said.

On August 10, 1963, the Orioles' Brooks Robinson had played in 462 straight games. It was the longest active streak in the majors. But his manager, Billy Hitchcock, gave him the night off against the Washington Senators. "I wasn't hitting. The thinking was, 'OK, sit out a game and watch; maybe you'll come back better,'" Robinson recalled years later.

He wound up entering the game as a pinch hitter in the eighth inning, and Hitchcock put him back in the lineup the next day and played him every day for another three weeks. Then, on September 2, Hitchcock held him out of the second game of a doubleheader in Boston, and he never got in, ending his streak at 483 games. That stood as the Orioles' franchise record until Ripken came along.

Robinson was hitting .259 when he sat out the game in Boston, and it was a brief respite, as he returned to the lineup the next day and played in every game for the rest of the season. His average dropped to .251 by the time the season was over, so sitting out a game did not help him at the plate.

"When you didn't play, the fact is, you still came to the park, put on the uniform, and took infield. You just didn't play. Big deal," Robinson said. "I mean, sometimes I would sit out a few games and come back just as horrible as I was before. But then there were other times when I sat out a game or two and came back totally refreshed."

Does a day off help?

"I don't know that anyone has the answer to that," Robinson said.

· · ·

As America moved from the buttoned-down 1950s into the psychedelic 1960s, baseball experienced a similarly seismic swing. It had undergone significant changes by the time Billy Williams began his playing streak. The major leagues had expanded from 16 to 20 teams. The regular season was eight games longer. Teams flew between cities when on the road. As of 1965, one team even played indoors, in a climate-controlled dome, on plastic grass. The Dodgers were in Los Angeles, the Giants in San Francisco. African American stars such as Hank Aaron, Ernie Banks, and Frank Robinson dominated the National League.

The challenge of playing a full season of games was no harder, but different. During his streak, Williams would play in California, Texas, Canada, and indoors. Gehrig never experienced any of that. A slender, circumspect African American from Whistler, Alabama, Williams would help fans grow more accustomed to seeing black players wearing major league uniforms.

His original deal with the Cubs, signed in 1956, contained no signing bonus, just a celebratory cigar for his father and guarantees of $150 a month and $2.25 a day for meals. On his rise through the minors, Williams briefly quit the game when several restaurant doors were slammed in his face in San Antonio, in 1959. But that year, he had the opportunity to play every day because his manager, Grady Hatton, a former major leaguer, did not believe in platoons. A left-handed hitter, Williams fared well against pitchers from both sides. By 1961, he was the Cubs' starting left fielder.

When he struggled early that season and was benched, "it gave me a chance to take stock, and I vowed that when I got back in the lineup, they would have to tear my uniform off to get me out again," Williams said for this book. He wound up hitting .278 with 25 home runs and 86 runs batted in, a performance that earned him the National League Rookie of the Year award.

The next year, he still had to stave off a half-dozen challengers in spring training to keep his job. The Cubs handed him nothing. "You had to be tough. There were always good players in the minors who were ready to take your job if you slipped. You didn't want to be the next Wally Pipp," Williams said. "The thinking was, 'If you take yourself out of the lineup, even just for a day, someone will take your job.'"

That was especially true for black players. Although baseball was becoming more open-minded, some teams used few black players, and others did not mind replacing them if the opportunity arose. Williams vowed not to give the Cubs that chance. He became a consistent contributor, dependable at the plate, solid in the field, an everyday presence. While sitting out just two games in 1962, he hit .298 with 22 homers and 92 runs batted in. In 1963, he missed one game.

The Cubs were also-rans. After making six World Series appearances between 1918 and 1945, all ending in defeat, they finished in the National League's second division for 15 straight seasons. In the 1950s, having the chance to watch Ernie Banks, their All-Star shortstop, was about the only benefit to rooting for them. For several seasons in the early 1960s, they tried using a rotation of "head coaches" rather than one manager, but they continued to lose.

The arrival of Williams, third baseman Ron Santo, and outfielder Lou Brock brought hope. Batting in front of Banks, Williams hit .312 with 33 home runs in 1964 while playing in every game. He was even better the next year. By the end of the 1965 season, he had played in 332 straight games.

Ironically, though his baseball era was marked by change, Williams was on the last major league team to play its home games during the day. The Cubs would not install lights at Wrigley Field until 1988. That meant Williams, like Gehrig, played mostly in midday heat, making his consecutive-game streak all the more impressive, Tim McCarver observed.

"It's a lot of games in a row, especially when you're playing during the day at Wrigley Field, as Billy did," said McCarver, who played dozens of games against Williams. "Everything after his era took place when night games became prevalent and guys were no longer playing in the heat of the day all the time. With Billy, you should probably tack on another 300 games to his number to get to the point of how difficult it was for him to do what he did."

In 1966, the Cubs hired Leo Durocher as their manager. "Leo the Lip" had previously managed the Dodgers and Giants in the 1940s and 1950s, becoming a controversial staple of the New York baseball scene. Earning a reputation as a loudmouth who stood up to authority, Durocher, now 61 years old, had been out of the majors for a decade but had lost none of his feistiness. "I'm not the manager of an eighth-place team," he said when the Cubs hired him. He was right. The Cubs finished 10th in 1966.

But as more young talent arrived, including catcher Randy Hundley, second baseman Glenn Beckert, and shortstop Don Kessinger, Durocher's Cubs improved. They won 87 games in 1967, with Durocher parceling out occasional rest to the regulars, especially Banks, now a first baseman with creaky knees.

Williams was the exception. By the end of the 1967 season, he had played in every game since September 22, 1963 — 656 straight.

"Players on other teams would come up and say, 'Man, why don't you get some rest?' They thought I was showing them up. They figured if I did it, they had to, too," Williams recalled. "There were plenty of days when I could have taken off, when I was tired or sore. But I wanted to be out there. Not many guys are wired that way. Most guys like a day off now and then. But a guy who never sits out, his mind is geared up for it, his body is geared up for it. If he's not out there, he's a miserable soul. That was me."

Durocher was impressed. "Billy Williams never gets excited. Never gets mad. Never throws a bat. You write his name down in the same spot every day and forget it. He will play left. He will bat third. Billy Williams is a machine," Durocher said.

The manager thought Williams's streak was important and vowed to keep it going after he broke Ashburn's record for outfielders in 1968. "Billy's got a good chance of topping Musial's [National League] record. I'll rest him occasionally, but when I do, I'll always have him go up and pinch-hit so he can keep his record going," Durocher said.

The Cubs' developing talent coalesced in 1969, producing the franchise's best team in years. They won 24 of their first 35 games to move into first place in the National League East — it was the first year of divisional play — and built a nine-game lead by June. A decade after the White Sox's pennant-winning season, the Cubs owned Chicago.

When the season began, Williams had played in 819 straight games, 76 short of Musial's record. His pursuit burbled in the background of the Cubs' triumphant season.

On June 13, the Cubs played the Reds on a Friday night in Cincinnati. Williams was 18 games shy of Musial. Batting in the top of the sixth, he swung at a high slider, chopping his bat down. The ball caromed awkwardly off his bat and hit his right instep. "One of the hardest balls I hit all season; it felt real bad," Williams said later.

Able to continue playing, he hobbled to the plate in the top of the ninth, took two pitches, and swung hard at a fastball, making contact. The ball soared over the infield and disappeared beyond the right-field fence. The Cubs erupted in their dugout, but Williams limped around the bases, returned to the dugout, and told Durocher, "Get me out of there." The next morning, he could barely walk.

Fortunately, a night game was scheduled, giving Williams all day to try to heal. A trainer applied a heat treatment and massage. Willie Smith, a reserve, took his place in the lineup, but Durocher wanted to keep Williams's streak going. So did Williams. He pinch-hit in the top of the sixth, drawing a walk. A pinch runner replaced him.

Williams's foot was still sore when the Cubs and Reds played a double-header on June 15. Another reserve replaced him in the lineup for the first game. Durocher planned on using the same strategy, letting Williams pinch-hit to keep the streak going. It almost backfired when rain began falling in the fourth inning with the Reds up, 3–0. Williams had not batted and remained on the bench as the Cubs went down in the top of the fifth. The game was official now. If it suddenly was called for rain, it would go into the books without Williams having played. But the rain stopped, and Williams hit with the bases loaded in the top of the sixth. He drew a walk, driving in a run, and was replaced by a pinch runner.

In the second game of the doubleheader, Williams again was out of the lineup, but he pinch-hit in the top of the sixth and drew a walk — his third walk in two days. The Cubs won, improving their best-in-baseball record to 41-19, and Williams was back in the lineup the next day for the start of a four-game series in Pittsburgh. He banged out seven hits in the four games. "Those days off seemed to help me," he said. "I might do it again if I start feeling tired."

First, he had to pass Musial. He was on schedule to do it on June 29, 1969, by playing in a doubleheader against the Cardinals. The Cubs organized a "Billy Williams Day" celebration. It was a sunny Sunday, and more than 41,000 fans, the largest crowd of the season, were in attendance to cheer on the first-place team and their durable left fielder. Another 10,000 fans reportedly were turned away. Williams had long subsisted in the shadow of Banks. Even Santo, a garrulous fan favorite, had a higher profile. But the quiet, dependable Williams finally was receiving his due.

The first game of the doubleheader was a scoreless duel for seven innings between a pair of future Hall of Fame pitchers, the Cubs' Ferguson Jenkins and the Cardinals' Bob Gibson. Williams started a rally in the bottom of the eighth, whacking a double down the right-field line. Banks singled him in, and Willie Smith followed with a two-run homer. The Cubs won.

When the game ended, a bank of microphones was set up by home plate. Williams had played in 895 straight games, tying Musial. Members of the Cubs' front office spoke. Williams was given a car, a boat, a puppy, and more. His high-school-sweetheart wife stood to his left, his mother to his right. When he stepped to the microphone, his soft voice was barely audible. "I want to thank the almighty God for giving me the ability to play major league baseball, and for protecting me over all these games I've played in," he said. The fans responded with a roar.

The second game was a rout. The Cubs scored four runs in the bottom of the first, as Williams singled and Banks hit a three-run homer. Williams went on to collect three more hits, giving him five for the day, and the Cubs completed the sweep. It was a great day to root for the Cubs, to play for the Cubs, to make history with the Cubs. They had an eight-game lead over the New York Mets, and their first trip to the postseason since World War II seemed certain. Meanwhile, Williams now owned the National League Ironman record. "What a beautiful day; it couldn't have been any better," he told reporters.

On August 16, the Cubs held a nine-game lead. But they started to slip, losing three in a row, then four in a row, while the Mets got hot. Their lead was down to five games in early September and disappeared entirely when they lost eight in a row. A glorious summer gave way to the grimmest of autumns. Durocher pulled every string imaginable. Nothing worked. The Mets pulled ahead, won the division, and went on to capture the World Series. The Cubs' 92-win total was their highest since 1945, but the season would be remembered only as a debacle, the year they completely collapsed.

Williams slumped down the stretch. He had spoken about possibly resting occasionally so he would feel fresher in September, but he was not going to sit out a game as the Cubs tried to save their season.

Early in 1970, he became the first National Leaguer to play in a thousand games in a row. It appeared his streak would not end soon. "By then, I wanted to keep it going," Williams recalled for this book. "I had never thought that much about it until I passed Ashburn. Then people started talking about Musial, and it got in the paper, and it got in my head, and you get where you want to do it. Once I had Stan's record, it was a matter of, 'Let's see how many games I can accumulate.'"

Seeking to bounce back from their 1969 disaster, the Cubs led their division for most of the first half of the season, until a 12-game losing streak sent them tumbling before the All-Star break. The Pirates passed them. So did the Mets. Williams kept them in the race almost by himself; he would end the season with 205 hits, 42 home runs, and 129 runs batted in, all career highs.

Durocher did not want to rest him. But in early August, with the Cubs on the road, the outfielder approached his manager. Always a man of few words, he said, "Leo, take me out."

Williams had gone as far as he could. "I was tired. It had become a struggle to do a lot of stuff," he recalled. "After you play in so many games, you might not go from first to third on a hit to right, or you might not catch up to a ball in the outfield, might be slow getting there. I wasn't playing at 100 percent. I figured with rest you could regenerate your body."

He asked out on August 6, after struggling during a series in Montreal. The Cubs traveled to Philadelphia, and Williams was out of the lineup on August 7. "Sometimes when I'm up at bat, I'm so bushed I feel like I've got nothing left," he told reporters when the lineup was posted before the game. "It's time for the streak to end. It's become too much of a big deal."

Reporters raced to the press box and filed stories about the streak ending at 1,092 straight games. Williams watched from the dugout as the Phillies built a lead and carried it into the late innings. But when the Cubs, trailing, 4–1, loaded the bases in the top of the ninth, Durocher sent Williams up to bat against a right-handed reliever. Williams lashed a pitch down the left-field line, foul by inches. He ended up striking out, and the Cubs lost, but his streak was alive.

That was enough rest, Durocher decided. The Cubs were in a pennant race. They needed him. Williams was back in the lineup the next day and stayed there. A little over a week later, he passed Joe Sewell's mark of 1,103 straight games, leaving only Gehrig and Scott ahead of him.

Inevitably, reporters asked about Gehrig. Could he go that far? He was 32 years old. To reach Gehrig, he would need to play almost seven more seasons without a break. The thought exhausted him. "When people started talking about Gehrig, I was like, 'No, I don't think I can do that,'" Williams recalled. "I had nowhere to go as far as another record."

In early September, the Cubs opened a three-game series against Philadelphia at home. They were closing in on first place, the stakes rising. But Williams went 0-for-6 in the first game, then 0-for-4 in the second. He was still hitting .317, but he "wasn't getting the bat around, wasn't performing at the plate," he said later. After the second game, he reiterated to Durocher that he would not mind missing a game.

The next day was September 4, a muggy late-summer afternoon in Chicago. When Williams arrived at the park, he was met at the clubhouse door by one of the Cubs' coaches, Joey Amalfitano. "Billy, Leo doesn't have you in the lineup," Amalfitano said gravely. "You can go home if you want. You don't have to be here for this."

Williams smiled. "No, I'm going to stay," he said.

He had been out of the lineup before, so it wasn't unusual for him to be in the dugout when Ferguson Jenkins tossed the first pitch at 1:30 p.m. But as the game unfolded, it became clear this day was different. The Cubs took the lead in the first. Jim Hickman hit a three-run homer. By the fifth, they had a 7–2 lead. "If we had been behind, I might have brought him in. But we weren't," Durocher said.

Williams moved around nervously, spent an inning in the bullpen, another in the clubhouse, and settled on the dugout bench. He had played in 1,117 straight games. "It is one of the most amazing individual feats in baseball history," one sportswriter had written. The fans at Wrigley Field were clued in to the situation. They started a chant in the seventh inning: "We want Billy!" Williams left the dugout for the clubhouse, vowing not to return. He flipped on a radio and listened to the final innings there.

"If I had stayed on the bench, I would have started thinking about maybe getting in there," he said.

Jenkins was due to bat in the bottom of the eighth, an ideal situation for Williams to hit. Durocher did not flinch. Jenkins struck out and then retired the Phillies in order in the top of the ninth. The last out was a ground ball to Kessinger, the shortstop. When his throw nestled in Banks's glove at first, the game was over, and so was Williams's streak.

"I have mixed emotions right now, part relief and part sadness," Williams told reporters. "But all I know is that if I start a new streak tomorrow, I want it to include some World Series games."

The Mets were coming to Chicago for a crucial series, part of Williams's rationale for ending the streak when he did. He wanted to focus on helping the Cubs get to the postseason and thought he might play better if he no longer had to think about the streak. "It just seemed like the right time," he said.

His strategy worked. He had two hits the next day and two more the day after that. Ending the streak seemed to energize him as the Cubs battled the Mets and Pirates for the division title.

But the Cubs faltered, losing three in a row, then four of five, and ended up in third place, out of the postseason for the 26th straight year. Williams finished second in the National League MVP voting.

Williams would play four more years for the Cubs, appearing in over 90 percent of the team's games, and then finish his career by switching leagues and playing for the Oakland A's for two seasons. In 1973, when his batting average dropped below .300 for the first time in four years, Williams was asked by *Chicago Sun-Times* sportswriter Edgar Munzel if he possibly had worn himself out by playing in every game for almost seven years.

"I don't really know," Williams replied. "But I'm certain of one thing. If I had it to do over again, I'd never get involved in it. When you get into an endurance streak like that, you go out there and play many days when you're hurt or not feeling well. And that does take something extra out of you."

Few players grasp the complex nature of a consecutive-game streak better than Dale Murphy, who fashioned a long streak while playing for the Atlanta Braves in the 1980s.

A slender, long-necked outfielder with a boyish grin, long dark locks, and a devastating right-handed batting stroke, he won the National League Most Valuable Player award in 1982 and 1983, then went on to hit 36 home runs in 1984 and 37 in 1985. By July 1986, he had the longest active consecutive-game streak in the majors, having played in more than 700 games in a row. Murphy was proud of the streak, but now he was in a horrid slump at the plate, feeling frustrated and frazzled. Murphy thought it might help to take a day off, just sit and watch, hopefully clear his head. But that would end his streak.

Murphy was a team leader, but Ted Simmons, the Braves' 37-year-old catcher, was higher up the chain of clubhouse elders. Though now a backup, Simmons had played in the major leagues since the 1960s and could offer counsel on just about any subject. Aware that Murphy was feeling conflicted, he approached the younger star in the clubhouse before a game.

"Let's have a heart-to-heart," Simmons said.

They found a quiet place to talk. "So, you've got a streak going. What's it mean to you?" Simmons asked. "If it means something to you, keep going. But if not, well, what are you feeling about it?"

Murphy paused. "I think I need a day off," he finally said.

He had not missed a game in almost five years, since September 25, 1981. For most of that time, he had abhorred the idea of taking a day off.

"I was young and healthy and wanted to be out there," Murphy recalled for this book. "This was baseball, a sport that, let's face it, isn't that physically taxing. A guy in his mid-20s, even his mid-30s, you should be able to go out there and play every day. Yeah, the travel is a bit of a challenge, but come on, you're flying on chartered planes, sleeping in the best hotels. Maybe the time-zone changes get you a little out of whack at times, but you can handle it."

He cared about his streak, making sure — with cooperation from his managers — to get into games on the rare occasions when he did not start. On August 19, 1982, he pinch-hit in the eighth inning. On July 20, 1983, he went in as a defensive replacement in the ninth. On May 22, 1985, he pinch-hit again late in the game.

Earlier in 1986, he had cut his right hand while trying to make a catch against the outfield wall. It took nine stitches to close the wound, and Murphy feared his streak was over. But taking batting practice the next day, he found the stitches did not keep him from swinging the bat normally. The Braves' manager, Chuck Tanner, kept him out of the lineup but used him to pinch-hit in the fifth. Murphy whacked a home run off the New York Mets' ace, Dwight Gooden.

But as his streak grew, Murphy began to notice he was struggling to stay fresh mentally. "Playing a full season is hard that way," he recalled. "It's a game of confidence, being mentally sharp at the plate and just as sharp in the field, and in a season so long, with so much failure bred into it, it's inevitable that there are times your confidence flags and you aren't as sharp; times when you say, 'Hey, I'm a little lost.' That's the honest truth. Sometimes it's hard to say, 'Hey, let's go get 'em.'"

He had observed St. Louis's manager, Whitey Herzog, resting certain Cardinals on Sundays before an off day on Monday and night game on Tuesday, effectively giving the players three straight days off. "It was almost like a mini–All-Star break for them," Murphy recalled. He was envious.

By the time Murphy and Simmons had their heart-to-heart talk in 1986, Murphy's streak was the 11th longest in major league history. Simmons advised him to tell Tanner that he wanted to sit one out.

"Your streak is long enough that whoever is managing you is not going to say, 'Hey, you're taking a day off.' You've got to be the guy to make the decision," Simmons said.

Murphy went to Tanner and said he was ready to sit out a game.

"Let's do it," Tanner said.

On July 9, 1986, Murphy watched from the dugout as the Braves scored a 7–3 win over the Phillies in Philadelphia. Tanner gave no thought to inserting him as a pinch hitter or defensive replacement. Murphy's streak ended at 740 games.

"It was a nice thing but not something I wanted to maintain," Murphy told reporters. "Now it's over with. It's better not to have it hanging over my head. It's better for the team. The streak was always on my mind."

Initially, he resumed his everyday habit, playing in 174 straight games after his night off. But for the rest of his career after that (he played until 1993 with the Braves, Phillies, and Rockies), he sat out a handful of games every year, becoming a proponent of the benefits of rest. He no longer believed in playing every day. It was not practical, he felt. A player needs a break now and then.

"When you get a day off, you get to just check out mentally for a day, relax, watch the other guys play, talk to someone about your swing, maybe take extra batting practice. It's amazing how you feel refreshed physically from getting the mental day off," Murphy recalled. "Since you're refreshed mentally, you're ready to go. You come back from that and you could go on a tear for two weeks. That's when a day off can help you."

Murphy actually performed better when playing without interruption. He hit 38 points higher during his streak than over the rest of his career, when he took breaks. Yet Murphy has no doubt, looking back, that he was right to end his streak when he did. He does not care what his statistics indicate.

"I had to end it. I was really struggling mentally. It was the right thing. It took a weight off," he said. "I came back and didn't take a lot of days off, but for the rest of my career, my managers had control of when I played, and that seemed smart. And I used the days off to get refreshed. I can't even imagine going on as long as Cal did. I don't know how he did it, or how Lou Gehrig did."

Six days after he ended his streak, Murphy represented the Braves at the 1986 All Star Game at the Astrodome in Houston. On the field before the game, he ran into Ripken.

"Hey, I see you ended your streak," Ripken said.

"Yeah," Murphy replied. "I just felt like I had to get out of there for my own sanity, for the good of the team."

Ripken nodded. He now owned the longest streak in the majors, more than 600 games in a row, but unlike Murphy, the Orioles' young shortstop was just getting started.

As Ripken's streak grew in the 1990s, Murphy watched with mixed emotions. They had started their streaks within months of each other in 1981 and 1982. Murphy could hardly believe Ripken was still going almost a decade later. "It's really unfathomable, what he did, and what Gehrig did," Murphy recalled.

But he cited what he believed was an important drawback. "When a streak becomes a big deal, the player can keep going for as long as he wants; he alone gets to decide when it ends. I know that from experience. That was my story. And that's messy," he said. "A manager should always have full control of his players, writing out the lineup, deciding who gets to play."

Also, Murphy said, a player's performance inevitably suffers if he plays every day for too long. He is firmly in the camp of believing players benefit from resting occasionally during a season.

"It's such an admirable thing that you hate to say anything other than positive things," Murphy said of Ripken's streak. "But the inside story is a little different. A consecutive-game streak is a paradox. You want to celebrate it, and it's great, but it has its costs. Everything about it isn't positive. It's a thing that has pros and cons."

19

Ripken

MAKING HISTORY

Several dozen reporters awaited Ripken when he arrived at the Orioles' spring training camp in Sarasota, Florida, in early April 1995. In the wake of a ruinous work stoppage, with Gehrig's record in sight, his streak was one of baseball's few positive stories.

At a press conference in a packed room, Ripken stepped to the podium, cleared his throat, and said, "I'm here to announce I'm retiring from baseball to pursue a career in the NBA." Laughter filled the room. A year earlier, basketball star Michael Jordan had retired at his peak to play pro baseball.

Ripken's playfulness reflected his altered view of his pending achievement. He had long felt defensive about the streak, but now he sensed support from all parties — the media, fans, opponents. It seemed everyone wanted to see him break the record.

He was optimistic that it would happen in a good year for the Orioles, who were coming off their most successful season in a decade — 63-49 before the strike — and had their core returning. But inexplicably, Angelos had fired Oates, the team's most successful manager since Earl Weaver, creating a sense of unease.

The new manager, Phil Regan, was a former major league pitcher whose baseball career dated to the 1950s. Though he had waited almost four decades for the chance to manage a big league club, he was knowledgeable, seemingly a solid hire. But he had never been around the Orioles or their players, and it was the wrong year to introduce a new man with new ideas. A shortened spring training gave teams less time to prepare for the regular season and fewer exhibition games. The Orioles, in the midst of a search for a permanent spring training home, rented a facility unequipped to host games, leaving them scrambling.

"We had five days of practice and maybe a dozen exhibition games, all on the road, before the season started. We were on a bus every morning in Florida," Regan recalled for this book, chuckling at the memory. "At a couple of places in Florida, they gave us a field for an hour before a game so we could practice bunt plays and relays. We didn't get much practice in, and the season kind of went from there."

The Orioles opened with three straight defeats and did not climb back to .500 until the season was more than half over and they were well back in the division standings. Regan bristled as his team struggled; his genial nature masked an intense competitive streak. He would last just one year on the job and often felt like an outsider. It took him several weeks, for example, to discover that Ripken occasionally called pitches for the Orioles' younger starters.

"I called in a catcher one day after a game and said, 'What were you thinking with that pitch?'" Regan recalled. "The catcher said, 'I didn't call it; Cal did.' My response was, 'He did?' The catcher told me, 'He doesn't call them all; maybe 15 or 20 a game.' I called Cal in and he said, 'I heard you were a little mad.' I wasn't mad, just wanted to know if [I could help in any way]. He kept doing it, and he called the plays in the infield, too. He was like a coach on the field."

Overall, Ripken, Regan recalled, was "one of the easiest guys to manage. He was always engaged. You never had to ask how he felt."

But while managing Ripken in 1995 was not stressful for Regan, it was a unique circumstance. As Ripken crept closer to Gehrig's record, so many reporters clamored for interviews that John Maroon, the Orioles' director of public relations, was compelled to devise a system. Ripken conducted a group interview in the dugout before the first game of every road series. Then he was off-limits for the rest of the series.

"It was a media crush that just went on and on. It was a lot of pressure on Cal. I thought he handled it well," Regan said.

An even greater obligation was the memorabilia requests from opponents who wanted Ripken to sign balls, bats, and other items — a form of professional courtesy common in the major leagues. As Ripken neared Gehrig's record, he was inundated.

"It could be a thousand items per series. Cal had said he would sign anything, and people took him at his word," Regan said. "We would wait until the last game of the series was over so all the requests were in, and then he would sit and sign. We would hold the bus [to the airport] until he was done. This happened all season."

Though his days were long, Ripken did not crumble under the burden, Regan said. To the contrary, Regan recalled him maintaining almost a childlike exuberance.

"Early in the season, we had an afternoon game at Tiger Stadium in Detroit, finished it, and then he and four or five guys went back out to the field for a pickup game," Regan recalled. "I asked Cal if he wanted us to hold the bus. He said, 'No, you go on ahead.' I think Brady [Anderson] went out there with him, maybe Mussina. They just wanted to play. You don't see that kind of thing anymore. Cal was like a guy from my day who just loved being around the game."

(What actually happened, Ripken said two decades later, was either he wanted to hit balls off a tee on a field as opposed to in a batting cage, or he and several teammates wanted to run sprints on the field. "Could be a combination," Ripken said. "I wish I could say we were playing a pickup game.")

It was not Regan's first experience with a record-setting Ironman. He had played with Billy Williams on the Chicago Cubs from 1968 through 1972, the period that included the years when Williams approached and passed Stan Musial's National League consecutive-game record and went on to play in 1,117 straight games.

Regan saw Williams and Ripken as similar. "Both were very easygoing, quiet, never really got upset about anything, but most of all, they just loved to play," he said. "I think that's what kept them going out there day after day. It's like when you were a kid in the backyard. You didn't think about fans or statistics or uniforms; you just had fun playing. Cal and Billy still had that mindset. Really, those guys were exactly the same that way."

The Orioles' season evolved into a valedictory tour for Ripken. At home and on the road, he was serenaded with applause and cheers, and signed autographs, sometimes for several hours, after the final pitch. One night in Minnesota, he was still signing at midnight as a line of fans snaked up an aisle in the lower deck.

No longer was there talk of Ripken's possibly undermining the Orioles' playoff chances by playing every day. The "take a day off" chorus had been silenced, partly due to the public's excitement over his pursuit of Gehrig's record, and also because Ripken played well enough in 1995 to quell the thought before it gained momentum. His average hovered around .290 and occasionally spiked over .300. In early June, he cracked a grand slam. In late July, he hit two home runs in a game. His strong defense continued. Though now in his mid-30s, Ripken would lead the American League's shortstops in fielding percentage for the fourth time in 1995.

On August 9, he drove a pitch over the left-field wall at Yankee Stadium, where so much of Gehrig's career had unfolded. The ball landed near the plaque honoring Gehrig in the Yankees' Monument Park, beyond the fence. It was almost as if Ripken were tipping his cap to the Iron Horse, dead now for 54 years. New York's savvy fans stood and cheered Ripken as he rounded the bases. Ripken later said the ovation gave him chills.

As much as he wanted to avoid being compared to Gehrig, he knew it was inevitable. As he crept closer to the record, *Sports Illustrated Kids* put Ripken and Gehrig together on its cover, photoshopping a smiling image of Ripken with his arm around Gehrig, as if they were pals. James Fiorentino, a young painting prodigy whose work was displayed at the Hall of Fame, produced a lithograph combining images of the two players. John Steadman, a sports columnist for the *Baltimore Sun,* wrote that Ripken and Gehrig "have a kinship that makes them baseball blood brothers for as long as the game is played."

The comparison was apt in many ways. Ripken and Gehrig were both known for their no-nonsense professionalism and played only for their hometown teams. They had quiet competitive streaks and tempers that occasionally boiled over, and preferred letting their play do the talking.

But while they played the same sport, largely by the same rules, they had inhabited baseball worlds that were different in fundamental ways. Thus their streaks were different. Was one somehow more substantial, a more significant achievement? The question became a quintessential barstool debate subject as Ripken approached Gehrig's record. One could hold their streaks up to the light for comparison using various metrics.

Schedule

The major league season was eight games shorter for Gehrig, but Ripken shrugged that off as a meaningful difference. "You're playing half the year straight through either way," he said. The truly meaningful difference regarding their schedules, Ripken said, was that Gehrig played only during the day, while Ripken mixed day and night games. (The first American League night game took place on May 16, 1939, weeks after Gehrig's streak ended.)

According to Ripken, Gehrig benefited from the unvarying routine. No matter if it was a weekday or weekend, or if he played at home or on the road, he got up, ate breakfast, went to the ballpark, played in the afternoon, came home, ate dinner, went to bed, and did it all again the next day. Ripken, on the other hand, played games that started anywhere from noon to 8:30 p.m. to suit television.

"That was the hardest part for me," Ripken said. "The schedule's roller-coaster nature, combined with travel, plays with your ability to feel good and play. You have 12:15 games, night games, Sunday night games, get-away games, Saturday day games, Saturday night games. So your body is up and down, up and down. To me, that's the biggest obstacle to playing a lot of games in a row now, the erratic nature of the schedule."

The perfect schedule for an Ironman, Ripken said, is "all night games or all day games. Then it's a routine. When you're in a routine, you train your body to get up at a certain time, eat at a certain time, and it responds."

Media Pressure

When Gehrig played, newspaper coverage dominated the lens through which the public viewed the game. Though the Yankees were immensely popular and covered by as many as a dozen beat writers, the coverage was not nearly as intense as it would become decades later, and much of it was supportive. Gehrig read relatively few discouraging words.

Newspaper coverage was still important during Ripken's career, most of which preceded the Internet, but the coverage was more questioning and at times sarcastic, making for fiercer scrutiny. Cable television and radio talk shows also had become an intrinsic part of the national baseball conversation, adding to the breadth — and volume — of the chatter accompanying the game.

Though Ripken became accustomed to hearing he needed a day off and was selfish to keep going, it created a mosquito-like buzz in his ear that he could not swat away. "I had to cope with everyone saying I was specifically chasing the record, which in my mind was never the case," Ripken said. "The scrutiny was of a different flavor [for Gehrig]. It seemed like the press was more of an ally with the team. The reporters and players all traveled together and kept secret whatever they did the night before, even when it might affect a player's ability to perform. It was just more of a partnership."

Field Surfaces

Gehrig played only on natural grass, the most forgiving surface, while Ripken played hundreds of games on artificial turf in domes and dual-purpose (football-baseball) stadiums built in the 1960s and 1970s — stadiums that were later replaced partly because their fields were little more than a thin layer of carpet over concrete.

In a 1992 University of Iowa study, AstroTurf, an early artificial surface constructed of nylon, was shown to cause more knee injuries, sore muscles, concussions, sprained ankles, and turf burns in pro football players than natural grass. Baseball players experienced similar problems. "Artificial turf shortened a lot of careers," Steve Garvey said. "That's the prime reason why guys like me have two replaced hips, because of the pounding that we took playing on AstroTurf, which started at the beginning of my career."

Playing on artificial surfaces certainly did not make Ripken's life easier, especially when he dealt with back trouble late in his career. Playing on those surfaces could have exacerbated Gehrig's chronic lumbago in much the same way. He was fortunate to have avoided that version of "progress."

Positional Demands

Ripken played the majority of his streak at shortstop, one of the game's most physically challenging and dangerous positions, where collisions are common. But he does not believe he endured a greater injury threat than Gehrig, who played first base, a position supposedly less challenging. "I could make the case that first base is more demanding than shortstop," Ripken said. "You've got a runner coming to first on every ground ball that is a potential collision. You've got throws up the line, throws that are high. Yes, at shortstop you have guys coming in to break up double plays, but I would argue that between my size and having the runner in front of me, I was protected. Meanwhile, you're in every play at first base. It has its own demands, maybe more. I see it as a wash."

Streak Integrity

Ripken started every game of his streak with the intention of playing nine innings. Unlike every other modern player who forged a long streak, he never used a pinch-hitting appearance or late-game defensive stint to keep his run going.

Gehrig and his managers, meanwhile, undertook contortions to keep his streak going on several occasions. He barely played in a handful of games, most notably in Detroit on July 14, 1934, when he led off the game, singled, and came out. In a 1975 paper, Raymond J. Gonzalez, a member of the Society for American Baseball Research, reported that Gehrig "was relieved by a pinch hitter eight times, by a pinch runner four times, and at first base 64 times" during his streak.

But though Ripken's streak was purer in that sense, one can argue that playing Gehrig every day made more sense. He averaged 58 more runs batted in per season than Ripken. His career batting average was 64 points higher. His bat was so vital to the Yankees that they *needed* him every day. Ripken's defense, power, and general dependability also made him essential, but it can be argued, at least, that a day off now and then might have helped him during his protracted slumps.

Travel

Although Ripken and Gehrig both traveled to half of their teams' games every year, their road lives were vastly different.

Gehrig traveled only on trains, and though the accommodations were luxurious by that era's standards, with the players holed up in private cars, removed from the public, trips took many more hours than they would when teams began flying between cities several decades later. Early in his career, Gehrig spent many nights in cramped sleeper cars that were not air-conditioned. Gehrig also never went west or south of St. Louis due to the limited geography of the major leagues in his era. He played in just two time zones.

By the time Ripken came along, baseball had experienced several rounds of expansion, altering its geography, and the nature of travel had changed. Ripken played on the West Coast and in Texas, the upper Midwest, and Canada. He traveled strictly by plane, taking commercial flights early in his career, then charters later. The living was good, especially on charters, which could feature gourmet meals and unlimited drinks, depending on a team's rules.

Which travel era provided a better platform for playing in every game for more than a decade? Steve Garvey, an independent arbiter in the case of Ripken v. Gehrig, laughed at the idea of a comparison of *any* kind.

"To measure one streak against the other is complicated and, frankly, an exercise that's never going to have a firm conclusion," Garvey said for this book. "I mean, travel, facilities, surfaces, game times — everything is different. Gloves were a lot smaller when Gehrig played. You can go on and on. I prefer what you can say definitively, that both were the only ones to do it within their era. Whatever circumstances each faced, it was hard to play in that many games, a huge challenge, and no one else came anywhere close to doing it for as long as they did."

Ripken's streak reached 2,100 consecutive games on August 5, leaving him just 30 away from Gehrig. Angelos wanted to fire Regan after the Orioles' disappointing season reached a nadir with four straight losses in Boston, but the owner held off, thinking a change would detract from the streak celebration soon to occur. Ripken's record had become the team's priority.

After playing 10 games on the West Coast in late August, the Orioles flew home for the nine-game homestand that would contain the record-tying and record-breaking games. The front office wrestled with how to commemorate the achievement on those nights, even asking Ripken, who admitted he was stumped. "I just go out and play a game. How do you celebrate that?" he said.

Several brainstorming sessions produced a plan. After the top of the fifth inning of every game of the homestand, a summary of the rule declaring the game official would appear on Camden Yards' giant video board, accompanied by "Day One," a soaring pop instrumental by composer John Tesh. When the music built to a crescendo, four 10-foot-high, orange-and-black banners, aligned on the B&O Warehouse overlooking the park, would unfurl, revealing the streak's latest number now that the game was official.

The scene debuted during the first game of the homestand, on August 29. As Ripken took the field in the bottom of the fifth, "Day One" played and the "official game" rule appeared on the scoreboard, stating that "a game is official and all stats count when a) the trailing team has batted five times, or b) the score is tied after five innings." The music built to a crescendo, and the banners on the warehouse unfurled, revealing the number "2,123." That was how many consecutive games Ripken had now played in.

The fans had little reaction that night, but they caught on quickly. By the third game of the homestand, they were standing and cheering throughout the fifth-inning commemoration, sending a palpable emotional charge through the ballpark.

The streak reached 2,128 games on September 3, a sunny Sunday afternoon, with the Orioles playing the finale of a weekend series against the Seattle Mariners. As the game began, Ripken lightheartedly raced Brady Anderson onto the field, then made the first putout of the game, ranging back and to his right to catch a pop-up down the left-field line. In the bottom of the first, he batted with one out and runners on first and second, worked the count full, and fouled off three pitches. On the 10th pitch of the at-bat, he singled to right-center, driving in his 67th run of the season.

In the top of the second, he charged onto the infield grass for a slow roller, grabbed the ball, and flipped it to Rafael Palmeiro, the Orioles' first baseman, in time to beat the runner. In the bottom of the inning, he grounded out with two runners in scoring position. As the game continued, Ripken grounded out to first, grabbed a hard-hit bouncer and started a double play, flied out to center, and singled in another run. Though it was just a typical day of ups and downs, everyone in the ballpark, including the players, knew they were witnessing history. The Mariners stood on the top step of their dugout and applauded along with the fans when the game became official in the middle of the fifth inning.

"There's a lot of power in that moment," Ripken said after the game. "I'm appreciative, but I don't know what to do. I become lost on the field. You stand there and start reflecting on your career. It's hard not to get teary-eyed."

Though they would miss the record-tying and record-breaking games, the Mariners were excited they had participated in the final buildup. "I'm so glad we were here to see his. I get goose bumps during that ceremony," Seattle infielder Rich Amaral said. "What Cal has done is amazing. We all have so much respect for him."

At the end of the day, Ripken spoke to reporters before heading off to another photo shoot. His stat line: two singles, two runs batted in, two putouts, and six assists in a 9–6 loss.

"How are you holding up?" a reporter asked.

He had batted close to .400 over the past week and was averaging almost one run batted in per game over the past month.

"I think I'm doing OK," he said with a smile.

Speaking to the media before the series finale against Seattle, Regan inadvertently caused a stir. During a discussion about what happens to players as they age, he noted that Alan Trammell, the Detroit Tigers' All-Star shortstop, played less now that his career was winding down. Ripken, two years younger than Trammell, eventually would benefit from that, Regan said.

"I think as Cal goes on, it would help him to take a day off. Not before the sixth [of September], though," Regan said.

Several media outlets reported that Regan had implied Ripken would get a day off soon, which prompted newspaper headlines, which set off the radio talk shows. Regan was eviscerated for daring to suggest he had any say in Ripken's feat.

Exasperated, Regan explained the next day that he had meant Ripken would surely get a day off *eventually*, not now.

"I didn't say I'm going to give Cal a day off," he said. "I'm not going to sit him down unless, like Lou Gehrig, Cal decides he needs a day off."

The lesson of the incident was that the streak belonged to Ripken. He alone would decide when it ended.

As Ripken pulled within one game of Gehrig's record during an afternoon game against the California Angels before 42,149 fans on September 4, a propeller plane flew over Camden Yards pulling a banner that read GOD BLESS CAL. It was Labor Day, certainly the right holiday to celebrate, given the circumstances.

The crowd demanded a curtain call after Ripken hit a home run in the third, and the ovations continued for each of his at-bats. In the seventh, a rookie reliever for the Angels, Troy Percival, tossed a 95 mph fastball inside, sending Ripken sprawling to avoid getting hit. Ripken stood up and dusted himself off, his irritation evident as boos rained down. He swung hard at Percival's next pitch and made contact, hoping to exact revenge, but the ball flew to left for a routine out.

His history-making moment arrived the next night. Scalpers were asking $1,500 for the best seats to consecutive-game No. 2,130. Supplemental box seats funding ALS research went for $5,000. Stores and kiosks around the ballpark sold Ripken memorabilia. In the home clubhouse, players filmed the pregame scene with camcorders and begged Regan for the chance to play and appear in a box score destined for the Hall of Fame.

Though Ripken spent the night on the field, playing shortstop, he was surrounded by family and friends. His parents watched from a private box overlooking the field. His wife and children were in front-row seats by the Orioles' dugout, alongside his brother Bill, who now played for the Buffalo Bisons, the Cleveland Indians' Triple A affiliate. The Bisons were letting Bill miss a playoff game so he could see his brother make history. "I asked some [Buffalo] teammates if they minded whether I went, and they all said, 'You're crazy not to be in Baltimore,'" Bill recalled. "It was weird to have a ticket and walk through the front gate, but once I did, you knew something special was happening."

Ben McDonald, Ripken's Orioles teammate, also had needed special permission to witness the game in person. He had missed the past several months with a shoulder injury, and now that it was improved, the team wanted to send him on a rehab assignment to Rochester, New York, where the Orioles' Triple A affiliate played. McDonald could pitch there as a prelude to returning to the Orioles, the thinking went. But he balked.

"When Phil Regan called me in and told me that was the plan, I said, 'Are you serious? I'm going to miss the biggest record-breaking moment in the history of baseball? For a rehab assignment? When we're 20 games out?'" McDonald recalled. "I told Phil, 'I'm not going. You can kick me off the team, but I'm not going.' He thought about it for a second and said, 'OK, you can go next week.' If we'd been one game out, I would've gone, no problem. But we were 20 out. So I got to stay and be there."

The Orioles hoped to celebrate the occasion by putting on a show . . . and they did. Leading off the bottom of the second, catcher Chris Hoiles hit a home run. One out later, third baseman Jeff Manto also hit a ball over the fence. The two batters who followed Manto, Mark Smith and Brady Anderson, *also* hit homers, giving the Orioles three in a row and four in the inning.

One of the Orioles' best pitchers, Scott Erickson, took a 7–0 lead into the top of the fifth. The fans stood in anticipation as Erickson retired the Angels in order. When a soft fly to center nestled in Anderson's glove for the third out, the game was official, Ripken had tied Gehrig, and the fans loosed a roar.

Ripken jogged toward the dugout with a purposeful expression but smiled when his teammates swarmed him on the top step. A flurry of images of Ripken and Gehrig flashed on the video board. Emerging from the home dugout, Ripken waved his arms, mouthed the words "thank you," and lifted his gaze to the private boxes overlooking the field. He located Senior, who was back at Camden Yards for the first time since the Orioles fired him three years earlier. Ripken acknowledged his father with a wave, and Senior waved back.

"Day One" built to a crescendo, and the banners on the warehouse dropped, leaving the number Gehrig had made famous — 2,130 — standing 10 feet high. The cheers continued, prompting Ripken to take a second curtain call, then a third. Al Clark, the home-plate umpire, tried to restart the game several times but gave up. This was an important moment for baseball, Clark thought, especially after the strike the year before. Rather than end the moment, he let it play out.

After a 10-minute delay, the game resumed. An inning later, Ripken led off the bottom of the sixth. He took a strike, then a ball. The Angels' pitcher, Mark Holzemer, hurled a fastball over the plate. Ripken swung and connected, launching a drive that soared over the infield and the outfield, then cleared the left-field wall. As more roars echoed, Ripken practically sprinted around the bases. "I'm not in the business of screenwriting, but if I were, this would have been a pretty good one," he said later.

Following the game, which the Orioles won, 8–0, there was a ceremony on the field. Ripken received gifts and testimonials from sports and entertainment figures such as Johnny Unitas, the Baltimore Colts' legendary quarterback; Hank Aaron, baseball's all-time home run king; Gary Williams, the men's basketball coach at the University of Maryland; actor Tom Selleck; Bonnie Blair, an Olympic gold medalist in speed skating; pro basketball star David Robinson; and rock star Joan Jett, a Maryland native and avid Orioles fan.

One gift touched Ripken deeply. When his streak began on May 30, 1982, and the Orioles lost to the Angels, Jim Gott, a tall rookie right-hander for the Angels, recorded his first major league win. Gott kept a ball from that game, and now, more than 13 years later, Ripken was stunned when Gott walked onto the field at Camden Yards and gave Ripken the ball commemorating Gott's first win but also the beginning of Ripken's streak.

"You don't have to do this," Ripken told him, but Gott, still pitching in the majors at age 36, took the microphone and told the crowd it was an honor just to be part of the streak.

After the ceremony, Ripken met with the media and said he felt "a little easing of the pressure" now that he had equaled Gehrig. He did not leave for home until after 2 a.m. and was back up within hours to take his daughter to her first day of first grade. It had been a joke in their family that Rachel and her father both had important events planned for September 6.

That morning, a proclamation honoring Ripken was read on the floor of the U.S. House of Representatives. Secret Service agents swarmed

Camden Yards when Ripken arrived in the afternoon. President Bill Clinton and Vice President Al Gore both were coming to watch the game. If Ripken had never grasped how much his achievement meant to the public, he surely did now.

Clinton and Gore went to the Orioles' clubhouse upon their arrival at the ballpark. Ripken visited with them, then headed out to the field for batting practice. As a sunny late afternoon became a clear-blue early evening, musicians Bruce Hornsby and Branford Marsalis performed a wordless national anthem that bordered on a jazz riff. The historic game began.

The Orioles trailed, 1–0, when Ripken batted for the first time in the bottom of the second. He acknowledged the fans' ovation, stepped into the batter's box against California's starter, Shawn Boskie, and popped out. When he batted again two innings later, Bobby Bonilla had just hit a home run to give the Orioles a 2–1 lead. Boskie, seemingly rattled, threw Ripken three straight balls, then left a fastball over the plate. Ripken swung and connected. The ball soared above the infield. California's left fielder, Garret Anderson, began to sprint back, then stopped chasing it. The ball cleared the wall and landed 10 rows into the outfield seats. For the second straight night, Ripken had cracked a home run on a history-making occasion.

Noise swirled as he circled the bases. Television cameras caught Clinton with a wry grin, as if he could not believe what he had just witnessed. "I nailed that pitch, and what a thrill that was. Going out in style, so to speak; that was extra sweet, no doubt about it," Ripken later wrote.

After Boskie retired the next three batters to end the inning, the Orioles' starter, Mike Mussina, took the mound for the top of the fifth. The first California batter, Rex Hudler, hit a soft line drive to left that was caught. The second batter, Jorge Fabregas, was out on a routine ground ball to second. That brought outfielder Damion Easley to the plate. On a 3-1 pitch, Easley swung at a breaking ball and lifted a pop to short right field. The Orioles' second baseman, Manny Alexander, drifted under it, waited, and snagged it.

The game was official. Ripken owned the consecutive-game record.

As he jogged toward the dugout, the now-familiar mid-game ceremony began. "Day One" played. The appearance rule went up on the video board. The banners on the warehouse dropped, revealing the number "2,131." Thousands of flashbulbs popped. An Orioles intern, Kristen Schultz, released hundreds of orange and black balloons, which flew into the night. Schultz would eventually become the team's director of community relations and promotions, never forgetting her small role in the historic event.

The fans stood, cheered, and did not stop. Ripken emerged from the dugout, waved, walked over to his family in the front row, pulled off his jersey, and handed it to them. He kissed his daughter, picked up his son, and shook hands with his brother. Behind him, the Angels took the field for the bottom of the fifth, and Boskie threw his requisite warm-up pitches, thinking the game might soon resume. But it did not.

Ripken continued to wave and tap his chest, letting the fans know he was touched. When he returned to the dugout, the crowd continued to roar. Ripken came back out on the field for a curtain call, and still the noise continued. A few minutes later, Bonilla and Palmeiro pulled him out of the dugout and pushed him down the right-field line. His lap around the ballpark began.

The entire sport had stopped to cheer Ripken. ESPN's broadcast from Baltimore was intermittently shown on video boards in other major league ballparks. In Arlington, Texas, where the Texas Rangers played the Chicago White Sox, "they would cut in, and when he had the record and went on the lap, everyone kind of stopped to watch and appreciate what they were witnessing," recalled Mickey Tettleton, who played for the Rangers.

Johnny Oates, who had been hired as the Rangers' manager within weeks of being fired by the Orioles, found himself on the verge of tears as he watched the scene in Baltimore on a video board halfway across the country. "I had played catch with Junior when he was a six-year-old with a runny nose and Senior was my manager in the Instructional League," Oates later recalled. "I probably never would have made it to the major leagues as a player without that family. Watching Junior on the video board that night, I got very emotional. But then, I think a lot of people did."

Rex Hudler could barely believe he was on the field for this historic game. Mussina was a right-hander, and Hudler, a 35-year-old journeyman, only played against left-handed pitching. Yet he was in California's lineup and, in fact, had also played the night before when Ripken had tied the record and Erickson, another right-hander, had pitched for the Orioles. "My manager did me a favor on those nights, pure and simple," Hudler said years later in an interview for this book.

Hudler had told Marcel Lachemann, the Angels' manager, that he and Ripken had been friends since they were teammates on the Orioles in the 1980s. Lachemann knew Hudler would be touched by the chance to play in Ripken's historic games. "I still thank [Lachemann] every time I see him," Hudler said.

Hudler was, indeed, thrilled. In fact, he was so excited before the September 6 game that he approached Larry Barnett, the home-plate umpire, and asked if he could have one of the game balls.

Barnett turned him down. The balls would become valuable commodities; several were destined for the Hall of Fame in Cooperstown. "If you want a ball from this game, you're going to have to catch a third out," the umpire said.

Hudler was disappointed. He had a memorabilia collection at his house in California, and a ball from this game would make a swell addition. He also had been asking Ripken all year for an inscribed bat, wanting to hang it on the wall next to another bat signed by Pete Rose. He had mentioned the bat to Ripken every time the Orioles and Angels had played that year, and Ripken had promised to sign one for him. But he had not done it, and now Ripken was swamped. Hudler was not optimistic about leaving town with a bat.

Once the game began, Hudler forced himself to focus on his job. He struck out in the second inning and handled several plays at second base without incident. But he kept wondering how he could get a ball. Barnett was right: his best chance was to record the third out of an inning in the field.

After the 22-minute interruption in the middle of the fifth — the break that included Ripken's "victory lap" — the game resumed, with the Angels in the field for the bottom of the inning. Boskie walked the first hitter, then quickly recorded two outs. But the Orioles' Rafael Palmeiro singled, and Bobby Bonilla reached on an error, loading the bases. Ripken stepped to the plate. It was hard to say who was more exhausted, Ripken or the fans, but the fans rose again, hoping to see a grand slam. Boskie fired a fastball. Ripken swung and made contact. The ball looped high into the air in shallow right-center field.

Hudler saw an opportunity. This was his chance to record a third out. He scrambled desperately after the pop-up. "I ran and ran and ran," he recalled, "and the ball hung up there like my personal eight-carat diamond in the Baltimore sky." As it plummeted to the ground, the fans shrieked, thinking Ripken was about to drive in more runs. But Hudler, on the dead run, swooped in and grabbed it for the third out.

As the fans groaned, Hudler raised his arms in triumph. "Everyone immediately started booing. They thought I was showing up Cal," Hudler said. "They had no idea I had just caught the souvenir ball of a lifetime."

He turned and headed for the dugout, still on the dead run. His teammates, anxious to congratulate him for the fine defensive play, waited for him on the top step. But Hudler sprinted past their outstretched hands and dashed into the tunnel leading to the clubhouse. "I ran straight to my locker, got out my briefcase, put the ball it in, and locked the briefcase," he said. Then he returned to the dugout. "My teammates were like, 'Hud, what the hell?'" he recalled. "I told them, 'Hey, dude, I got my ball.' I was just so happy."

Years later, Fred Tyler, the visitors' clubhouse manager that night at Camden Yards, still smiled about Hudler. "He just came bursting into the clubhouse like the biggest thing had happened," Tyler recalled. "A few other guys on the Angels also got balls when they made a third out that night. Everyone wanted a keepsake."

After the game, as Hudler recounted his ball story to a gaggle of reporters, a batboy approached him with a bat in hand. "Excuse me, Hud, this is for you. It's from Cal," the batboy said. It was the bat Hudler had been asking for, signed by Ripken.

"I said, 'Oh, my God! He did it! He kept his word!' I was so thrilled he remembered me on that special day," Hudler said.

When the Angels flew back to California that night, Hudler carried his bat, opened his briefcase, took out his ball, and gripped both items. They were destined for his living room wall.

"That night was the highlight of my career," he recalled, "and I went 0-for-4."

The Orioles were off the next day. No one needed a break more than Ripken, but the celebration of his achievement continued with a parade in his honor in downtown Baltimore, put on by the city. Ripken, his wife, and their kids sat atop a float carpeted with 2,131 baseballs. Ripken wore his white home jersey, which glistened in the noonday sunshine. Thousands of fans lined the route and cheered as he rode by.

At the end of the parade, Ripken stepped onto an outdoor stage at the Inner Harbor, Baltimore's iconic waterfront development. Reprising the postgame ceremonies of the previous two nights, he listened patiently to praise from team officials, local politicians, and business leaders. Then it was his turn. With his son asleep in his wife's lap, Ripken spoke for nearly 20 minutes.

"Somebody just said I should run around the harbor; I barely had enough energy to make it around that little ballpark last night," he said, drawing laughs.

He continued: "This has been one of the most overwhelming experiences of my life, so much it's hard for me to put in my words some of my feelings about the sentiments you all have expressed to me. All I ever wanted to do was be a baseball player and all I ever wanted to do is be a baseball player in this city."

Toward the end of his remarks, he admitted there had been times over the years when he had wondered if he needed a day off.

"What would Baltimore want me to do?" he asked.

The crowd answered as one: "Play!"

Before the Orioles' next game, the opener of a weekend series in Cleveland, Ripken took the lineup card out to the umpires, and Eddie Murray, now playing for the Indians, brought out their lineup card. Fans gave the close friends a standing ovation.

Ripken continued to receive cheers and ovations for the rest of the season. He had become baseball's feel-good ambassador. The commissioner asked him to throw out the ceremonial first pitch at the opening game of the World Series, a moment rich in symbolism after the strike the year before. Before Game 1 between the Atlanta Braves and New York Yankees on October 25, 1995, Ripken emerged from the home dugout in Atlanta, strode to the mound, and threw a strike. The fans roared. It was almost as if the holder of baseball's Ironman record *was* the game.

20

Ironmen

THE TRUE BELIEVER

Steve Garvey watched ESPN's broadcast of Ripken's record-breaking game with a mixture of admiration and frustration. Now 46 years old, the retired All-Star first baseman for the Dodgers and San Diego Padres had once played in 1,207 straight games, setting the National League consecutive-game record. Unlike Ripken, who insisted he was not pursuing Gehrig's record, Garvey had readily admitted he wanted to break it. But an injury ended his chance, and now someone else had passed Gehrig.

"I had no intention of stopping," Garvey said for this book years later. "When my streak was long enough that the press started asking me about Gehrig, I said it was the ultimate record in sports as far as individual performance, the ultimate commitment by a team sport player. I said I would be honored if, over a long period of time, I could catch Lou Gehrig and go by him."

Garvey was a true believer in the Ironman principle, the importance of playing every day. When his 19-year major league career ended in 1988, he owned a league record and two franchise records for consecutive games played. There was no doubt where he stood on the question of whether it was a good idea to play every day year after year. "You want to be a good teammate, be productive, be a leader, set an example," Garvey said. "That culminates with the feeling of, 'Do you want to be the person who is always there for your teammates?'"

Growing up in Florida in the 1950s, Garvey was around the Dodgers. His father drove their team bus during spring training in Vero Beach, and Garvey served as a batboy, picking up balls and bantering with the players, including his favorite, first baseman Gil Hodges. Slightly more than a decade later, the Dodgers made him their first-round draft pick in 1968. Though he stood just five feet ten, he had a thick trunk and huge forearms — he had played football at Michigan State — and could turn on a pitch.

In a quick rise through the Dodgers' minor league system, Garvey clouted 50 home runs. But once he made the big league club, the Dodgers could not find a position for him. He lacked the speed to play in the outfield, and the Dodgers' infield was set, with Bill Buckner playing first base, Davey Lopes at second, Bill Russell at shortstop, and Ron Cey at third.

Walter Alston, the Dodgers' manager, an avuncular former high school science teacher, wanted Garvey's bat in the lineup and gave him extended looks at second base and third base in 1971 and 1972, but Garvey's defense was too shaky. Finally, between games of a doubleheader in Cincinnati on June 23, 1973, the manager asked Garvey a question a Little League coach might ask of a 12-year-old: "Son, you ever play first base?"

Von Joshua, the Dodgers' left fielder, was out with a broken hand, and Alston wanted to replace him with Buckner, who was athletic enough to play the outfield. Could Garvey step in for Buckner at first? "Sure," Garvey replied. In truth, as far as he could remember, he had played only one game in Little League and another in Triple A at the position. But his positive reply encouraged Alston to give him a shot. In the second game of the doubleheader, he singled, doubled, and dug a couple of throws out of the dirt, and the Dodgers won. Alston kept him at first base in the coming days, and pretty soon the arrangement was no longer an experiment. Garvey was the Dodgers' first baseman.

In 1974, Garvey was so productive at the plate, dependable in the clutch, and solid in the field that he made the National League All-Star team as a write-in candidate with more than a million votes. Then he won the league's Most Valuable Player award after hitting .312 for the season and driving in 111 runs. His story was almost too hokey for Hollywood — a team's former batboy becoming a star at his hero's position — but it was real.

The Dodgers had been in a rut; they had not won 90 games in a season or made the postseason since the mid-1960s. Garvey's emergence changed their fortunes. In 1974, they won the National League West and defeated the Pittsburgh Pirates in the league championship series. After Alston retired, they won two more pennants, in 1977 and 1978, under their new manager, Tommy Lasorda, a talkative showman who entertained movie stars in the clubhouse. Although they lost to the Oakland A's in the 1974 World Series and also lost to the Yankees in the 1977 and 1978 Series, the Dodgers ruled Southern California's sports scene. Their attendance jumped from 1.8 million in 1972 to 3.3 million in 1978.

Garvey was a vital piece of their renaissance, hitting .319 in 1975, clouting 33 home runs in 1977, and leading the league in hits in 1978. He almost seemed a fictional creation, so perfect he could not be real. Aside from his strong play, he had magazine-cover looks — with coiffed dark hair, a square jaw, and a bright smile — and a beautiful wife and two young daughters. Media members who asked for his time received a firm handshake and thoughtful responses. Fans loved him. Advertisers loved him more. A Southern California suburb even named a junior high school after him. Columnists speculated he might have a future in politics.

Once he had a starting spot, Garvey never wanted to take a day off. Though he had come of age in the turbulent sixties and shaggy-haired seventies, he was a child of the fifties, old-fashioned about his work responsibilities. He believed the Dodgers paid him to lead the team and perform for the noisy crowds that filled their ballpark. In 1974, his MVP season, he sat out six games. The next year, he missed two, in early September, with the flu. His replacement struck out three times, and Garvey was back in the lineup on September 3, 1975, the starting date for his endurance streak. He completed a full schedule of games for the first time in 1976, Alston's final season, and Lasorda handled him the same way in 1977, starting him in 160 games and twice using him as a pinch hitter.

In 1978, Garvey started every game, surpassing 500 in a row late that season. "It kind of crept up on you," he recalled. "You win the first-base job in 1973, have a good year in 1974, and start playing every game. After a while, you notice you have a streak. Alston or Lasorda would say, 'Why don't you sit one out?' Or 'You're struggling, why not sit and watch?' I had no interest in that. Are you kidding? How am I going to make adjustments sitting on the bench? I make adjustments in the context of one at-bat to the next. You can't do that from the bench."

In 1980, he played in every game for the fifth straight season, starting all but one. In the second game of a doubleheader on May 26, he pinch-hit in the ninth inning to keep his streak going. By the end of the season, he had played in 835 straight games.

"It takes over your life. You dream about it," he recalled. "In my dream,

I would be on the freeway at 3:30 in the afternoon, turn on the radio, and the Dodger game was on. It was the bottom of the eighth, and I'd go, 'My God, it's a day game today!' I'd rush to the stadium and get dressed just in time to see the last out, a pop-up, and that was it, the streak was over."

But that only happened in his dreams. In his waking hours, his endurance was part of what seemed a perfect baseball life. Then cracks formed. Some teammates soured on his wholesome act, believing it was calculated. One day in the clubhouse, when pitcher Don Sutton insulted his wife, Garvey grabbed him and they wrestled. In 1981, Garvey's wife left him, claiming he had cheated on her. He played on through the turmoil, never missing a game.

"I had migraines, the flu, hairline fractures, hamstrings. I was still able to go out and perform," he recalled. "Maybe I was slowed down a rung or didn't quite have the same bat speed as usual. But I could do the job defensively, get the runner over offensively, do the things a teammate needs to do. I was not going to be the guy who sat out because of an upset stomach or a little headache."

When his production declined, some commentators and fans suggested he should start taking more days off.

"I tried not to think too much about the critics," he recalled. "Unless you played the game, you can't comprehend it. To criticize someone who wants to play every inning of every game, you're doing what your contract says, what your franchise wants, what your responsibility to the fans is. The critics know not of what they speak. There's always going to be adversity. You just play through it."

Several hours before the Dodgers played the Atlanta Braves on June 8, 1982, Garvey entered the home clubhouse at Dodger Stadium and checked the lineup. His name had been scratched out. Rick Monday was playing first. Garvey blinked. "For a second, I really wondered what was going on," he said later. Then he realized it was a joke. His consecutive-game streak was due to reach 1,000 games that night. Lasorda was not about to sit him.

That night, 44,714 fans gave him an ovation when his achievement was announced. Only four other players in major league history had extended playing streaks this long: Gehrig, Everett Scott, Joe Sewell, and Billy Wil-

liams. "It's a source of pride, the ability to produce every day of my contract, almost every inning," he told reporters.

Garvey was 33 years old, hitting .250, his bat lukewarm enough that
Lasorda had ended his streak of almost 300 straight starts earlier in the
season. (Lasorda did make sure to get him into the game as a pinch hitter
to keep his playing streak going.) Garvey's contract was up at the end of
the 1982 season, and there were whispers he might not return. The Dodgers had a top prospect, Greg Brock, ready to play first base. Although
they offered Garvey a long-term deal in July, he sensed tepid interest and
turned it down. In the final game of the season — his final game with the
Dodgers, it turned out — he collected three hits while running his streak
to 1,107 straight games.

When he hit the open market as a free agent that winter, the San Diego Padres, Chicago Cubs, and San Francisco Giants all pursued him. He
ended up signing a five-year deal with the Padres worth $8.56 million.
Having experienced just one winning season since their birth as an expansion team in 1969, the Padres hoped he could help them change their
fortunes.

When he joined the Padres, Garvey was just 10 games short of Billy
Williams's National League consecutive-game record. Dick Williams, the
Padres' manager, was going to make sure he passed that threshold. But
around the batting cage one day in spring training, Williams told report-
ers he might rest Garvey "now and then" after Garvey set the National
League record.

Garvey overheard the comment. "Please don't do that, Dick. Gehrig's
record is only six years away," Garvey said.

Dave Anderson, a *New York Times* columnist, was standing nearby and
asked Garvey if he really thought about Gehrig's record. "It's a long way
away," Garvey replied with a smile. "God would have to visit me and say,
'Steve, I'm going to keep you healthy.' But it's in the back of my mind."

He was familiar enough with the numbers to quickly calculate the
math. "At 1,107, I need another 1,024 to break it," he told Anderson. "With
162 games in a season, that's six more and part of a seventh."

Garvey believed he had a chance. Although he was 34 years old, he
stayed in terrific shape and had batted .292 with 86 runs batted in the
year before. The Dodgers might not have tolerated his desire to play every
day for much longer, but the Padres surely would. Garvey gave them an

identity. Their season ticket sales were up. The marketing staff could not believe how helpful he was.

His move to San Diego set up a theatrical scene early in the 1983 season. He would tie and pass Billy Williams's record during a series in, of all places, Los Angeles, on his first trip to Dodger Stadium as an opponent.

He conceded he felt "very strange" as he drove to the stadium on April 15, 1983, before he tied the record that night. He had to remind himself to go to the visitors' clubhouse rather than the one he had inhabited for so long. A small mountain of flowers, balloons, and gifts awaited him at his locker, along with a chocolate fudge cake from Dodgers pitcher Jerry Reuss and his wife, which came in a box inscribed SLUGGO, AT LEAST 1,117 CALORIES IN EVERY BITE, BECAUSE WE LOVE YOU.

During batting practice, Garvey exchanged strained greetings with Lasorda and crossed paths with Brock, his replacement. Fans behind the visitors' dugout unfurled a banner reading THE DODGERS BLUE IT. WE LOVE YOU, STEVE.

When he batted in the top of the first, the sold-out crowd stood and cheered for more than a minute. Standing outside the batter's box, Garvey hoisted his bat aloft and slowly turned in a circle while blowing kisses and waving, making sure he directed his affection to every corner of the park. The next night, he became the National League's all-time Ironman, and in a sporting gesture, the Dodgers commemorated the feat, holding a "night" for their estranged star. Garvey was presented with plaques, scrolls, and gifts after the game. He gave an emotional speech and thanked the fans. "I consider you the tenth player," he said. "There aren't many words to describe how I feel, but there are three, and 'I love you.'"

The Padres had flown his parents in from Tampa for the occasion. Billy Williams also was present. "Only he and I know what you have to go through, playing hurt, staying lucky," Williams told the crowd. "I don't think he has a chance to catch Gehrig. But then, Garvey's kind of special."

More than 40 years had passed since Gehrig's streak ended. It was thought to be among the safest of records. Gehrig had played when teams did not travel as far, seasons were shorter, the media was more complicit. It was hard to imagine a current player not missing a game for 13 years. Between cross-country flights, weird start times, and a critical media braying in your ear, there was more to overcome. Billy Williams's streak had been the longest since Gehrig's, and Williams had barely made it halfway to the record. Now Garvey was slightly more than halfway there, but unlike Williams, he wanted to keep going.

Dick Williams heeded Garvey's directive to continue playing him every day after he set the record. On July 29, 1983, he ran his streak to 1,206 straight games as the Padres lost in Pittsburgh. Garvey was hitting .292, and the Padres were in the middle of the pack in the National League West.

Back in San Diego, on July 31, they took on Atlanta in a doubleheader. Garvey singled in the bottom of the first of the opening game, then took third on a subsequent single. The Braves' starting pitcher, Pascual Perez, an erratic right-hander, hurled a wild fastball over the next batter's head. It sailed past the Braves' catcher, Bruce Benedict, and Garvey dashed for home as Benedict scrambled to retrieve the ball and Perez raced in to cover home plate.

It appeared Garvey was going to score easily, until the ball caromed sharply off the backstop directly to Benedict, who turned and flipped it to Perez. The pitcher grabbed the throw and bent to tag Garvey with his feet straddling the plate.

As he came down the line, Garvey saw the sharp carom and knew his only hope was to avoid Perez's tag and touch the plate. But Perez's position forced him to make a decision. "They never teach you to straddle the plate like he did on that play," Garvey recalled. "My split-second decision was whether to go into his knee and maybe hurt him, or go around and try to tag the plate. I went around."

As he dove headfirst and reached out for the plate, his hand hit Perez's heel, bending his thumb awkwardly. Perez tagged him out, ending the inning. Garvey rose to his knees, holding his thumb with his other hand. He knew something was wrong; his thumb was numb. But he held out hope as the Padres' trainer came out to take a look. "My thought was, 'Maybe I can ice it, tape it, pinch-hit in the second game [of the doubleheader],' and we would get it ready for tomorrow," Garvey recalled.

But when Garvey took his other hand away, his thumb drooped like a strand of cooked spaghetti. The trainer gasped. Garvey knew what it meant. He stood and walked slowly to the dugout. "I stepped inside the tunnel [to the clubhouse], and it hit me: this is it. I started to sweat, went to my knees. It almost felt like something had left your body. Seven and a half years of total commitment, and it was over," he recalled.

A teammate, Kurt Bevacqua, passed him in the tunnel. "He was squatting. I couldn't see the extent of the injury, but I didn't have to ask how bad it was. There was disappointment on his face," Bevacqua said. As the game continued, Garvey went to the nearby Scripps Clinic for X-rays, which revealed the thumb was dislocated. Leaving the emergency room wearing an elbow-length cast, he told reporters, "It's as low as I've felt in many, many years."

He returned to the ballpark and sat on the bench during the second game of the doubleheader. His streak, the fourth longest in history, ended at 1,207 straight games.

"As long as he was healthy, he was doing the job, day in and day out," said one of his former Dodgers teammates, shortstop Bill Russell, upon hearing the news. "What more can you ask? I hate to see a streak like his come to an end. He did a lot during that streak."

Lasorda also expressed disappointment. "It's a shame, too bad," the Dodgers' manager said. "But I didn't think he had a chance at Gehrig's record."

The next day, Garvey learned he had torn ligaments in the thumb and needed surgery. "We'll put a pin in. You'll be ready in three months," a surgeon said.

"There's no way I can play through it?" Garvey asked.

"Not unless you want to bunt every time," the surgeon said.

He dove into his rehab program and was ready the next year. Although he could not muster much power and hit just eight home runs, his career low, he played in every game except one, led the Padres in runs batted in, and did not commit an error. The Padres suddenly had a potent blend of experience and youth with Garvey; a pair of former Yankees, closer Rich "Goose" Gossage and third baseman Graig Nettles; and second baseman Alan Wiggins, shortstop Garry Templeton, and outfielder Tony Gwynn. The franchise's first division title resulted.

Taking on the Cubs in the league championship series, they dropped the first two games in Chicago, but the rest of the best-of-five series was in California, giving them hope. They won Game 3 and were tied, 5–5, going into the bottom of the ninth of Game 4. Facing Lee Smith, the Cubs' star closer, Gwynn singled, bringing Garvey to the plate. He had already driven in three runs, and with the crowd cheering, he launched a drive to right-center that cleared the fence, winning the game. The Padres completed the comeback the next day, winning Game 5 to take the pennant. Garvey was named the Most Valuable Player in the series. Although the Padres lost to Detroit in the World Series, it had been a season unlike any other in San Diego.

Though now in his late 30s, Garvey played two more full seasons and part of a third for the Padres before injuries ended his career. From September 23, 1984, until September 6, 1986, he played in 305 straight games, the longest streak in Padres history. His record stood for more than two decades, until another first baseman, Adrian Gonzalez, surpassed it in 2009. Garvey's Dodgers franchise record of 1,107 straight games remains unchallenged. The second-longest streak in that franchise's history belongs to Matt Kemp, an outfielder who played in 399 straight games.

No one has come within 400 games of Garvey's National League record in the three decades since he set it.

"One person out of 20 would look at your career and say that [streak] was Steve's high point, but it's my favorite subject to talk about," Garvey said for this book. "Wanting to play every inning of every game, you realize, as you start to get deeper, there's tremendous stress physically, mentally, and spiritually. To play every day, you have to do a lot of things to get to the starting line, play a game, and be ready for the next day. One thing leads to another, it consumes you, and it ends up defining who you are, your philosophy about the game. You can't have a better legacy, as far as I'm concerned."

21

Ripken

A DAY OFF, AT LAST

Although Ripken's historic games ranked among the Orioles' proudest occasions, their owner was not happy about the rest of the 1995 season. Peter Angelos had not paid $193 million for a team to watch it finish 15 games out of first place. Intent on engineering a quick reversal, he spent freely during the off-season, hiring a new manager, Davey Johnson, and signing several premier free agents, including an All-Star second baseman, Roberto Alomar; a top closer, Randy Myers; and a versatile veteran, B. J. Surhoff. Johnson was a popular hire, having played second base on the Orioles' World Series–winning team in 1966 before becoming a manager and guiding the New York Mets to a World Series triumph in 1986.

But Angelos's most important hire was a new general manager, Pat Gillick, the former Orioles pitching prospect who had played with Senior in the minors in the 1960s. Gillick's playing career had fizzled, but he had become a respected roster architect and talent evaluator, building a Toronto team that had won back-to-back World Series titles a few years earlier.

With Gillick and Johnson in charge of a reinvigorated roster, Baltimore fans hoped the Orioles would become contenders again and maybe even make the playoffs for the first time in 13 years.

Amid the many changes, Ripken's role initially seemed unchanged. He had been the Orioles' shortstop since 1982 and was still the shortstop in 1996. Gillick had no issue with seeing Ripken's name in the lineup every day. "He was still a good player," Gillick said for this book. "He could hit. His range in the field wasn't as good as it had been, but his positioning was good. He had been in the league so long that he knew where to play and got to balls."

But Gillick had always believed Ripken was a more natural third base-man. "Because of his size," Gillick said. "Even when he was a kid, I viewed him as more suited to third. He wasn't a prototypical shortstop like Luis Aparicio and those guys who were like little ballerinas. Junior did it in a little different fashion. For me, he just profiled better at third."

Now that Gillick ran the Orioles, he had a say in where Ripken played. He mentioned to Johnson the idea of moving Ripken to third, clearing the way for Manny Alexander to play shortstop. A 25-year-old from the Dominican Republic, Alexander was a slick fielder who had hit .300 in spring training and added speed to the Orioles' lumbering lineup.

"I thought it might take a little pressure off Junior," Gillick recalled. "Playing third, you're not quite as active as you are at shortstop. You're not involved in as many plays."

When Ripken slumped at the plate early in the season, Johnson pub-licly floated the idea, telling reporters it was possible Ripken would change positions. Johnson knew Ripken would not like it, but after managing in New York, with its tumultuous tabloid culture swirling at the ballparks, he was accustomed to controversy and unafraid of clubhouse tension.

On May 1, Johnson sent Alexander in to pinch-run for Ripken in the bottom of the eighth with the Orioles down by a run to the Yankees be-fore a packed house at Camden Yards. Ripken was shocked; he had not been pulled from a game in doubt since 1981. A few weeks later, the man-ager pulled Ripken from another game, then briefly dropped him to sev-enth in the batting order. Fans wondered if Johnson was signaling that the streak might end soon.

As if challenged, Ripken responded in his typical fashion, with actions rather than words. In a 12–8 win on May 28 in Seattle, he clouted three home runs and drove in eight runs. In early June, he hit balls over the fence in three straight games.

But while he continued to play every day, his younger brother Bill, back with the Orioles in a reserve role after playing for Texas and Cleve-land, noticed a subtle change in Junior's routine. "He had always taken batting practice every day when I was on the team before, but when I came back, he would take a BP off now and then," Bill recalled. "We also weren't taking infield every day, so there were days when he showed up later. It was his way of taking a mental break to clear his head when he wasn't faring well at the plate."

The idea of taking a real break, a day or two off, never crossed Ripken's mind. If he ended the streak now, so soon after passing Gehrig, he believed it would indicate that he had played every day just to set a record, which, in his mind, was not the case.

Baseball fans in America assumed Ripken was the game's greatest Ironman, but a Japanese major leaguer, Sachio Kinugasa, actually had a longer streak, having played in 2,215 straight games for the Hiroshima Carp between 1970 and 1987. His "world record" streak was 85 games longer than Gehrig's. Ripken was due to tie and pass it during a series in Kansas City in mid-June 1996.

There was little buzz as Ripken neared the record. The focus in Baltimore was back on the Orioles' playoff prospects rather than Ripken's endurance. Everyone, including Ripken, was "streaked out." But when the time came, Kinugasa flew into Kansas City, ate lunch with Ripken, and met up with him at the Orioles' hotel bar after a game. Though an interpreter had to sit with them to keep their conversation going, they hit it off.

Balding and diminutive, Kinugasa was older than Ripken by more than a decade. Talking to him, Ripken was transported to another time. "It was how I perceived talking to Lou Gehrig would be like," Ripken recalled. "I thoroughly enjoyed it. There's just a small club of people who know what it is like to have played in so many games in a row."

Kinugasa, who had played third base and first base for Hiroshima, had a lot in common with Ripken as a player. Both were adept in the field and powerful at the plate. Kinugasa hit more than 500 home runs. Ripken was closing in on 400. Kinugasa's .270 career average was almost identical to Ripken's .267 figure at that point.

Kinugasa's story was familiar to Japanese fans. His father was a black American serviceman who had been stationed in Okinawa after World War II and abandoned the family after fathering a child. Kinugasa had dark features and endured taunts as a youngster because he was not 100 percent Japanese. Neither of his authorized biographies mentioned his parentage, a painful subject. Kinugasa learned English in hopes of being able to communicate if his father ever returned, but he never needed it.

His ethnicity impacted his playing style. In a country where short, compact batting strokes were the norm, he favored a long, American-style swing, taking such aggressive cuts that he gave himself whiplash. His coaches tolerated it because, as one said, Kinugasa "was not Japanese so it could not be helped."

As a young man, he liked fast cars and late nights on the town. He spent his signing bonus on a Ford Galaxy. But he also spent hours in front of a mirror with a bat in his hands, practicing his swing. He started out as a catcher, but at five feet nine and 180 pounds, he took such a pounding that the Carp switched him to the infield. Kinugasa would go on to play in 13 All-Star Games.

His consecutive-game streak began in 1970, at the end of his third season as a regular. He was 23 years old and would play until he was 40 without missing a game. The Japanese season consisted of 130 games, 32 fewer than the American season in Ripken's era. But spring training began in January in Japan, and players endured rigorous pregame and off-day physical training, ratcheting up the physical demands.

Kinugasa's streak survived several close calls. Known for crowding the plate, he led the league in getting hit by pitches and suffered five broken bones over the years. In August 1978, he was hit in the back, diagnosed with a shoulder blade fracture, and told not to play. He had appeared in more than 1,100 straight games. The next day, he showed up at the park and swung his bat as hard as ever in the cage before the game. The manager let him play. "If I swung the bat, the pain in my shoulder would last only an instant. If I had to stay home and watch the game on TV, I would hurt all over for three hours," Kinugasa explained.

It took him 18 years to accomplish what Gehrig did in 13. When he passed Gehrig on June 13, 1987, Japan celebrated wildly, much as it did when slugger Sadaharu Oh passed the home run totals of Babe Ruth and Hank Aaron. Hiroshima's ballpark was packed, and the game was halted for a long ceremony that included a parade and a confetti shower.

Clyde Haberman, the *New York Times*' Tokyo bureau chief, explained Kinugasa's appeal: "He is a rock of consistency, and, as such, the salariman's hero. The salariman [a Japanese word for 'salary man'] is Japan's average Joe. He is the guy who puts on a blue suit every morning, rides the train to work for an hour and a half, puts in 10–12 hours, drinks late into the night with his colleagues, then heads home for a few hours' sleep so that he can start all over again the next day. Like the salariman, Kinugasa is there as promised every day."

After playing in every game for the rest of the 1987 season, Kinugasa retired. Now, nine years later, as Ripken and Kinugasa became acquainted in Kansas City, Ripken was surprised to discover that his own approach borrowed heavily from the guiding philosophy of Japanese baseball, where the team comes first. "There, it is seen as an honor to play every day. It is seen as your obligation and responsibility. That's exactly how I felt," Ripken said. Having felt compelled to defend his motivation for so long, he was excited to come across a kindred spirit. He felt he would be understood in Japan, as Kinugasa was, and not face accusations of selfishness.

"You're a baseball player, doing something everyone else in the country would love to do. Your obligation is to come and play. It's the manager's job to make out the lineup. The manager created that thing called the streak by putting you in there. You responded," Ripken said.

He broke Kinugasa's record in Kansas City on June 14, 1996. On the surface, it did not compare with 2,131 as an occasion. There were thousands of empty seats at Kauffman Stadium. No banners dropped, no soaring music played, and Ripken did not take a victory lap. But it was moving in its own way. Ripken and Kinugasa exchanged gifts on the field before the game and shared the commemorative first-pitch honors. Kinugasa took a ball to the mound, raised his arms in triumph over his head, unbuttoned his jacket, and threw a strike to Ripken as the fans cheered.

After the top of the fifth, the game was official. The crowd stood and cheered, and Ripken came out of the dugout and waved his cap. He retreated to the dugout, emerged again, waved his cap again, and sought out Kinugasa, who was applauding in a seat by the Baltimore dugout. Ripken walked to the railing, and Kinugasa shuffled past several fans to meet him. They shook hands.

After the game, they met with reporters. A large Japanese media contingent was covering the event.

"Was there any way this night could have compared to the night you passed Gehrig last September?" Ripken was asked.

He chuckled. He knew no one else thought it compared. But he looked over at Kinugasa and smiled.

"In some ways," he said, "this was more fulfilling."

· · ·

Shortly after the All-Star break in 1996, the Orioles lost five straight games and dropped 10 games behind the first-place Yankees. Gillick and Johnson made the move they had discussed, announcing that Ripken would move to third base so Manny Alexander could play shortstop.

Ripken was not happy. He did not believe the Orioles were better with Alexander at shortstop. But Gillick and Johnson were adamant, so on July 15, 1996, after playing in 2,216 straight games at shortstop, he played third base against Toronto at Camden Yards.

The Blue Jays' first two batters tried to bunt, blatantly challenging him. Ripken smiled and gestured to Toronto manager Cito Gaston. "I said, 'Take off the bunt sign, would you?'" Ripken recalled. The first ball that came his way was a sharp grounder down the line, hit by Toronto catcher Charlie O'Brien in the top of the third. Ripken dove, speared the ball, rose to one knee, and threw across the diamond, beating O'Brien. As cheers echoed, Ripken stared ahead with a drop-dead expression, looking as if he wanted to give the world the middle finger.

The Alexander experiment failed. Paralyzed by the prospect of replacing his famous teammate, Alexander went hitless for a week and returned to the bench. Ripken moved back to shortstop and ended the season with a .278 average, 26 home runs, and 102 runs batted in — his best numbers in five years.

The Yankees won the division, but the Orioles also qualified for the playoffs with a late surge, making it as a wild card, the second-place finisher with the best record. After upsetting the favored Cleveland Indians in a first-round playoff series, they lost to the Yankees in the league championship series. No one suggested Ripken was tired. In his first playoff appearance in 13 years, he batted .342.

After Ripken finally ended his consecutive-game streak near the end of the 1998 season, the *New York Times*' Buster Olney, formerly the Orioles beat writer for the *Baltimore Sun*, wrote that the Ironman record had become "an albatross" for the team since Ripken passed Gehrig. Ripken had resisted change, Olney wrote, and challenged suggestions that his skills were declining, making life difficult for his superiors.

It certainly was true that the Orioles' managers had to play him in 1996, 1997, and 1998. Even though Ripken steadfastly claimed otherwise, his Ironman record was so popular and important that neither the manager nor the front office had any say in when the streak ended. "You knew it wasn't a decision you were going to make. He was going to make it. I don't think there was anything we could have said to influence him," Gillick recalled.

But Gillick did not recall the streak as being horrendously damaging to the team's fortunes. "The fact that he was so committed to being out there every day was wonderful," Gillick said. Advanced statistics, calculated years later in some cases, indicated that he continued to perform at his customary levels at least through 1996. His WAR (wins above replacement) figure, reflecting how many wins he was worth compared to a statistically average player, was higher in 1996 than in 1993.

Seeking to control as much about the situation as he could, Gillick finally achieved his goal of moving Ripken to third base in 1997. He signed Mike Bordick, a veteran free-agent shortstop known as a dependable fielder. Ripken had not wanted to move to third to make way for Manny Alexander, but it was hard to quibble with making way for Bordick, who was five years younger.

"Ripken and Bordick could have been brothers. They had the same approach to the game — just put your head down and grind it out," Gillick said. "I'm not sure Junior was crazy about moving, but he liked Bordick, and that made it easy."

Changing positions did not change Ripken's approach to playing every day. The Orioles led their division all season in 1997 and finished with 98 wins. Ripken, after playing on so many losing teams, relished contributing to a winner.

As the season unfolded, though, playing every day became harder. Ripken experienced back stiffness and soreness, which he initially dismissed as the by-products of playing a new position that required him to crouch and lunge more. He steeled himself and kept going, but when he woke with a dull ache in his left hip on July 14, he knew his position was not the issue. Although he played that night, collecting three hits, he could not sleep after the game and wound up seeing the sunrise from the hot tub on his deck. He called Richie Bancells, who consulted with the team's doctors. They all met at Johns Hopkins Hospital a few hours later. X-rays and an MRI identified a herniated disc in Ripken's back.

The good news, Ripken was told, was if he took an anti-inflammatory injection and rested for six weeks, he probably would be fine in September and could play in the postseason.

But there also was bad news: "You can't play with this," one doctor said. "You're going to have to sit out the six weeks after taking the injection."

Ron Shapiro was present for the meeting. "There was a whole group of doctors," Shapiro recalled, "and the conclusion was, Cal couldn't play."

The conversation's significance was not lost on anyone in the room. It seemed Ripken's famous streak was about to end. But Ripken was dubious. "Why can't I play?" he asked.

"It's too painful," one doctor said.

The Orioles were playing Toronto that night at Camden Yards. Shapiro and Ripken spoke with John Maroon, the Orioles' director of public relations, about holding a press conference before the game to announce the streak was over. "I can't remember who called who, but there was definitely a conversation about that," Shapiro recalled.

As Ripken took the anti-inflammatory injection, his mind whirred through his options. Before leaving Hopkins, he asked a doctor if he could further injure himself by playing. No, the doctor said, if you can stand the pain, you can play. Ripken mulled that over as he and Shapiro left the hospital and shared a ride to Camden Yards. "We were in his Tahoe," Shapiro recalled. "He was sort of doubting the decision not to play. He already owned the consecutive-game record, but he was still the Ironman."

Maroon never called a press conference. "When we got to the stadium, he went straight into the batting cage and started to hit off a tee, and then he started to stretch," Shapiro recalled. In the end, he played even though his leg ached, going 0-for-4 and making four plays in the field without an error as the Orioles built an 8–2 lead.

Johnson knew what Ripken had experienced that afternoon and could tell he was struggling. "Is it hurting?" the manager asked.

"A little bit," Ripken replied.

Knowing that was a major admission, Johnson took him out before the top of the eighth. "I was trying to preserve him," Johnson said later. "I figured he'd had enough. He has said he'd let me know when that was the case. But I've come to know that, with him, he never lets you know."

Despite pain he later described as "a fire inside your leg," Ripken continued to play every night. It was easily the toughest physical challenge he had faced during the streak. His back was stiff. His leg throbbed. One night, he lunged for a ground ball and his leg gave way, sending him tumbling. It was a discouraging moment; he could not even reach for a ball. "This really might be the end," he thought. "There was a door behind home plate, and I visualized myself calling time out and walking straight through that door, and that was going to be how the streak ended," Ripken recalled.

But he did not leave the game. "I was leading off the next inning [after I tumbled], and I went, 'Well, let me at least give it a try at bat,'" he said. He hit a line drive to left for a single, and as he ran to first, he thought, "Well, I guess it's OK."

It was not. After a six-hour charter flight from Baltimore to Oakland at the end of July, his back was so stiff he could barely walk off the plane. Before playing against the A's the next night, he underwent hours of therapy hooked up to an electronic stimulator, with node patches all over his back. He easily could have ended the streak then, but Johnson "practically begged me to play," Ripken said later. The Orioles led the division, but with Alomar on the disabled list and outfielder Eric Davis taking chemotherapy treatments after a shocking cancer diagnosis, the team needed the stability Ripken provided, Johnson felt.

The disruption to Ripken's normal pattern of nerve signals was so severe that it caused his leg to atrophy. "I wound up losing an inch of size off my left thigh and an inch of size off my left calf," he recalled. "Somehow, some way, I made it through."

It took some ingenuity. Instead of sitting on the bench between innings, he went into the clubhouse and draped himself over a chair, stretching his back. "Standing, it hurt. Sitting down, it hurt. Laying down, sleeping, it hurt. But I found that one position that didn't hurt, against a chair. That was the one position that gave me some relief," Ripken recalled.

Brady Anderson just shook his head as his teammate pressed on. "There was no way most guys would play through anything like that. That was brutal to watch," Anderson said. "So, yes, he was durable and all that, but he also was really tough."

In early August, Ripken's back was so sore one day that he contemplated sitting out. "You have to try," Anderson told him. "If it hurts too badly, you can come out in the third inning."

Ripken elected to give it a shot, "but I'm only doing that once," he told

Anderson. "If it keeps hurting, I'm not going to keep going out there for the sake of the streak."

He played the whole game.

His determination would impact several teammates. In July of that season, Anderson, wanting to play in every game, eschewed a doctor's recommendation that he undergo an appendectomy. He wound up missing just two games. Several years later, Surhoff played back-to-back seasons without missing a game.

Few outsiders knew the extent of Ripken's struggle as he played through the pain in 1996, partly because he hit .320 in the six weeks after he took the injection. "Knowing you had an issue really increased your focus," he recalled. After the pain abruptly vanished, as promised, around Labor Day, his bat cooled, and he hit just .156 in September. "I had used up so much energy to focus on getting through the pain. Maybe your guard is let down, and the urgency isn't there as much," he recalled.

Predictably, his late-season slump promoted a flurry of second-guessing. "Ripken is hurt, and he's hurting the Orioles. If he doesn't rest his back before the postseason, he might even hurt them when it counts the most," *Baltimore Sun* columnist Ken Rosenthal wrote, renewing a familiar talk-show debate.

On the last day of the regular season, Ripken doubled in his first at-bat, walked in the top of the third, and came out of the game in the fourth. His season was over. For the 15th straight year, and the last time, he had played in every game.

As the postseason began, some columnists wondered whether he should have ended the streak to rest up for the playoffs. But his back and leg felt fine now, and it showed. The Orioles played two series that October, defeating Seattle in the divisional round before losing to Cleveland in the league championship series, and Ripken was productive, collecting 15 hits, including four doubles and a home run. He had now played in 28 straight postseason games, hitting .336.

Despite their back-to-back playoff seasons, the Orioles were in chaos. Angelos had strong opinions about who should be on the roster and what the manager and general manager should do. Weary of being overruled, Gillick could hardly wait until his contract expired after the 1998 season. Johnson departed even sooner. When he asked for an extension and Angelos balked, he resigned on the day he was elected 1997 American League Manager of the Year.

Ray Miller, the pitching coach, took over as manager. The Orioles went 10-2 to start the 1998 season, then sank into a tailspin that included a nine-game losing streak. By Memorial Day, they were 15 games out. Ripken, now 37 years old, still played solid defense every day, but his offense tailed off. He would end the season with 14 homers, matching his lowest total in a non-strike season. His 67 runs batted in were his fewest in a full season. His streak reached 2,500 straight games on April 25, but he began to think about ending it. While he had never believed his managers were "trapped," forced to play him, he could see Ray Miller did not need this.

"You always felt you had support for playing every day, and then, all of a sudden, you felt like you didn't; you were losing some support for that," Ripken recalled. "My thought was, 'If we fall out of the race, this would be a good time to end it.'"

After the Orioles lost 10 straight games in August to end their playoff hopes, Ripken plotted the streak's end. His initial idea was to do it in the Orioles' season finale at Fenway Park in Boston. "The statement that would make is, 'I could have played 162 if I wanted, but let's put it to bed,'" Ripken recalled.

Kelly talked him out of that. "You should do it at a home game, where everyone has followed you," she said.

Ripken saw that she was right. Only his wife, parents, and a few friends knew of his plan. He wanted to avoid the hoopla he knew would occur if he announced he would sit out a game.

Before the game on September 17, Ripken approached Miller in the manager's office and mentioned he was contemplating ending the streak before the season ended. But he did not indicate that he had a plan in mind. When the *Baltimore Sun*'s Joe Strauss asked him about the possibility, Ripken coyly replied, "You'll have to watch and see."

On September 20, the Orioles played their final home game of the 1998 season. It was a Sunday night affair against the Yankees, televised nationally on ESPN. Several hours before the first pitch, Miller wrote out a lineup with Ripken batting sixth and playing third. But Ripken approached the manager after batting practice and said simply, "I think it's time."

At first, Miller thought it was a joke. But he quickly realized Ripken was serious and reworked the lineup, replacing Ripken with Ryan Minor, one of the Orioles' top infield prospects.

Ripken called Angelos to give the owner the news personally. "He is an amazing athlete," Angelos told the *Baltimore Sun* later that evening. "I don't think there will ever be another Cal Ripken or anyone capable of accomplishing what he has accomplished."

Minor did not find out he was playing until 15 minutes before the game, when Miller gave him the news in the dugout. "So you're in there at third base," Miller said.

"Does he know?" Minor said, eyes widening.

Miller smiled. Yes, the Ironman knew his streak was ending.

"The funny thing was, Ryan didn't want to take the field because he thought it was a prank," Ripken recalled. "He was a rookie, thinking he was going to go out there and everyone would laugh at him and then I would come out and play. I went, 'Ryan, this is for real. Go play.'"

The Orioles took the field with Minor stationed at third. There was no announcement. The game just began. The Orioles' starting pitcher, Doug Johns, threw a pitch to Chuck Knoblauch, the Yankees' leadoff hitter, who grounded out to shortstop. It seemed the 48,013 fans were unaware of what was happening. But the Yankees were well aware of it. After the first out, they gathered on the top step of their dugout and applauded. Then the crowd understood and began to applaud. A ballpark camera found Ripken sitting in the dugout. Seeing himself on the scoreboard, he acknowledged the cheers and motioned for Johns to get on with the game. He had played in 2,632 straight games, a number destined for the history books.

"Doing it at home made it what it should have been, a celebration," Ripken recalled. "What the Yankees did was very cool. And everyone relates to the discipline of playing every day, coming to work, what's important to them. So it turned out to be more of a celebration of that value than anything. I was right to do it at home."

As the game proceeded, he signed some balls for teammates in the dugout and wandered around the ballpark, spending an inning in the clubhouse and several innings in the bullpen. Before the bottom of the sixth, he exchanged warm-up tosses with the outfielders.

"I wanted to experience some things I had never experienced before," he recalled. "People asked me what it felt like. It felt like I was on the outside of the game looking in. You had always been on the inside, and now you weren't. I didn't care for that."

After the game, reporters asked why he had ended it now. "The emphasis should be on the team," Ripken said. "There have been times during the streak when the emphasis was on the streak. I was never comfortable with that. It was time to move the focus back to the team."

Shortly after the streak ended, Senior was diagnosed with lung cancer. He died six months later, just before the start of the 1999 season.

As his father declined, Ripken lost himself in his off-season routine, overdid it, injured his back, and went on the disabled list for the first time after trying to play on Opening Day. He rehabbed the injury and came back strong, batting .340 with 18 home runs in 86 games.

The milestones rolled by. He clouted his 400th career home run and closed in on his 3,000th hit. But the back pain persisted. He was diagnosed with stenosis, a narrowing of the spinal column that caused chronic nerve irritation. He went back on the disabled list at one point, and then slipped while running the bases in Boston in early September and felt a stabbing pain. That night, he called Bancells at 3 a.m. and said he was flying to Cleveland to see his back specialist. Within days, he underwent a surgical procedure, a decompression, which relieved the inflammation.

After rehabbing all off-season, Ripken was in the lineup on Opening Day 2000, batting sixth and playing third base. He collected his 3,000th hit on April 15, but back pain put him on the disabled list from late June through August. When he returned in September, he told himself he would base a retirement decision on how he hit that month. He hit .307 and drove in 13 runs in 20 games; he even batted cleanup once. That convinced him to play another season.

On June 19, 2001, he announced he would retire at the end of the season. He was 40 years old, in his 21st season, hitting .210. A farewell tour commenced. In every city, fans stood in long lines for his autograph, and he received ovations during games. Opposing teams showered him with gifts. The Toronto Blue Jays gave him a painting of himself and Gehrig. The Boston Red Sox gave him a dark green No. 8 Fenway Park box seat. The New York Yankees gave him a framed enlargement of the commemorative ticket to his final game in the city, which featured pictures of Ripken and Gehrig. The Florida Marlins gave him a framed team picture of the 1979 Miami Orioles, his Class A team. The Texas Rangers retired his locker in the visitors' clubhouse. Teams also contributed to the Cal Ripken, Sr. Foundation, a baseball-centric nonprofit Ripken had started to honor his father.

Though it was a response befitting royalty, it was not all cheers. In an ESPN.com column, sportswriter Bill Simmons took issue with the idea that he needed to take advantage of this last chance to see Ripken on the playing field. While conceding that Ripken, "statistically, may be the greatest shortstop of all time," Simmons wrote that he had "just chugged along" for most of his career, piling up high career totals without producing the "electric" moments other famous players engineered. And actually, Simmons wrote, his stats were average except for those for a couple of seasons.

As for the consecutive-game record, it was "more luck than anything," Simmons wrote, adding that he was "still waiting for somebody to explain why it benefits a baseball team to have its franchise player playing 162 games a year for 16 consecutive seasons. If winning is the bottom line, and it's proven that baseball players perform better when they are rested occasionally . . . well, isn't that the most counter-productive record of all-time?"

Simmons, who would become his generation's most popular sportswriter, was voicing familiar criticisms of the streak on the Internet, fast becoming the dominant media. A new century was under way, momentous changes were in motion, and Ripken, even while still in uniform, already seemed like a time traveler from another era. He had played in every game for more than 16 years on principle, not because it was always practical or statistically sensible. The rationale was either old-fashioned or beautiful, depending on one's point of view.

Simmons's desire for "electric" moments also was a familiar refrain. Fans had longed for baseball players to wow them since Babe Ruth started slugging home runs after World War I. More recently, the ubiquity of nightly highlight packages on television had elevated the public's craving for outstanding individual plays.

But indelible moments are not baseball's basic currency. This is a sport that rewards consistency and perseverance. Its truths crystallize gradually rather than immediately, over weeks, over months, sometimes even over years. Ripken's record was a reflection of that subtle sensibility, its value becoming evident almost imperceptibly, inning by inning, game by game, year by year. He delivered indelible moments, none more enduring than the night he passed Gehrig, but what mattered, what constituted the very essence of baseball, was his consistent presence, his dependability, the simple fact that he was *there*, always there.

He did not need to defend himself. His career ranked with the greatest ever witnessed, and his signature achievement, though certainly open to interpretation, was perched in the first rank of the sport's history. Ripken played his final game on October 6, 2001, and when he went into the Hall of Fame in 2007, his bronze testimonial plaque began with these words, which cast his legacy: "Arrived at the ballpark every day with a burning desire to perform at his highest level. Dedication and work ethic resulted in a record 2,632 consecutive games played from May 30, 1982 through September 19, 1998, earning him the title of baseball's 'Iron Man.'"

Those spare, poignant sentences said it all.

Ironmen

A PHILOSOPHICAL CHANGE

On September 20, 1998 — the day after Ripken's streak ended — baseball had a new active consecutive-game leader for the first time in more than a decade. It was Albert Belle, a surly slugger for the Chicago White Sox. He had played in 327 straight games, leaving him 2,305 shy of the record. Even if he played in every game for the next 14 seasons, he would trail Ripken.

After that season, Belle, coincidentally, signed with the Orioles as a free agent and became Ripken's teammate. He stretched his streak to 392 games before it ended ignominiously on June 9, 1999, when the Orioles' manager, Ray Miller, suspended Belle for a game for failing to run out a ground ball.

The end of Belle's streak meant Vinny Castilla, a third baseman for the Colorado Rockies, now had the longest active streak in the majors — 303 straight games. But within a week, Jim Leyland, the Rockies' manager, gave Castilla a day off, explaining simply that Castilla appeared to need a break. Another Oriole, B. J. Surhoff, then became the active major league leader, having played in 225 straight games.

Surhoff would eventually play in 445 straight games for the Orioles and Atlanta Braves before sitting one out after taking a fastball to the ribs. Several other players put together similar streaks as the new century began, but they all stopped well short of 500. The Cubs' Sammy Sosa played in 388 straight until a bad back forced him to miss a game on September 19, 2000. Shawn Green played in 415 straight for the Blue Jays and Dodgers before sitting out a game on September 26, 2001, in observance of Yom Kippur, the Jewish holiday.

Consecutive-game streaks were experiencing a palpable decline, both in length and renown. But actually, Ripken's notwithstanding, they had been in decline for decades.

In the first half of the twentieth century, major leaguers routinely achieved the fundamental element of a streak, playing an entire season without missing a game. On average over those five decades, 9.66 players per year did it. But the per-year average dropped to 5.92 in the second half of the twentieth century despite the major league population nearly doubling due to expansion. Fewer seasons of perfect attendance inevitably meant fewer streaks.

Once the new century began, the decline in perfect attendance accelerated. In 2004, only two National Leaguers and two American Leaguers played all season without missing a game. Only 2.6 major leaguers per year did it between 2009 and 2013. Hunter Pence, an outfielder for the San Francisco Giants, was the only major leaguer to play in every game in 2013 and 2014.

What caused the philosophical shift on endurance that has resulted in consecutive-game streaks becoming an endangered species?

Higher Salaries

In 1975, the year before free agency was instituted, the average major league salary was $44,676. By 2012, it was $3.2 million, and 20 players earned at least $20 million per season. The spike in pay altered how both players and teams viewed the conundrum of whether to play through an injury or sit out.

"With that kind of money on the table, the mindset of the player is, 'If I'm injured and not 100 percent, I'm not going to let the injury affect my future earnings. I'm going to sit out until I'm healthy.' I hate to say that, but it's true," said Doug Melvin, the Milwaukee Brewers' general manager from 2002 through 2015.

Ripken agreed. "Now a player gets praised if he recognizes he has an injury and takes himself out for the sake of the team. Needless to say, I looked at that situation differently," he said.

Teams exhibit similar caution, preferring not to see high-priced players risk the team's large investment in them by playing when less than fully healthy.

"There's a protective nature on the part of clubs when contracts are so big," Ripken said. "Teams don't want to risk a guy getting hurt when they're paying him so much. If he's borderline to play, money is a major factor in the decision."

Guaranteed Multiyear Contracts

Before free agency, most players signed one-year deals and worried about playing well enough to secure another contract the next year. That encouraged them to play whenever possible, almost out of fear. The story of Wally Pipp echoed in many players' minds. Pipp took one day off and lost his job to Lou Gehrig forever.

But now many more players are on multiyear contracts that are fully guaranteed. They can feel secure about their jobs even if they take a day off.

"Today, there are guys who look for days off, who say, 'This hurts' or 'That hurts.' They're very comfortable playing 120 games a year. But when guys were on one-year contracts, very few felt comfortable playing 120 games. Someone would take their job if they sat out," Tim McCarver said.

He continued: "In those days, your salary for the next year depended on your performance, and part of your performance was playing every day. It makes it that much more unbelievable that Ripken played in more than 2,600 straight games. He was on guaranteed contracts the whole way, so why play? Cal deserves credit."

Richie Bancells, the Orioles' head trainer and a veteran of countless decisions about whether a player should take the field, said the change has come quickly. "It's since Cal played. There is just so much more money on the table and so many guaranteed contracts, all of which behooves one to be conservative," Bancells said. "Agents get involved, and they're very, very protective of their investment."

Smarter Sports Medicine

Thanks to the evolving use of techniques such as MRI and arthroscopy, team doctors and trainers can now diagnose more injuries and have a better grasp of their potential harm. For instance, it is now known that hip and back pain can result from ligament and labrum tears rather than just sprains and bruises. As a result, more players choose to sit out games rather than play when injured.

"I had a conversation with our former team doctor not long ago," Doug Melvin said. "I said, 'Doc, it's a good thing you're not a doc in today's baseball world. You'd be real busy.' He said, 'I was a doctor for 25 years and I never treated one oblique [rib] muscle injury. Now every team deals with oblique injuries every year.' I asked, 'Why is that?' He said, 'Today, with all the MRIs and exams at our disposal, diagnosis of injuries goes way, way beyond what used to be the norm.'"

Increased Statistical Analysis and Specialization

The more information a manager has, the more he is liable to tailor his use of certain players to certain situations, inevitably resulting in fewer of them playing every day.

This strategy has long been part of the game. As early as the 1800s, it was evident that left-handed hitters fared better against right handed pitchers, and vice versa. Shortly after World War II, the Dodgers' Branch Rickey hired a full-time statistician to evaluate players' performance. Beginning in the 1960s, Earl Weaver managed with the help of index cards containing his batters' performance against different pitchers.

Today, with the rise of sabermetrics since the 1970s, there is a veritable avalanche of sophisticated statistics and performance analytics. When making out his lineup, a manager can study how hitters fare in different ballparks, how pitchers perform on different counts, how much ground players cover in the field, how often batters put the ball in play — enough information to make him dizzy. Inevitably, it produces more specialization and fewer players appearing in the lineup every day.

"It used to be that you played your best guys because they gave you the best chance to win, but now there's a mindset that, with the help of analytics, you can fare just as well without a guy by using more chess pieces, as long as you use them correctly," Ripken said.

General De-emphasis

Although Ripken's streak will always be applauded as a remarkable feat, consecutive-game streaks have long generated an opposing view best summed up as "Who cares?" That view finally has prevailed, it seems.

"Being an everyday player just isn't as valued as much as when I played," Ripken said. "A full season — I think that's something like 145 games now."

A signature moment quietly occurred early in the 2010 season when Evan Longoria, a third baseman for the Tampa Bay Rays, had played in 131 straight games. A redoubtable, broad-shouldered infielder with home run power and a sure glove, Longoria was emerging as his generation's version of Ripken. Already a two-time All-Star at age 24, he liked to play every day.

One Sunday in late May, he came to the ballpark feeling "under the weather," according to the *Tampa Bay Times*. He wanted to play, but Joe Maddon, the Rays' manager, kept him on the bench all day.

"We're not looking for the next Cal Ripken right now in regards to number of games in a row played," Maddon explained. "I just want to keep him well and healthy and on the top of his game."

Maddon, considered one of the game's shrewdest managers, then issued what amounted to a death knell for playing streaks.

"I do believe if you were to permit him to play 162 games, I bet he could," he said of Longoria. "But I don't think it is in his best interest or ours."

Two decades after Ripken passed Gehrig, it is difficult to imagine any player producing a consecutive-game streak so long. Yet several players in those decades have possessed a Ripken-like desire to play every day.

Ichiro Suzuki, a Japanese outfielder who spent most of his major league career with the Seattle Mariners, played in either 161 or 162 games in every season but one between 2004 and 2012. Before that, as a young player in Japan, he played in 763 consecutive games. Juan Pierre, another outfielder, appeared in 821 straight for the Rockies, Marlins, Cubs, and Dodgers between 2003 and 2007. But since he only pinch-ran on June 3, 2005, he could not claim what would have been one of the 10 longest streaks ever. Instead, he was credited with two shorter streaks of 434 and 386 games.

Hideki Matsui, another Japanese outfielder, played in his first 518 games in the major leagues after the Yankees brought him to America in 2003. Before that, he played in 1,250 straight for the Yomiuri Giants, a Japanese club, giving him a combined streak of 1,768 straight games in Japan and America before a wrist injury ended his run on May 10, 2006.

Prince Fielder, a slugging first baseman, played in 547 straight games for the Brewers, Tigers, and Rangers between 2010 and 2014. He stopped only because of a herniated disc in his neck, which required surgery.

"Only a few guys have that mindset, that sense of responsibility to their job and their teammates, like Cal and Gehrig, obviously, and a few others more recently, like Matsui. Prince had that mindset," said Doug Melvin, who was the Brewers' general manager when they drafted Fielder, in 2002. "They come to the park, they enjoy playing, they have fun doing it, and they never want to come out. When they're hurt or sore, they just go beyond it. There's a mental toughness about them."

Fielder's father, Cecil, had also been a prolific slugger, swatting 319 home runs, mostly for the Tigers, in a 13-year major league career. At five feet eleven and 275 pounds, Prince was rounder than his father but could hit the ball just as far.

Once he became a regular with the Brewers, Fielder missed just five games in 2006, four in 2007, and three in 2008. But even after he smacked 50 home runs in 2007 to establish his credentials as a power hitter, the Brewers' manager, Ned Yost, rested him several times each season.

Fielder bristled at the days off. "Every time I missed a game, it pissed me off," he recalled. "I hated being sat, just didn't ever want to sit at all. I was a young guy and made it into something personal. I said that when I put in enough time and did well enough that I had the chance to dictate it and play every day, I was going to do that, play every single day. That's what I wanted."

Criticism from fans and the media helped shape his philosophy. Fielder constantly heard and read that he was not in shape and was bound to break down because he did not take care of his body. His response was to try to play every day.

"A lot of people didn't think I'd be able to do it. I heard that from my rookie year on — 'He's too big, too all that.' At the time, I probably was," Fielder said. "But I've been big all my life. It's not like it popped up on anybody. I'm big. But that doesn't mean anything. I'm stubborn. Because they said I couldn't play every day, I wanted to."

He finally played a full season in 2009. In 2010, he sat out just one game, the nightcap of a doubleheader on September 14. That ended a streak of 327 straight games for him, and it was the last game he would miss for almost four years.

"Unless it's bleeding or broken, I'm going to play," Fielder told reporters when he reached 500 games in a row while with the Tigers in 2013.

The Tigers' manager, Jim Leyland, appreciated Fielder's approach. "Prince is a very proud guy," Leyland said. "On most occasions, he runs to first base as hard as anybody we've got. He likes to play. He likes to be in the lineup. He knows he gets paid to be in the lineup, and that's what he does. I give him the utmost credit."

That winter, Fielder was traded to the Rangers. He never took a physical, according to Jon Daniels, the Rangers' general manager, and was in the Opening Day lineup, batting fourth and playing first base. Much was expected of him. He was in his prime, 29 years old, and had hit between 25 and 50 home runs for eight straight seasons.

From the outset in 2014, though, Fielder struggled. Instead of lashing the ball with his fierce left-handed swing, he hit weak grounders and struck out. His batting average plummeted and Texas fans grumbled, until Fielder admitted in early May that his neck was stiff and sore. When doctors investigated, they found the herniated disc.

At first, Fielder tried to play through the pain. He had the longest active consecutive-game streak in the majors and was stubborn about playing every day. "I didn't care if I was 0-for-50 or whatever, I was going to play," he said.

But his struggles persisted, and it soon became clear he could not keep going without receiving medical attention that would force him out of the lineup. After playing in 547 straight games, he sat out a game on May 17, 2014, received an injection of painkiller, and said he hoped to return in a few days. He had just turned 30.

As it turned out, his season was over. The injection did not provide relief, and Fielder wound up undergoing surgery. With good cheer, he tweeted, "I'll be back!"

When he returned to the Rangers in 2015, he hit .305 with 98 runs batted in and made the American League All-Star team. But he made sure he took occasional games off. His feelings about playing every day had changed, reflecting the shift in attitude throughout the sport that had occurred during his career.

"I'm feeling really refreshed," Fielder said, smiling, in the middle of the 2015 season. "I'm proud of the streak I had, but looking back, I'm thinking a day off now and then would have done me good. That was just me being stubborn. A day off or two isn't going to hurt me."

In 2016, his neck issues resurfaced, prompting more surgery. He had played in 98.9 percent of his team's games between 2006 and 2013 and achieved perfect attendance four times, but it was doubtful he would ever set foot on a major league diamond again.

Although Ripken's record is widely regarded as unbreakable, Ripken himself has doubts about its permanence. "People say it's an unbreakable record, but I did it, so somebody else can," he said. "How you evaluate an everyday player now might have changed a bit, but still, there are plenty of guys who can play one season of 162. It's a streak of consecutive seasons playing 162, so a lot of things have to go right, and you have to be worthy of being in the lineup, but I don't look at it as an unbreakable record."

If any player since Ripken has had a chance, it was Miguel Tejada, a muscular shortstop who compiled the fifth-longest streak in major league history while playing for the Oakland A's and Orioles between 2001 and 2007.

"With him, more than anything, it was pure love of the game," said Art Howe, who managed Tejada in Oakland. "He loved to play baseball. He couldn't wait to get on the field and compete. If he was healthy, he was going to be in the lineup. I guess you have to be lucky not to get hit by a pitch or sprain an ankle. He left his feet a lot, dove for balls. Fortunately, he never came up lame and never had any really bad collisions."

A native of Los Barrancones, a tiny village in the Dominican Republic, Tejada grew up in poverty, the youngest of 11 children in a home without electricity or running water. Rather than attend school, he helped provide for his family, at different times shining shoes, making garments in a factory, and working construction.

In the afternoons, he played baseball, a passion he shared with many

Dominican boys. He played shortstop, a position rich in tradition on the island, but he was so thick through his chest and trunk that he lacked natural grace. Several of his friends glided after ground balls, made effortless throws across the diamond, and signed pro contracts before him. Finally, Juan Marichal, a Hall of Fame pitcher who scouted for the A's, saw enough potential to sign Tejada.

He rose through Oakland's minor league system, exhibiting surprising power, and made the majors in a few years. The A's were not a large-market franchise, leaving their general manager, Billy Beane, with limited funds to pursue free agents. Beane had no choice but to construct a roster with homegrown talent, drafted and developed by the club. Fortunately for Beane, his system produced Jason Giambi, a powerful slugger, and pitchers Barry Zito, Tim Hudson, and Mark Mulder as well as Tejada — a group that would lead the A's to four straight division titles beginning in 2000.

Once Tejada had the shortstop job, he gripped it tightly, playing with almost frightening fierceness. He swung hard at pitches and drove himself relentlessly, never wanting to rest. Howe occasionally asked Tejada if he wanted to take a day off. "He gave me a look like, 'Are you kidding?'" Howe recalled.

The American League shortstop roster included Boston's Nomar Garciaparra, Texas's Alex Rodriguez, and New York's Derek Jeter. Tejada elbowed his way into their starry company. Playing a full season of games for the first time in 2001, he batted .267 with 31 home runs and 113 runs batted in. The next year, he again played in every game and hit .308 with 34 home runs and 131 runs batted in. The A's suffered a first-round playoff defeat for the third straight year, but Tejada was voted the league's Most Valuable Player.

The playoff disappointments prompted Howe's firing, but Oakland's new manager, Ken Macha, continued to play Tejada every day. When he became a free agent after the 2003 season, which ended with another early playoff defeat for the A's, Tejada had eye-popping offensive statistics for a shortstop and had played in 594 straight games. The Orioles signed him to a six-year, $72 million contract.

Baltimore fans hoped Tejada could lead their club back to glory. The Orioles had not finished over .500 since 1997. As a durable middle infielder with home run power, he was, in a way, a reincarnation of Ripken. His approach certainly was similar: Tejada did not even rest in the off-season, instead playing winter ball in the Dominican Republic. A day without a game was unfathomable to him.

"He didn't even want a day off in spring training," recalled Dave Trembley, a manager in the Orioles' minor league system when Tejada joined the club. "Most veteran guys are always looking for that, a day off in the spring, especially when a long bus ride is involved. Tejada would hop on the bus and say, 'Let's go!'"

In 2004, he played in every game and batted .304 with 34 home runs and 150 runs batted in—a spectacular season. But the Orioles still languished, finishing 23 games out of first. Early in 2005, they surprisingly shot to the top of the division, with Tejada leading the way. In July, he hit a home run in the All-Star Game and was named the game's MVP. The fans had elected him a starter over Jeter, Garciaparra, and Rodriguez.

But the Orioles crashed hard in the final months of 2005. Rafael Palmeiro, back with the club at age 40, tested positive for a banned steroid and claimed Tejada had provided it in a tainted vitamin B12 supplement. Tejada admitted giving Palmeiro a shot of B12, a legal vitamin, but denied it contained a performance-enhancing drug. A panel overseeing baseball's drug-testing program exonerated Tejada, but the specter of steroids would haunt him for the rest of his career.

Early in 2006, he hyperextended his right knee, and fans criticized him for not hustling down the line on some ground balls. But he played on, never taking a day off. The Orioles' manager, Sam Perlozzo, suggested he serve as the designated hitter on days when his knee hurt. Tejada liked the idea. He would DH more than a dozen times in the next two seasons, utilizing an option unavailable in Gehrig's era to keep his playing streak going. He considered those "DH days" his days off, Tejada said later.

On July 1, 2006, in the midst of yet another last-place season for the Orioles, his playing streak reached 1,000 straight games. He could not suppress a smile as he spoke to reporters in the clubhouse. "It is not easy to play in a thousand games in a row. I know how Cal Ripken feels," he said.

He had not missed a game since June 1, 2000. Asked how he was holding up, he said, "I feel fine. I am happy. For me, this streak is not important. I don't worry about 1,000 games, 2,000 games. I just worry about one game at a time. I play every day because I like to play baseball."

Perlozzo had no plans to rest him. "When I come to the ballpark, it's the one given I have. His name is in the lineup and you don't even think about it," Perlozzo said, echoing a line several Orioles managers had voiced about Ripken.

By the middle of the 2007 season, Perlozzo had been fired, and Trembley was Baltimore's manager on an interim basis. The Orioles were back in last place and contemplating trading Tejada to bolster a rebuilding effort. Although he was hitting .306, he was no longer an MVP candidate. The Orioles were ready to deal him if they could find a team willing to give up quality prospects in return.

On June 20, Tejada played shortstop and batted cleanup against the Padres in San Diego. He doubled in a run in the first, and the Orioles took a three-run lead into the eighth. Facing reliever Doug Brocail, Tejada took a first-pitch strike. Brocail then came inside with a pitch and hit Tejada on the left wrist. Tejada grimaced and rubbed his wrist as he took first base. He came around to score as the Orioles put the game away with a big inning, but when he reached the dugout, he told Trembley he needed to come out. X-rays revealed a fractured radius at the juncture of his wrist and forearm.

"The doctor and I had to sit him down and tell him it was broken. His look was one of sheer disbelief," said Richie Bancells, still working for the Orioles. "His response was, 'No, I'll be fine, it's not that bad, I'll be OK.' You have to have a conversation with him at that point: 'Miggy, it isn't a matter of how tough you are. If you play through this, you could damage your hand for life.' You have to have conversations with people like that. They have a different mental outlook, sort of a childlike disbelief that anything could be wrong with them, that something like this could happen."

The Orioles played another game in San Diego the next night. Trembley was in a difficult position. He had taken over for Perlozzo just the day before, and this was his first major league managing job. Tejada told him during batting practice that swinging the bat did not hurt his wrist. Trembley knew Tejada was injured but gave him a shot out of respect, batting him fourth in an early version of the lineup before moving him to second so he could bat in the first inning.

After the Orioles' Brian Roberts led off the game with a single, Tejada approached the plate. His wrist hurt when he took his practice cuts, so he squared around and bunted the first pitch from San Diego's pitcher, David Wells. The ball rolled to Wells, who picked it up and threw to second to force Roberts. Tejada was safe at first on the fielder's choice, and Trembley replaced him with a pinch runner.

"We were very much aware of his streak. He was very much aware of it. It was very important to him. He said he could play. He was cleared to play. But he really couldn't swing the bat. He could in BP, but in the game, with the velocity of pitches, you could tell it was bothering him," Trembley recalled. "He was crushed. His teammates, his coaches, everyone knew he had the streak. Everyone knew it was really important to him. The night he got hit, he was determined he was going to keep playing. He gave it a shot. It was an unfortunate thing."

Wells criticized Trembley after the game for letting Tejada employ a gimmick to extend his streak to 1,152 straight games. It was similar to the gimmick Gehrig and the Yankees had employed to extend Gehrig's streak in 1934.

Trembley explained his thinking. "It's been a tough day, a real tough day," he told reporters after the game. "We wanted to show Miguel we care about him, not only as a baseball player, but as a person. Now he needs to go get well."

The streak was over. Tejada wore a soft cast on his wrist before the Orioles' next game, against the Arizona Diamondbacks. Consigned to the disabled list, he appeared lost as he wandered through the clubhouse knowing he would not play.

"I'm really proud of myself to play so many games in a row," he told reporters. "I don't want to end it like this. What can I say? There's nothing I can do. Right now, I can't help the team. This is better for me and for the team to have somebody in there who can help the team."

Given the respect he commanded and his approach to playing, he could have gone years without missing a game had he not suffered an injury. But even after compiling the fifth-longest streak in history, he was less than halfway to Ripken's record. To get that far, Tejada would have needed to play 9 more full seasons consecutively, plus part of a 10th . . . almost another decade.

"It makes you realize how special Cal was," Trembley told reporters in 2007, "and how no one will ever even come close to touching that."

. . .

When Tejada returned to the Orioles' lineup in 2007 after missing almost a month while his wrist healed, he played in every game for the rest of the season. In December, the Orioles traded him to the Houston Astros for five players.

"He plays every inning of every game," Houston's general manager, Ed Wade, told the local media in explaining why he made the deal.

Coincidentally, the Astros had recently signed Brocail, the reliever whose pitch injured him. They would play together for two seasons. It became a difficult time for Tejada. A day after he was traded, Major League Baseball released the Mitchell Report, a grim document resulting from a 21-month independent investigation — led by former U.S. senator George Mitchell — into the use of performance-enhancing drugs in the major leagues. The report stated that in 2003, while in Oakland, Tejada had conversations about steroids with a teammate who also obtained the drugs for him. The report did not say Tejada used the drugs. But his name had appeared in two books on the subject, and although he denied using such drugs, many fans assumed he did.

The Mitchell Report was not his only problem. In 2008, ESPN discovered he had lied about his age when he first signed with Oakland and was, in fact, three years older. In 2009, he pleaded guilty to a charge of lying to congressional investigators about steroid use in baseball and received a year's probation.

But while many fans believe his off-field problems sullied his accomplishments, those who played with him and managed him did not view him so negatively. His Latin teammates called him "La Gua Gua," Dominican slang for "the Bus," because he carried everyone with his play on the field.

"If you ask people who played with him, they'll tell you he was the best teammate they ever had," Trembley said. "He was absolutely loved by his teammates and coaches wherever he went."

In 2014, Trembley was employed by the Astros as a bench coach. Square-jawed and broad-shouldered, he was a foot soldier with a general's bearing, having worked in professional baseball for three decades, mostly as a minor league coach and minor league manager with the Cubs, Pirates, Padres, and Orioles. His only chance to manage in the majors had come in Baltimore and lasted less than three years. The Orioles fired him in 2010.

Trembley had watched Tejada from afar for many years before managing him in Baltimore in 2007. "I saw him as a kid in the California Instructional League. I managed against him in the Southern League. I saw him in Oakland. In every case, he exhibited an extreme exuberance for the game," Trembley said. "When I came to the Astros in 2013, the trainer said he was the best teammate they ever had there. I think that's the case in a lot of places. Tejada just loved to play. He took responsibility for how he played. He played with enthusiasm. He played hard. All the time, he played hard."

Trembley said Tejada's approach contrasted with those of many current players, helping explain why Ripken's record might stand forever. "There's a different culture now. I'm not sure a streak like that is significant to a lot of people. Just a handful of guys play 162. We don't have many," Trembley said. "To think someone might do it even for one year, and then for so many, it's hard to fathom. I don't see it happening. What Ripken did, what Gehrig did, what Tejada did, it's rare now. The game has changed, and how players view the game has changed. There are a lot of people who like it, but not many who really, truly love it. Tejada really, truly loved baseball, like Ripken. He just got hurt, unlike Ripken."

Epilogue

He rode his bicycle to a lunch meeting in Canton, a downtown Baltimore neighborhood east of the Inner Harbor. When the meeting ended, Cal Ripken Jr. jumped back on his bike and pedaled away. He had to get home, get ready, and get back downtown for the Orioles' game that night. The team was commemorating the 20th anniversary of the night he passed Lou Gehrig's consecutive-game record. Ripken, now 55, was scheduled to hold a press conference and throw out the first pitch.

The date was September 1, 2015. Though somewhat thicker than when he played, Ripken still had a broad, strong frame and got in his sporting kicks cycling around Maryland on everything from rural trails to city streets. Leaving his lunch in Canton, he estimated he had plenty of time to make the game, so there was no rush. But he misjudged a curb, struck it, and when his bike came to a sudden halt, Ripken flew over the handlebars and crashed to the sidewalk, landing hard on his right shoulder.

Embarrassed, he quickly stood up, got back on his bike, and rode off. But as the afternoon progressed, he realized he could not lift his right arm above his shoulder without experiencing searing pain. Something was not right.

Having long ago transitioned from baseball to the business world, Ripken oversaw a thriving baseball empire that included a pair of minor league teams, a stadium in his hometown, youth baseball complexes in three states, camps and clinics, a nonprofit named for his father, and an annual worldwide tournament for 12-year-olds. It all went under the umbrella of an entity called Ripken Baseball, which he described as the "business of Cal."

His divorce from Kelly the following year, ending a 29-year marriage, would reveal that his life was not without difficulties, but all in all, Ripken's post-playing world was seemingly happy and prosperous. "The business of Cal is bustling," *Fortune* magazine wrote in a 2014 profile.

After he fell off his bike, though, Ripken was abruptly taken back to a predicament from his playing days: could he overcome an injury, get on the field, and perform?

He drove to Oriole Park at Camden Yards, where he seldom ventured now. The "2,131" banners were back on the B&O Warehouse wall, and a video from his historic night played on the stadium video board during batting practice, conjuring up memories for Ripken, who admitted to feeling tearful when the camera focused on his late father. "We lost dad much too soon," he told reporters.

During the press conference, he sheepishly admitted he had injured himself earlier that day, and before he headed to the field to throw out the first pitch, he explained the situation to his designated catcher, Brady Anderson, his former teammate, now a front office executive with the Orioles.

"Dude, I hurt myself real bad," Ripken told Anderson.

Ever the planner, he told Anderson he would stop on the grass between the mound and home plate and throw a shorter first pitch. He feared he could not make the throw from the mound and did not want to bounce a feeble toss that ESPN's anchors could, and surely would, mock.

Dressed in a sports jacket and slacks, he was announced to the crowd, emerged from the dugout, and waved — with one arm. If any fans wondered why he stopped on the grass and made a shorter throw to Anderson, it did not stop them from cheering for Ripken and his consecutive-game achievement.

Upon leaving the field, he mentioned his injury to the Orioles' team doctors in the home clubhouse. They X-rayed his shoulder and told him to get an MRI. Indeed, something was not right. The MRI confirmed what the team doctors saw: Ripken had ripped two tendons from his rotator cuff when he landed on his shoulder.

"The tendons had come clean off the bone," Ripken recalled. "This wasn't going to heal."

The irony was not lost on the Ironman: on the day he celebrated his streak, he suffered an injury that would have ended it. He underwent surgery within days.

"There was no way I could have played through it," he said. "It was kind of funny and painful at the same time."

The accident illustrated the good fortune that visited Ripken throughout his streak. He experienced his share of mishaps, but none ended his run.

The accident also emphasized the unlikelihood of another major leaguer playing in every game for more than 16 years in a row, even if he wanted to try. Major league games were as full of physical risks as ever, and as Billy Williams said, "stuff happens" off the field.

After Everett Scott's playing streak ended in 1925, it was widely believed the little shortstop would always hold the consecutive-game record. Who else would want to try such a stunt? Scott's achievement "will be equaled only through another miracle the equal of his own," the *New York Times* wrote. But that "miracle" took place soon. Gehrig passed Scott eight years later.

Like Scott's record, Gehrig's was also deemed unbreakable, this time for longer. "When I started playing [in the 1950s], the two records everyone saw as unbreakable were Gehrig's and Ruth's," Brooks Robinson said. "How were you going to hit more than 714 home runs? And how were you going to play in more games in a row than Gehrig? That was just incredible."

But Hank Aaron broke Ruth's career home run record in 1974, and Ripken passed Gehrig in 1995. Now Ripken's streak of 2,632 straight games is widely viewed as likely to stand for as long as baseball is played.

"That's one record where you have to say, 'Well, no one is going to break that.' Because, I mean, no one is going to," Robinson said.

Numerous other records are deemed unbreakable. Pitcher Cy Young's career record of 511 wins, set when arms were not treated nearly so carefully, certainly appears safe; it would take twenty-five 20-win seasons just to get close. Connie Mack's career mark of managing 53 major league seasons surely will never be topped. On the night the Orioles celebrated the 20th anniversary of 2,131, the team's current manager, Buck Showalter, cited Hack Wilson's single-season record of 191 runs batted in, set in 1930, as a mark "nobody will ever touch."

Though set much more recently, Ripken's record already seems similarly preposterous.

"Trust me, nobody's going to touch it," Showalter said.

"We may never see anyone get to a thousand again, much less to what

Gehrig or Cal did," Steve Garvey said. "There's a mindset of not needing to play every day, of managers not wanting guys to play every day. You have to overcome the challenge of that philosophy to have a streak."

Garvey played every day, he said, because of "a philosophy, an attitude of wanting to always be there for your teammates, be dependable, uphold the terms of your contract. I'm not sure you're going to see that anymore. Now we're in the era of, 'I'll take $20 million a year, but don't ask me to play more than 140 games.' My response is, 'Wait, you don't want to play every game?'"

When teams reported to spring training before the 2015 season, Hunter Pence, an outfielder for the San Francisco Giants, had the longest active consecutive-game streak in the majors — 383 straight games. Tall, curly-haired, and known as an aggressive, high-energy player, Pence possessed an old-fashioned determination to play through aches. He had missed just 24 games in seven seasons since becoming a regular in 2008.

When he stepped to the plate in an exhibition game against the Chicago Cubs in Surprise, Arizona, on March 5, 2015, it seemed certain his streak would continue when the regular season began. But a Cubs pitcher, Corey Black, threw a fastball that sailed inside and hit him on the left wrist. "I had a feeling it wasn't good," Pence said.

Sure enough, his ulna was fractured. Doctors estimated he would miss two months, including the first weeks of the 2015 regular season. His streak was over.

"Lost for words. Hope you heal fast @hunterpence. Hitting someone is never a good feeling. Hurting someone is even worse," Black posted on Twitter.

Pence good-naturedly responded with this tweet: "It happens, my friend. Thanks for the concern. It's a part of the game we love. No slowing down!"

With Pence out, the two longest active streaks belonged to Freddie Freeman, a first baseman for the Atlanta Braves, and Kyle Seagar, a third baseman for the Seattle Mariners. But several months later, within hours of each other on June 18, 2015, Freeman sat out a game because of a wrist injury, ending his streak at 234 straight games, and Seagar was a late scratch due to food poisoning, ending his run of 192 straight.

On the day Ripken fell off his bike, Manny Machado, a young third baseman for the Orioles, had the longest active streak in the majors, having played in 132 consecutive games — exactly 2,500 fewer than Ripken. Completing even one season of games was deemed a mountain too high for most players, and the idea of doing it for a period of years had become a relic from baseball's past, as outdated as exaggerated pitching windups and twi-night doubleheaders.

Yes, Ripken's Ironman record was safe, probably forever.

Author's Note

Of all my books, this one took the longest to complete, making it something of an Ironman feat in itself. Fortunately, no one kept track of the days.

As always, I had a lot of help. In the midst of the project, I took a job as a columnist at Baltimoreravens.com, the website for the National Football League team in Baltimore, where I live. I worked on the book when I wasn't covering the Ravens, and I thank Michelle Andres, the team's vice president of digital media, for understanding the balance I needed to strike to get my various jobs done.

My thanks also go to Scott Waxman, my agent, who helped get the project off the ground and provided invaluable counsel at key times; Susan Canavan, my editor at Houghton Mifflin Harcourt, who gently explained why and how an early version of the manuscript needed help and then had a terrific vision for the final version; and Barbara Jatkola, whose careful copyediting made the manuscript more accurate and polished.

Along the way, I celebrated several wedding anniversaries, including No. 30, with Mary Wynne Eisenberg, whose patience, understanding, and support make it possible for me to undertake these (long) projects. MW, I love you so much.

To write about the history of baseball's consecutive-game record since the 1870s, I relied on interviews and research.

I interviewed these people for the book, either in person or on the phone: Brady Anderson, Richie Bancells, Al Clark, Prince Fielder, Al Fultz, Steve Garvey, Pat Gillick, Art Howe, Rex Hudler, Adam Jones, Tim McCarver, Ben McDonald, Doug Melvin, Dale Murphy, Phil Regan, Bill Ripken, Cal Ripken Jr., Frank Robinson, Fred Roussey, Ron Shapiro, John Shelby, Ken Singleton, Mickey Tettleton, Dave Trembley, Fred Tyler, and Billy Williams. I thank them all for their time and memories and also thank Steve Brener, Dan Connolly, Bob Ibach, John Maroon, and Bill Stetka for helping me get in touch with some of them.

The quotes and information from Roland Hemond, Davey Johnson, Johnny Oates, Rafael Palmeiro, and Brooks Robinson in this book are taken from interviews that occurred in 1999 during my research for *From 33rd Street to Camden Yards,* my oral history of the Baltimore Orioles, published in 2001 by Contemporary Books.

As for the research, I tapped my usual suspects: old newspapers and magazines, previous books that covered the same terrain, and websites. I also used my own coverage of Cal Ripken Jr. and the Baltimore Orioles. As a *Baltimore Sun* sportswriter and columnist from 1984 to 2007, I was on hand for many of Ripken's highs and lows.

My best resource for old newspapers and magazines was the library at the National Baseball Hall of Fame in Cooperstown, New York, where just about every player who ever suited up in the major leagues has a file. The library's vast collection of Lou Gehrig material, which includes Eleanor Gehrig's scrapbooks, was especially helpful. Most of the material on Gehrig and other players was easily identifiable, but several clippings that I used lacked a date or a source. I sought to identify them as best I could in both the text and the chapter-by-chapter discursive notes that follow, using the HOF (Hall of Fame) designation in the latter when I was unable to pinpoint a source.

To access newspapers going back to the 1800s, I used the microfilm rolls at the Library of Congress in Washington, D.C.

The books that I used are listed in the bibliography, but several warrant special mention. *Luckiest Man: The Life and Death of Lou Gehrig,* by Jonathan Eig, was invaluable in helping me construct scenes from Gehrig's life. I also could not have proceeded far without *The Iron Men of Baseball,* by Marty Friedrich, which contains lengthy capsules focusing on the consecutive-game streaks of every player who ever had the longest active streak in the major leagues. Marty's painstaking research was hugely helpful.

Another book that helped with Gehrig was *Iron Horse: Lou Gehrig in His Time,* by Ray Robinson. Books that helped with the Ripken sections were *The Only Way I Know,* by Cal Ripken Jr. and Mike Bryan, and *The Ripken Way: A Manual for Baseball and Life,* by Cal Ripken Sr.

I covered baseball for many years for the *Baltimore Sun,* long enough to become a lifetime member of the Baseball Writers' Association of America. I tended to focus on narrative more than numbers in my coverage, but this is a book about numbers as well as narrative, and taking it on convinced me to join the Society for American Baseball Research. I was in touch with a handful of its members as I reported and wrote, and they all offered encouragement and help, sometimes with the smallest of details.

My one truly indispensable resource was Pro-baseball-reference.com, the website for scores, statistics, and records going back to the 1870s. I used it whenever I needed a stat, date, lineup, or just about anything involving a number. Information from the site is all over just about every page in this book. I'm a big fan.

I have strived for 100 percent accuracy, knowing that is difficult to attain, if not impossible. For any mistakes, I take full responsibility.

— JOHN EISENBERG

Source Notes

Introduction

Quotes from Adam Jones and Steve Garvey from author interviews.

Chapter 1

Quotes from Bill Ripken, Cal Ripken Jr., Regan, Bancells, Shapiro, Hudler, Clark, Roussey, and Fultz from author interviews. Palmeiro quotes from 1999 author interview. Dugout conversations during ovation from author interview with Cal Ripken Jr. Olney comment from *Bowdoin Orient*, October 23, 2009. "World's largest outdoor insane asylum" from sportswriter Cooper Rollow's obituary, *Chicago Tribune*, April 1, 2013. "Devil on earth" from E. M. Swift, "Now You See Him, Now You Don't," *Sports Illustrated*, December 10, 1986. "I locked eyes" from Tim Kurkjian, "Twenty Years Later, Ripken's Feat Remains Unforgettable," ESPN.com, September 4, 2015. Maroon essay from *Baltimore Business Journal*, September 2, 2015.

Chapter 2

Text of DiMaggio speech from *New York Times*, September 8, 1995. Ripken quotes from author interview. "People were mad" from Tim Kurkjian, "Twenty Years Later, Ripken's Feat Remains Unforgettable," ESPN.com, September 4, 2015. Angelos quote about DiMaggio from *Baltimore Sun*, September 7, 1995. "Lou Gehrig Appreciation Day" from Eig, *Luckiest Man*; *New York World-Telegram*, August 4, 1937; *New York Times*, August 4, 1937; and *New York Herald Tribune*, August 4, 1937. Samuel Goldwyn background and *The Pride of the Yankees* from Berg, *Goldwyn*; IMDb.com; and PBS.org. Eleanor Gehrig quote about Gary Cooper from Eleanor Gehrig scrapbook, National Baseball Hall of Fame (hereafter cited as HOF). Text of Ripken's speech from *Baltimore Sun*, September 7, 1995.

Chapter 3

Pheidippides's background from USATF.org, Findingdulcinea.com, and Eyewitnessto history.com. Spyridon Louis and inaugural Olympic marathon from Olympic.org and Sports-reference.com. Boston Marathon history from History.com, Runningpast.com, and BAA.org. Matthew Webb and English Channel crossing from Kingofthechannel. com; History.com; and Express.com, December 15, 2015. Henry Sullivan from Skinner inc.com and *Montreal Gazette*, August 7, 1923. Luderus "new 'Iron Man'" from *Philadelphia Inquirer*, August 4, 1919. Early baseball history from *Total Baseball*. Early set-lineup statistics and Hornung background from Friedrich, *The Iron Men of Baseball*. *Spalding's Base Ball Guide*s from LOC.gov. Pinkney background and scenes from Friedrich, *The Iron Men of Baseball*; Shafer, *When the Dodgers Were Bridegrooms*; Greater Peoria Sports Hall of Fame, Peoria, Illinois; *Brooklyn Eagle* online archives; *Sporting Life* archives; *Peoria Journal Star*, January 2005; and SABR.org.

Chapter 4

Quotes from Bill Ripken, Cal Ripken Jr., Hudler, Shelby, Gillick, Tyler, and Bancells from author interviews. Ripken family history from *Baltimore Sun*, September 4, 1995; *Aberdeen Museum Review*; and Cal Ripken Sr., *The Ripken Way*. Senior's background from Ripken, *The Ripken Way*; Cal Ripken Jr. and Mike Bryan, *The Only Way I Know*; author interviews with Cal Ripken Jr. and Bill Ripken; and SABR.org bio. "I'm taking you out" conversation from author interview with Cal Ripken Jr. "Lack of fluid mobility" scouting report from Barry Petchesky, "Very Cool: Cal Ripken Jr.'s High School Scouting Report as a Pitcher," Deadspin.com, January 3, 2014. Tim Norris quotes from *PressBox*, June 26, 2007.

Chapter 5

Steve Brodie background from *Baltimore Sun*, July 29, 2015; *Roanoke Times and World-News*, February 2, 1992; Brodie family presentation for consideration as a Hall of Fame inductee, Brodie file, HOF; *Sporting News*, December 19, 1925; "Death of Steve Brodie," *Sporting News*, 1935, Brodie file, HOF; and SABR.org bio. "As fast on his feet as a Kansas grasshopper" from *Roanoke Times and World-News*, February 2, 1992. Al Munro Elias background and history of statistics from Schwarz, *The Numbers Game*; Moreland, *Balldom*; Lanigan, *The Baseball Cyclopedia*; and Jewishsports.org. Elias column referenced in *Baseball Magazine*, March 1918. Luderus-Elias streak-extension scene from *Philadelphia Inquirer*, June 4 and June 5, 1919, and *New York Times*, June 4, 1919. Luderus ceremony from *Philadelphia Inquirer*, September 25, 1919.

Chapter 6

Scott background from Friedrich, *The Iron Men of Baseball*; *New York Times*, April 6, 1922; "The Durable Deacon," *Yankees Magazine*, December 17, 1992; and SABR.org bio. Scott ties and sets record from *Boston Globe*, April 26 and April 27, 1920, and *Philadelphia Inquirer*, April 27, 1920. Ruppert background from Appel, *Pinstripe Empire*, and SABR.org bio. Ruth's standing with the Red Sox and circumstances that led to trade from Stout, *The Selling of the Babe,* and Appel, *Pinstripe Empire.* "My transfer to New York," from Cava, *Indiana-Born Major League Baseball Players.*

Chapter 7

"Look, we traded DeCinces" from author interview with Ripken. Jackson comment to Ripken from author interview with Ripken. "I'm putting you there" from author interview with Ripken. "If only I had moved" from Cal Ripken Jr. and Mike Bryan, *The Only Way I Know.* "That's just how he stands" from author interview with Ripken. Ripken quotes cited as written from Ripken and Bryan, *The Only Way I Know;* all others from author interview. Senior quotes cited as written from Cal Ripken Sr., *The Ripken Way.* Story about crutches from Tim Kurkjian, "Twenty Years Later, Ripken's Feat Remains Unforgettable," ESPN.com, September 4, 2015. "20-run homer" from *Baltimore Sun,* September 15, 1987. Dugout conversation in Toronto between Senior and Junior from author interview with Ripken. Quotes from Bill Ripken, Bancells, and Singleton from author interviews.

Chapter 8

Scott's trip from Indiana to Comiskey Park from *New York Times,* September 15, 1922, and *New York Sun,* September 28, 1922. First game at Yankee Stadium from *Sports Illustrated,* April 22, 1963. Scott's 1,000th straight game from *New York Times,* May 2 and May 3, 1923; *New York World-Telegram,* May 3, 1923; *Washington Post,* May 3, 1923; *Washington Star,* May 3, 1923; *Sporting News,* May 5 and May 12, 1923; and *Christian Science Monitor,* May 1923. Yankees dissatisfaction with Scott in 1922 World Series from unidentified clipping, October 26, 1922, Scott file, HOF. Scott background from Friedrich, *The Iron Men of Baseball; New York Times,* April 6, 1922; "The Durable Deacon," *Yankees Magazine,* December 17, 1992; SABR.org bio; Sid Mercer clipping, April 23, 1937, Scott file, HOF; and *New York Times,* March 19, 1922. McGraw "beer legs" comment from *New York Times,* March 27, 1939. Gehrig background from Eig, *Luckiest Man;* Robinson, *Iron Horse;* Appel, *Pinstripe Empire;* Friedrich, *The Iron Men of Baseball;* SABR.org bio; and Niven Busch, "The Little Heinie," *The New Yorker,* August 10, 1929. Yankees scouting of Gehrig and Yankee Stadium batting practice from Weintraub, *The House That Ruth Built,* and Eig, *Luckiest Man.* Pipp background from SABR.org bio and Bruce Anderson, "Just a Pipp of a Legend," *Sports Illustrated,* June 29, 1987. End of Scott's streak from *New York Times,* May 7, 1925, and *New York Times* 1925 Year in Review, Scott file, HOF. Yankees 1925 lineup makeover from *New York World-Telegram,* June 10, 1935.

Chapter 9

Gehrig background and scenes from Eig, *Luckiest Man;* Robinson, *Iron Horse;* Appel, *Pinstripe Empire;* SABR.org bio; clippings in Gehrig file and Eleanor Gehrig scrapbook,

HOF; and Lougehrig.com. Statistics on playing every day in 1920s from Friedrich, *The Iron Men of Baseball.* Ripken quote from author interview. Ruth's 60th home run from *New York Times,* October 1, 1927; Appel, *Pinstripe Empire;* and Creamer, *Babe.* Barnstorming background from Eig, *Luckiest Man,* and press release, n.d., Gehrig file, HOF. Huggins death from SABR.org bio and Eig, *Luckiest Man.*

Chapter 10

Quotes from Cal Ripken Jr., Bill Ripken, Robinson, Anderson, Singleton, Shapiro, McDonald, Bancells, and Tettleton from author interviews. Hemond quotes from 1999 author interview. Lucchino quote from *Baltimore Sun,* July 28, 1988.

Chapter 11

Sewell background from Friedrich, *The Iron Men of Baseball;* Sewell interview with Cleveland Public Library, 1977, archived at http://cplorg.cdmhost.com/; William E. Brandt, "Players of the Game," *New York Times,* 1931, Sewell file, HOF; SABR.org bio; Harry T. Brundidge, "Joey Sewell, Summoned to Fill Ray Chapman's Place in 1920," *St. Louis Star,* n.d., Sewell file, HOF; *New York Times,* March 8, 1990; *Sporting News,* May 8, 1930, and October 20, 1932; *New York Daily News,* February 19, 1977; *New York World-Telegram,* May 4, 1939; and *Baseball Magazine,* Hall of Fame edition, 1977. Sewell rests in Chicago from *Cleveland Plain Dealer,* September 8, 1922. Streak ends from *Cleveland Plain Dealer,* April 29, April 30, May 3, and May 4, 1930. Sewell rooms with Gehrig from Associated Press obituary, March 7, 1990. Postponed Yankees game from Eig, *Luckiest Man.* Daniel conversation with Gehrig from *New York World-Telegram,* n.d., Gehrig file, HOF. Gehrig keeping box score in wallet from Eig, *Luckiest Man,* and *New York Times,* September 8, 2009. Gehrig passes Scott from *New York Times,* August 13, 1933; John Kieran, "The Man Who Is Known as Lou," *New York Times,* August 13, 1933; Sid Keener, "Lou Gehrig and His Phenomenal Iron-Man Record," Gehrig file, HOF; *Christian Science Monitor,* August 18, 1933; and *New York Times,* August 17, 1933. Courtship and marriage of Eleanor and Gehrig from Eig, *Luckiest Man,* and Rud Rennie, "Gehrig Confirms Reports of Betrothal," *New York Herald Tribune,* June 20, 1933.

Chapter 12

Gehrig letter titled "Gehrig Says It Was Luck," *Sporting News,* n.d., Gehrig file, HOF; Japan injury from Eig, *Luckiest Man.* Quotes from Williams and Garvey from author interviews. "A good percentage of luck" from "Luck Helps Make Endurance Record," *New York Times,* April 6, 1922. Garvey calculus from *Los Angeles Times,* August 16, 1995. Suhr background from Clifford Bloodgood, "The National League's Iron Man," April 1937, Suhr file, HOF; *Sports Collectors Digest,* May 27, 1994; *San Francisco Chronicle,* March 15, 2003; "Suhr Keeps His Streak Intact," May 21, 1935, Suhr file, HOF; Associated Press, "NL Endurance Mark Sought by Suhr," May 14, 1935, Suhr file, HOF; and "Suhr Shooting for Brown's Record," January 3, 1935, Suhr file, HOF. End of Suhr's streak from *Sporting News*, June 10, 1937. McCarver quotes from author interview. Fox background and scenes from *Saturday Evening Post*, May 14, 1955; *Congressional Record* commentary on Fox, November 12, 1975; *Sporting News*, November 18, 1959; and Associated Press coverage of end of playing streak, obtained via Google News. Rose background and scenes from Friedrich, *The Iron Men of Baseball;* Yahoo Sports, "Big League Stew," interview, November 23, 2011; William Leggett, "Charlie Hustle Gives Twelve Dimes on the Dollar," *Sports Illustrated*, May 27, 1968; *Baseball Magazine*, April 1980; and Associated Press coverage of his streaks, obtained via Google News.

Chapter 13

Quotes from Cal Ripken Jr., Bill Ripken, Frank Robinson, and Clark from author interviews. Coble ejection from author's coverage for *Baltimore Sun*. Brooks Robinson quote from 1999 author interview. Ripken being "fundamentally sound" from *Washington Post*, May 17, 1991. Oates comment about Ripken not missing batting practice in 10 years from ESPN.com, September 4, 2015. Ripken trying to catch Horn home runs from ESPN.com, September 4, 2015.

Chapter 14

Gehrig appreciation from John Kieran, "The Man Who Is Known as Lou," *New York Times*, August 13, 1933. Fractured toe from *New York World-Telegram*, June 1, 1934. Norfolk beaning and aftermath from Eig, *Luckiest Man; New York Post*, June 30, 1934; *New York World-Telegram*, June 30, 1934, and *New York Times*, August 28, 2010. "You can't hurt that guy" from *New York American*, June 30, 1934. Detroit lumbago scene from Eig, *Luckiest Man;* Robinson, *Iron Horse; New York World-Telegram*, July 14, 1934; *New York Times*, July 14, 1934; Stanley Frank, "Baseball's Gibraltar," n.d. Gehrig file, HOF; and Sid Keener interview, n.d., Gehrig file, HOF. Ruth final years from Creamer, *Babe*, and Eig, *Luckiest Man.* Gehrig ascendance post-Ruth from *Sporting News*, July 2, 1936. Grantland Rice, "The Real Iron Man," n.d., Gehrig file, HOF. Gehrig reaches 1,600 from United Press International, August 8, 1935. Gehrig reaches 1,700 from *New York Journal-American*, June 6, 1936, and *New York Sun*, June 6, 1936. Scott quote from Cava, *Indiana-Born Major League Baseball Players.* Ruth criticism from Bill Corum, "The Iron Horse Rolls On," *New York Journal*, March 4, 1936. "Tea party" from Eig, *Luckiest Man; New York Journal*, February 1, 1937; and *New York World-Telegram*, February 1, 1937.

Chapter 15

Yost background and streak from Friedrich, *The Iron Men of Baseball;* SABR.org bio; Associated Press coverage, obtained via Google News; 1953 Washington scorecard, Yost file, HOF; Arthur Daley, "Walking Delegate," *New York Times*, March 25, 1959, Yost file, HOF; *Sports Collectors Digest*, January 18, 2002, Yost file, HOF; Shirley Povich, "Young

Iron-Man Yost Keeps Strolling," *Sporting News,* 1955, Yost file, HOF; and Yost obituary, *New York Times,* October 19, 2012, Yost file, HOF. Details of Yost shenanigans from box scores at Baseball-reference.com. Yost streak ends from *Washington Post,* May 14, 1955. Musial background and streak details from Friedrich, *The Iron Men of Baseball;* SABR .org bio; Associated Press coverage, obtained via Google News; and *Sporting News,* April 25, 1956; June 19 and June 26, 1957; and May 11, 1960. Use of starting-lineup loophole from *Sporting News,* June 19, 1957. Dead-ball era zeros from email exchange with Trent McCotter, SABR records committee. Consecutive-game rule-book timing and language from *Sporting News,* March 3, 1973, and February 2, 1974, and Leonard Koppett, "The Rulebook Is a Mess," *Sporting News,* May 1, 1976.

Chapter 16

Brawl from *Baltimore Sun,* June 7, 1993, and author interview with Ripken. Ripken conversation with Kelly from author interview with Ripken. Bancells quotes from author interview. "Cal might not make it tonight" from 1999 author interview with Hemond. Steinbach quote from *Baltimore Sun,* August 20, 1995. Bonds quote from *Baltimore Sun,* September 24, 1993. Oates "rain" quote from *Los Angeles Times,* March 16, 1993. "I wanted him in there" from 1999 author interview with Oates. Ripken hotel arrangements from Tom Verducci, "Solitary Man," *Sports Illustrated,* June 28, 1993. Quotes from Anderson and McDonald from author interviews. Miller quote from *Baltimore Sun,* September 24, 1993. Tettleton quote from author interview. "They really got into it" and "I was pleasantly surprised" from Cal Ripken Jr. and Mike Bryan, *The Only Way I Know.* La Russa quote from *Baltimore Sun,* March 27, 1995.

Chapter 17

Gehrig conversation with Eleanor from *New York Times,* July 18, 1993, and Eig, *Luckiest Man.* Gehrig reaches 2,000 from *New York Times,* June 1, 1938; Associated Press, June 1, 1938; *New York World-Telegram,* June 1, 1938; and *New York Sun,* June 1, 1938. Fractured thumb from Eig, *Luckiest Man,* and Edward T. Murphy, "Iron Man Refuses to Rest," *New York Sun,* n.d., Gehrig file, HOF. "No thumb at all" from *New York World-Telegram,* July 20, 1938. "Oh, it hurts" from Frank Graham, "Gehrig Looks Back," July 4, 1939, Gehrig file, HOF. Eleanor Gehrig unease from Eig, *Luckiest Man.* "I don't believe in making a practice" from *New York World-Telegram,* February 1, 1937. "Brain tumor" from Associated Press, April 30, 1974. Yankees doubts about Gehrig in 1939 spring training from Joe Williams, "McCarthy Admits Doubt," *New York World-Telegram,* March 16, 1939. Gehrig belief that he will get better from *New York World-Telegram,* April 28, 1939. "I can't help believe" from Steve Rock, "Gehrig Took His Final Swing in Kansas City," *Kansas City Star,* June 11, 1999. Streak ends from Eig, *Luckiest Man;* Robinson, *Iron Horse;* Creamer, *Baseball in '41* (McCarthy remembrance); *Sports Illustrated,* June 18, 1956; *New York Times,* September 24, 1997, and May 3, 1939; *New York Journal,* May

3, 1939; and Ford Frick, "The Day Lou Gehrig Quit," 1961, Gehrig file, HOF. McCarthy afraid to play Gehrig from unidentified clipping, Gehrig file, HOF. Pipp comments on Gehrig ending streak from *New York World-Telegram,* May 3, 1925. Gehrig speech from Eig, *Luckiest Man.* Gehrig speech scene from Eig, *Luckiest Man;* Robinson, *Iron Horse; New York World-Telegram,* July 5, 1939; *New York Times,* July 5, 1939; *New York Sun,* July 5, 1939; and *New York Daily Mirror,* July 5, 1939.

Chapter 18

"Head coaches" from Will, *A Nice Little Place on the North Side.* Williams streak from *Chicago Sun-Times,* February 8 and June 8, 1968; Associated Press, "Cubs Outfielder Says Streak Began Consciously," May 22, 1968, Williams file, HOF. Williams background from author interview; Edgar Munzel, "Bruins' Billy Born to Blast a Ball," *Sporting News,* July 4, 1964; SABR.org bio; *Ebony,* July 1967; Sandy Grady, "Aaron Gave Williams Idea," *Philadelphia Bulletin,* June 21, 1962; and Bill Gleason, "Billy Williams Is Hitter," *Chicago American,* June 9, 1963. Quotes from McCarver and Ripken from author interviews. Robinson quotes from 1999 author interview. Durocher quotes from *Ebony,* July 1967, and *Sporting News,* July 5, 1969. Williams breaks Musial record from *Sporting News,* July 5 and July 12, 1969; United Press International, June 28, 1969; Associated Press, July 8, 1969; Cubs press release, Williams file, HOF; and *Chicago Tribune,* August 29, 1970. Williams streak ends from Associated Press, September 4, 1970; *Chicago Tribune,* September 4, 1970; and *Baltimore Afro-American,* September 12, 1970. "I don't really know" from *Chicago Sun-Times,* August 25, 1973. Murphy background from SABR.org bio; *Philadelphia Daily News,* April 8, 1991; and *Philadelphia Inquirer,* September 6, 1995. Murphy conversations with Ripken and other Murphy quotes from author interview with Murphy. Murphy streak ends from Associated Press, July 10, 1986.

Chapter 19

Ripken spring training press conference from author coverage for *Baltimore Sun.* Regan and Ripken quotes from author interviews. Garvey quotes from author interview. Ripken being stumped on how to commemorate achievement from Cal Ripken Jr. and Mike Bryan, *The Only Way I Know.* Amaral quote from *Baltimore Sun,* September 4, 1995. "How are you holding up?" from author coverage for *Baltimore Sun.* Regan comments about Ripken needing a day off from *Baltimore Sun,* September 5, 1995. Quotes from Bill Ripken and McDonald from author interviews. Ripken "screenwriting" quote from author interview with Ripken. Ripken comment to Gott from author interview with Ripken. Details of 2,131 scene from author coverage for *Baltimore Sun.* "Going out in style" from Ripken, *The Only Way I Know.* Tettleton quote on Texas scene from author interview. Oates quote on Texas scene from 1999 author interview. Hudler 2,131 story from author interviews with Hudler and Fred Tyler. Parade details from *Baltimore Sun,* September 8, 1995.

Chapter 20

Garvey background from SABR.org bio; Friedrich, *The Iron Men of Baseball*; Porter, *Biographical Dictionary of American Sports: Baseball, G–P*; Peter Pascarelli, "Garvey: Class Act in an Era of Embarrassment," *Sporting News*, February 1, 1988; and author interview with Garvey. Garvey quotes from author interview. "Son, you ever play first base?" from author interview with Garvey. "Source of pride" from Associated Press, June 9, 1982. Garvey 1,000th game scene from Associated Press, June 9, 1982. End of streak of starts in 1982 from *Sporting News*, May 17, 1982. Garvey conversation with Anderson from *New York Times*, March 14, 1983. Garvey passing Williams scene from *Sports Illustrated*, April 25, 1983, and United Press International, April 16, 1983. End of consecutive-game streak from author interview with Garvey; *Washington Post*, July 30, 1983; and Associated Press, July 30, 1983. Quotes from Bevacqua, Russell, and Lasorda from *Los Angeles Daily News*, July 30, 1983.

Chapter 21

Quotes from Gillick, Bill Ripken, and Cal Ripken Jr. from author interviews. Details and quotes from Kinugasa visit to Kansas City from author's coverage for *Baltimore Sun*. Kinugasa background and streak details from Whiting, *You Gotta Have Wa*; *New York Times*, May 13, 1987; and Baseball-reference.com. Ripken comment to Cito Gaston from author interview with Ripken. "Albatross" from *New York Times*, September 21, 1998. "You can't play with this" from author interview with Ripken. Shapiro quotes from author interview. Johnson quotes from 1999 author interview. Anderson quotes and conversation with Ripken from author interview with Anderson. Ripken conversation with Kelly about ending streak from author interview with Ripken. Ripken-Miller interaction, "You'll have to watch and see," and Angelos quote from Joe Strauss, "Ripken Ends the Streak," *Baltimore Sun*, September 21, 1998. Minor dugout scene and conversation with Miller from author interview with Ripken. "Emphasis should be on the team" from Ripken postgame press conference, September 20, 1998. Simmons quotes from Bill Simmons, "Go See Cal? Hardly," ESPN.com, 2001.

Chapter 22

Quotes from Melvin, Ripken, McCarver, and Bancells from author interviews. Statistics on decline of playing full seasons from Friedrich, *The Iron Men of Baseball*. Longoria rests from *Tampa Bay Times*, May 23, 2010. Matsui streak from *New York Times*, May 12, 2006. Fielder quotes from author interview. "Unless it's bleeding or broken" from MLive.com, September 23, 2013. Leyland quote on Fielder from MLive.com, September 23, 2013. Howe quotes from author interview. Tejada background from Jockbio.com and Jorge Arangure Jr., "A Man, a Time, Intertwined," Sportsonearth.com, May 1, 2013. Trembley quotes from author interview. Tejada and Perlozzo on 1,000 straight games from *Baltimore Sun,* July 2, 2006. Tejada broken wrist in San Diego from *Baltimore Sun,* June 21, 2007. End of Tejada's streak from *Washington Post,* June 23, 2007. Tejada in the Mitchell Report from *Baltimore Sun,* December 14, 2007. "He plays every inning" from MLB.com, December 12, 2007. Tejada lying about his age from ESPN.com, April 17, 2008. Tejada pleading guilty of lying to Congress from Associated Press, February 11, 2009. "La Gua Gua" from Arangure, "A Man, a Time, Intertwined."

Epilogue

Ripken bicycle accident story from author interview with Ripken and *Baltimore Sun,* September 2, 2015. "Business of Cal" from "Iron Businessman," *Fortune,* May 19, 2014. Conversation with Anderson from author interview with Ripken. Robinson quotes from 1999 author interview. Showalter quotes from Peter Schmuck, "Twenty Years After 2,131, Orioles Celebrate Cal Ripken Jr.'s 'Superhuman' Accomplishment," *Baltimore Sun,* September 2, 2015. Garvey quotes from author interview. Pence injury from Yahoo.com, March 7, 2015. Twitter exchange between Pence and Black from *USA Today,* March 6, 2015. Freeman streak ends from Foxsports.com, June 18, 2015. Seagar streak ends from *Tacoma News Tribune,* June 19, 2015.

Bibliography

Allen, Lee. *The National League Story.* New York: Hill and Wang, 1961.

Appel, Marty. *Pinstripe Empire: The New York Yankees from Before the Babe to After the Boss.* New York: Bloomsbury, 2012.

Berg, A Scott. *Goldwyn: A Biography.* New York: Simon and Schuster, 1989.

Cava, Pete. *Indiana-Born Major League Baseball Players.* Jefferson, NC: McFarland, 2015.

Clark, Al, with Dan Schlossberg. *Called Out but Safe.* Lincoln: University of Nebraska Press, 2014.

Connolly, Dan. *100 Things Orioles Fans Should Know Before They Die.* Chicago: Triumph Books, 2015.

Creamer, Robert W. *Babe: The Legend Comes to Life.* New York: Simon and Schuster, 1974.

———. *Baseball in '41.* New York: Viking, 1991.

Eig, Jonathan. *Luckiest Man: The Life and Death of Lou Gehrig.* New York: Simon and Schuster, 2005.

Eisenberg, John. *From 33rd Street to Camden Yards: An Oral History of the Baltimore Orioles.* New York: Contemporary Books, 2001.

Friedrich, Marty. *The Iron Men of Baseball.* Jefferson, NC: McFarland, 2006.

Lanigan, Ernest J. *The Baseball Cyclopedia.* New York: Baseball Magazine Company, 1922.

Moreland, George. *Balldom: The Britannica of Baseball.* New York: Horton, 1914.

Porter, David L. *The Biographical Dictionary of American Sports: Baseball, G–P.* Westport, CT: Greenwood Press, 2000.

Ripken, Cal, Jr., and Mike Bryan. *The Only Way I Know.* New York: Penguin, 1998.

Ripken, Cal, Sr. *The Ripken Way: A Manual for Baseball and Life.* New York: Diversion Books, 2010.

Robinson, Ray. *Iron Horse: Lou Gehrig in His Time.* New York: Norton, 1990.

Schwarz, Alan. *The Numbers Game.* New York: Thomas Dunne Books, 2004.

Shafer, Ronald G. *When the Dodgers Were Bridegrooms.* Jefferson, NC: McFarland, 2011.

Stout, Glenn. *The Selling of the Babe.* New York: Thomas Dunne Books, 2016.

Thorn, John, and Pete Palmer. *Total Baseball.* New York: Warner Books, 1989.

Vecsey, George. *Stan Musial: An American Life.* New York: ESPN Books, 2011.

Weintraub, Robert. *The House That Ruth Built.* New York: Little, Brown, 2011.

Whiting, Robert. *You Gotta Have Wa.* New York: Macmillan, 1989.

Will, George. *A Nice Little Place on the North Side.* New York: Crown, 2014.

Index